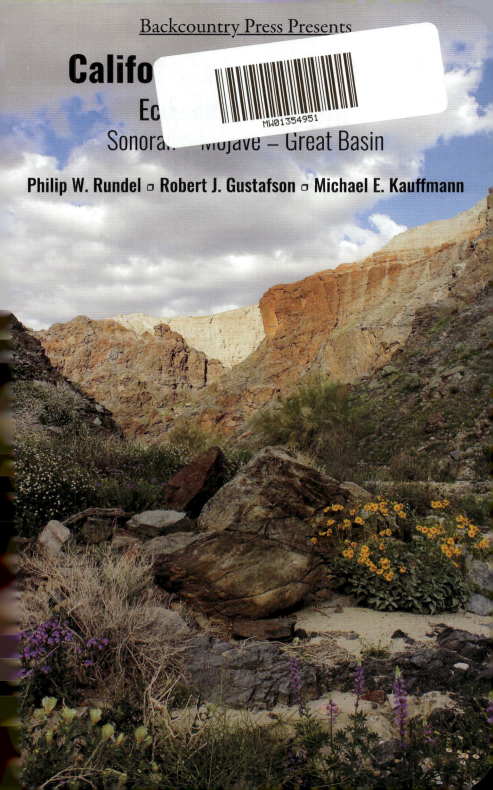

Backcountry Press Presents

California
Ec...
Sonoran – Mojave – Great Basin

Philip W. Rundel ▫ Robert J. Gustafson ▫ Michael E. Kauffmann

Datura wrightii, Solanaceae, sacred datura. Photo by Anita Bauer Arnold.

In Praise of **California Desert Plants**

> *California Desert Plants* is a rich, nuanced, and accessible exploration of plant relationships and adaptations. This book gives the context in which plants make sense, and helps us to see relationships between species, across families, and in response to place.
>
> — **John Muir Laws,** Author of *The Laws Guide to the Sierra Nevada*

> I am marveling at *California Desert Plants*! This book is packed with incredible information and beautiful images—from the ecosystem level to individual species. It will be cherished and enjoyed by both the seasoned ecologist and the budding botanist. A must have for any desert lover.
>
> — **Naomi Fraga,** Director of Conservation Programs, CA Botanic Garden

> Finally a book that summarizes all the botanical natural history of the deserts of California by combining ecology, taxonomy, and identification. Read it as you wander through California's deserts and these places will never appear the same again.
>
> — **Jenn Yost,** Botany Professor, Cal Poly San Luis Obispo

> An amazing achievement, *California Desert Plants* is far more than a field guide—this essential resource distills the authors' deep, nuanced knowledge of desert plant ecology and natural history, and presents it in a beautifully compelling way.
>
> — **Bruce Baldwin,** Curator of the Jepson Herbarium

> Another gem from Backcountry Press. Those mesmerized by California's desert biomes will fall happily and deeply into this indispensable field guide which reveals not only the photosynthesizers but the geology, hydrology, and atmospheric spheres that help co-create the landscape.
>
> — **Mary Ellen Hannibal,** Author of *Citizen Scientist: Searching for Heroes and Hope in an Age of Extinction.*

> The authors have outdone themselves in providing a richly expansive overview of the ecological regions, landforms, and adaptations of desert plants residing in southeastern California. Their compilation of photographs and descriptive text make this an indispensable guide.
>
> — **Julie Evens,** Co-author of *Manual of California Vegetation*

Eureka Dunes sunrise, Death Valley National Park. Photo by Michael Kauffmann.

©Copyright 2022 • Backcountry Press
First Edition
9 8 7 6 5 4 3 2 1

All rights reserved. No part of this publication may be reproduced, stored, or transmitted in any form or by any means—electronic, mechanical, photocopying, recording, or otherwise—without written permission from Backcountry Press.

Front cover photo: Death Valley monkeyflower (*Diplacus rupicola*) by Matt Berger.
Back cover photos: *Nolina parryi* by Anita Bauer Arnold, sand dune by Dylan Neubauer.
Title page photo by Moe Donnelly
Table of content photo by Morgan Stickrod
Book layout and cover design by Backcountry Press
Published by Backcountry Press • Kneeland, California

ISBN 978-1-941624-14-2
Library of Congress Control Number: 2022932363

Order this book online: www.backcountrypress.com

California Desert Plants
Ecology and Diversity
Sonoran – Mojave – Great Basin

Philip W. Rundel
Robert J. Gustafson
Michael E. Kauffmann

With photos by
Matt Berger, Robert Gustafson, Stan Shebs, Michael Kauffmann,
Jim Morefield, Julie Evens, Morgan Stickrod, Joey Santore, Kjirsten Wayman,
Naomi Fraga, Dylan Neubauer, Robert Childs, Mark Bailey, James Andre,
Moe Donnelly, Jim Bartel, Mike Splain, Tim Messick, Todd Keeler-Wolf,
Robb Hannawacker, Len Mazur, Chris Clarke, David Greenberger.
Jon Rebman, Ryan Henson, Gina Radieve, Duncan Bell, Jesse Miller, Karen Orso,
Scott Harding, Allan A. Schoenherr, Allison Poklemba, and Phil Rundel

Table of Contents

- VI — **Preface and Dedication**
- 10 — Chapter 1 **Desert Environments**
- 18 — Chapter 2 **California Deserts**
- 38 — Chapter 3 **Ecological Strategies of Desert Plants**
- 50 — Chapter 4 **Creosote Bush Scrub and Joshua Tree Woodlands**
- 88 — Chapter 5 **Cactus and Succulent Scrub**
- 102 — Chapter 6 **Wash Woodlands and Arroyos**
- 126 — Chapter 7 **Desert Wetlands: Palm Oases, Riparian Woodlands, and Marshes**
- 140 — Chapter 8 **Saline Habitats: Playas, Saltbush Scrub, and Alkali Sinks**
- 154 — Chapter 9 **Sand Dunes**
- 170 — Chapter 10 **The Flowering Desert**
- 214 — Chapter 11 **Great Basin Shrublands and Woodlands**
- 242 — Chapter 12 **Conserving the California Desert**
- 262 — **Further Reading**
- 264 — **Index**

Preface

Desert environments have always held a fascination for many, their stark landscapes notwithstanding. At first glance these seemingly-lifeless landscapes are actually home to hardy woody shrubs and succulents with amazing adaptations to survive in harsh desert conditions. All of this changes, however, when the onset of winter rains bring carpets of brightly colored annuals and flowering shrubs.

For those interested in plants, there are obvious questions that come to mind when considering California's deserts. How do perennial plants survive high temperatures and drought every summer? How do superblooms happen? How are California's deserts unique compared to other desert areas of the world?

Although there are many excellent books on California's deserts and desert ecology, this contribution is unique in many respects. We strongly believe that desert ecology, and the traits of individual desert plants, are best understood in the context of desert landscapes and their ecological communities. We have chosen this context rather than the typical flower-color organization of most desert plant guides. In this way, the book not only provides a landscape and community perspective, but also remains a useful field guide to important species at any time of the year—regardless of whether they are flowering.

Having described that the book is organized around plant communities, it is important to add a disclaimer: desert ecosystems generally lack clear habitat boundaries. Consider that, for example, in coastal southern California it is relatively easy to see habitat differences and thus separate chaparral from oak woodland or sage scrub from grasslands. Desert plant communities are typically difficult to map because the visual boundaries are fuzzy and do not lend themselves to delineation. For example, creosote bush scrub may be transected by small arroyos or a broader wash system with linear extensions of wash woodland habitat. Alternatively, it may have localized sandy areas that support what are typically dune species. Broad wash woodlands with ephemeral water may grade into riparian wetlands or marshes where springs allow for continuous moisture. Similarly, the higher elevations of the

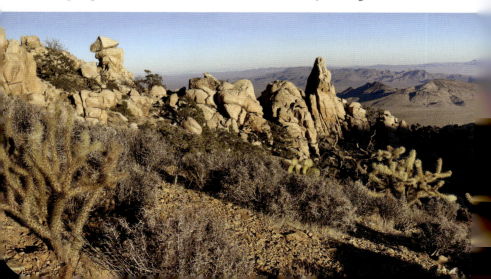

eastern Mojave Desert may exhibit a mosaic of creosote bush scrub, cactus scrub, Great Basin shrublands, and pinyon-juniper woodlands without clear boundaries.

This book begins with an overview of the physical geography of the desert environments globally (Chapter 1) and California deserts specifically (Chapter 2). In Chapter 3 we discuss a variety of adaptations that allow desert plants to survive, and thrive, in these harsh conditions. The next eight chapters focus on specific habitats within California's deserts and the key species that characterize those habitats. We start with creosote bush scrub and associated Joshua tree woodlands in Chapter 4, the most widespread community across our desert basins and bajada slopes. We then move on to cactus and succulent scrub with their often-rocky habitats in Chapter 5. The next four chapters treat specific desert communities as with washes and arroyos (Chapter 6), desert wetlands (Chapter 7), saline habitats (Chapter 8), and sand dunes (Chapter 9). Our one deviation from a focus on perennial plant species comes in Chapter 10 when we explore the flowering desert and its remarkable diversity of annuals and herbaceous perennials. These are invisible for much of their life cycle only to mature and flower when rains germinate seeds and allow the desert to bloom.

We move on from the warm desert communities of the Mojave and Sonoran deserts in Chapter 11 where we present an introduction to the cold desert shrublands and woodlands of the Great Basin areas of California. We close the book with an overview of significant conservation issues and the threats to the preservation of key desert habitats and plant species diversity in California's deserts (Chapter 12).

Dedication

The senior author dedicates this book to three mentors who pioneered understanding the quiet ways in which desert plants tell their stories to anyone who will spends the time to listen carefully.
- Dwight Billings
- Otto Lange
- Hal Mooney

Michael Kauffmann

Chapter 1
Desert Environments

Looking across creosote flats in Saline Valley, Death Valley National Park, to the Inyo Mountains. Photo by Michael Kauffmann.

Introduction

When deserts come to mind, most of us think of a hot and dry landscape with little vegetation (Fig. 1.1). However, there is no simple or all-encompassing definition of what constitutes a desert. Geographers will typically define deserts as regions that receive an average of less than ten inches of annual rainfall, producing arid conditions where rates of evaporation exceed the amount of rain. This rainfall limit is somewhat arbitrary, however. The difference in average annual rainfall between the coastal shrublands of southern California and the Mojave or Sonoran deserts is generally closer to 8 inches. Having said this, average annual amounts of rainfall are characteristically variable in desert regions, with irregular years much higher than normal—interspersed with years, or sequences of years, with little rainfall.

More practically speaking, however, we tend to point to deserts as aridlands. In southern California, for example, a transition from the Transverse and Peninsular ranges is seen from west to east where the typical chaparral shrubland and woodland floras of the southern California coast and foothills are replaced by species with a strong floristic relationships to the arid southwest. These desert species have adaptations to survive extended summer drought and include common shrubs such as creosote bush, burrobush, Joshua tree and various species of cacti, agaves, and mesquite. Areas of the southwestern San Joaquin Valley and inner Coast Ranges in southern California receive minimal rainfall that could be described as desert-like (4–6 inches per year) but are not generally mapped as desert because they lack the characteristic desert flora and fauna.

Fig. 1.1. Carrizo Badlands, Anza-Borrego Desert State Park. Photo by Moe Donnelly.

Many geography books draw a contrast between *warm deserts*, such as our Mojave and Sonoran deserts where low winter temperatures are moderated, with *cold deserts* such as our Great Basin or the Gobi Desert of Asia with cold winter conditions. Adding to the definition confusion, maps of global desert regions often include names that would seem to indicate a true warm desert habitat. Examples can be seen with the Kalahari Desert in Africa, Thar Desert in India, and Great Australian Desert. In fact, all of these areas typically receive more than ten inches of annual rainfall and are better considered as arid savannas or steppe habitats. At the other extreme are polar areas in the Arctic and Antarctica that could technically be categorized as cold deserts because of the low rainfall and cold conditions that limit water availability.

Desert environments exist due to one or more conditions that sharply restrict the rainfall reaching these areas. Most of the major deserts of the world occur in belts centered around the Earth at 30° north and south latitude (Fig. 1.2). These belts are characterized by a dominance of relatively stable high-pressure systems produced by global patterns of wind circulation that bring clear air and warm temperatures. A quick look at a globe shows the northern hemisphere belt contains the Sonoran and Chihuahuan deserts in North America, the Sahara Desert in Africa, and the Arabian and Thar deserts in Asia. The southern hemisphere belt includes portions of the Atacama and Monte deserts in South America and the Namib and Karoo deserts in Africa.

A second geographic factor promoting desert conditions is the presence of rain shadows, created when tall mountain ranges prevent the flow of moist air into interior continental areas. Rain shadow conditions are associated with warm deserts at lower latitudes either as a primary cause or a secondary factor—in addition to the low latitude desert belt. Our Mojave Desert, for example, is primarily a rain shadow desert, shielded from coastal precipitation by mountains to the west. Rain shadow conditions also influence aridity and thus extend the size of the Chihua-

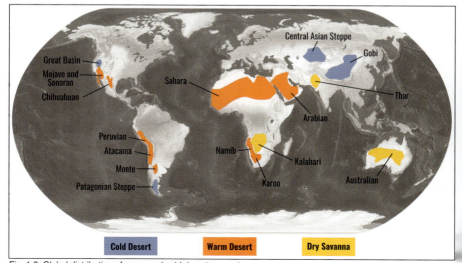

Fig. 1.2. Global distribution of warm and cold desert ecosystems.

huan Desert in Mexico and Monte Desert in Argentina. Where rain shadows occur in higher temperate latitudes, they produce arid conditions and what we call cold deserts—as with our Great Basin or the Gobi Desert area of Asia.

There is a third factor promoting arid desert conditions which has only a limited impact here in California—the presence of cold offshore currents. Under these conditions the cold ocean flow pulls moisture out the air producing frequent fog and leaving little water available for rainfall. Such conditions occur with the Humboldt Current along the west coast of South America. This produces the arid coastal zone of the Atacama and Peruvian deserts that extends for more than 2,000 miles from 30° S latitude in Chile to almost the equator in southern Ecuador. Similar conditions are present with the cold Benguela Current that flows from Antarctica up along the southwest coast of Africa—promoting the arid coastal conditions of the Namib Desert and portions of the Succulent Karoo. To a limited extent, such fog desert conditions are present along the Pacific Coast of central Baja California.

As described in more detail in Chapter 2, the California desert region has a Mediterranean-type climate regime with rainfall centered in the winter months coupled with dry summers. There are only three other areas of the world where there are winter-rainfall deserts. These are the Atacama Desert in Chile, Succulent Karoo Desert in South Africa, and northern Sahara Desert in Africa. All of the other warm desert regions of the world are characterized by a summer or biseasonal rainfall regime.

Desert Landforms

It is quite impossible to understand the patterns of desert plants and plant communities without some basic understanding of the significance of dynamic landforms and processes that impact the structure and dynamics of desert ecosystems. Geologic substrates, for example, have an influence on the rate of weathering and the nature and speed of soil formation. Metamorphic granite and gneiss, formed as much as 1.4–1.7 billion years ago, are resistant to weathering. This leads to spheroidal erosion and the formation of rounded boulders like those seen in Joshua Tree National Park (Fig. 1.3). Limestones formed beginning around 1.1 billion years ago when oceans covered our Southwest. In arid regions, limestone weathers slowly into blocky alluvium as water invades cracks and slowly dissolves the rock. Other desert landscapes are sedimentary and formed by the accumulation or deposition of mineral particles at the Earth's surface followed by cementation (Fig. 1.4). Volcanic rock, which can take many forms, includes intrusives which are relatively resistant to weathering. The age of the volcanic rock in California's deserts varies. Some are over a billion years while other, like Amboy Crater, date back only ten thousand years (Fig. 1.5).

Geomorphic and hydrologic processes produce a characteristic gradient of landforms and associated soil profiles taking place over millennia. In these sequences, steep rocky upland areas erode to produce rocky pediment slopes formed by irregular masses of erosional debris resting on the mountain parent material. When rains occur, desert storms may be locally intense with water runoff from the mountain slopes collecting into narrow arroyos that channel flow. This phenomenon transports large amounts of sediment and rock (Fig. 1.6). As these confined

Fig. 1.3. Weathered granite formations, Joshua Tree National Park. Photo by Michael Kauffmann.

Fig. 1.4. Sedimentary formations, Death Valley National Park. Photo by Michael Kauffmann.

Fig. 1.5. Amboy Crater is one of the youngest volcanic fields in the United States. Photo by Michael Kauffmann.

arroyos leave the uplands, they broaden widely—forming alluvial fans as they drop their sediment loads (Fig. 1.7). The change in channel morphology and flow velocity leads to debris flows with the deposition of large amounts of sand, gravel, and other sediments. The joining of multiple alluvial fans on the lower mountain slopes forms a broad fan-shaped surface across the lower slopes of the hills called a bajada (Fig. 1.8). All alluvial fans undergo cycles of deposition and erosion relating to patterns of rainfall variability. These processes have a strong influence on the establishment and survival of vegetation.

In a simple scenario, where the history of sediment transport has been regular and relatively simple, bajadas exhibit a regular gradation of particle sorting with coarser particles deposited upslope and finer particles moving down to the lower portions of the bajada. Under such conditions, the coarser soils on the upper fan have a more rapid infiltration of water into the soil during rain, intermittent surface flow, and a less tenacious hold on this water (higher soil water potentials) when compared to the finer-textured soils lower on the fan. These lower bajada slopes are

Fig. 1.6. Arroyo in Death Valley. Photo by Kjirsten Wayman.

Fig. 1.7. Alluvial fan with multiple flow patterns, Death Valley National Park. Photo by Tim Messick.

Fig. 1.8. Broad bajada formed from merging alluvial fans, Death Valley National Park. Photo by Kjirsten Wayman.

characterized by rapid rates of runoff and thus low rates of moisture infiltration. In addition, the fine texture of soil particles of the lower bajadas, and valley flats below, promotes capillarity. This draws moisture to the soil surface where it readily evaporates, further reducing soil moisture availability, decreasing soil water potential, and concentrating salts. These complex soil profiles, structures, and textures have profound impacts on rates of soil water distribution and, thus, plant growth.

Complicating these generalized patterns is the reality of the complex depositional history that affects most bajadas. Many of these erosional features date back to the Pleistocene. Due to this time frame, cyclical changes of depositional flows are superimposed over Holocene patterns. Thus, complex variation in the spatial pattern of debris flows in geologic and historical time has profound impacts on vegetation composition and structure.

Below the bajada the desert landscape changes to gently sloping plains across the broad valley basins (Chapters 4 and 5). As the bajadas grade into the valley bottoms there is a mixture of larger particles and sand at the surface of the plains. Slow wind erosion acts to gradually remove the finer particles leaving a size-sorted surface of small pebbles, called desert pavement (Fig. 1.9). Once formed and stabilized, slow action by bacteria on the surface of rocks often leads to the formation of a thin and shiny coating of clay minerals with magnesium and iron oxides, called desert varnish. These plains are cut by irregular braided washes that meander across the basin and channel heavier runoff flows from the mountains (Fig. 1.10; Chapter 6) or local springs with perennial water flow (Chapter 7). Under conditions of heavy flow, water may cross the desert plains and eventually collect at the low point of the basins. Here water accumulates but quickly evaporates to form dry lake beds called playas (Fig. 1.11; Chapter 8).

Fig. 1.9. Desert pavement, Milpitas Wash Wilderness. Photo by Ryan Henson.

Fig. 1.10. Braided washes meandering across a large desert basin. Photo by Chris Clarke.

Fig. 1.11. Badwater Basin, Death Valley National Park. Photo by Kjirsten Wayman.

Chapter 2
California Deserts

Looking across Death Valley National Park.
Photo by Kjirsten Wayman.

Introduction

North America has four major desert regions. The majority of the Mojave Desert lies within California, but only small portions of the Sonoran and Great Basin deserts are found here (Fig. 2.1). The Mojave and Sonoran deserts, together with the Chihuahuan Desert of southern Texas and north-central Mexico, are warm deserts because of their mild winter conditions and presence of plants and animals with strong affinities to the arid subtropics. The Great Basin is a cold desert because of its higher elevations, more extreme winter conditions, and flora and fauna linkages to the north-temperate zones.

Mojave Desert

The Mojave Desert is the smallest of the four North American desert regions. At 48,000 mi^2, it is roughly the size of the state of New York. About 80 percent of the Mojave Desert lies in California—extending beyond to cover portions of southern Nevada and small adjacent areas of southern Utah and northwestern Arizona. In a topographic sense, the Mojave Desert forms a transition between the higher and colder Great Basin Desert to its north and east and the warmer, lower elevation Sonoran Desert to its south and west. Valley basins in the Mojave Desert generally lie between 2,000–3,500 feet in elevation, although Death Valley is much lower. By comparison, Great Basin valleys are typical around 4,000 feet elevation and higher. Most valley basins in the Sonoran Desert within California have elevations below 1,300 feet, extending to below sea level in the Cahuilla Basin.

Landforms in the Mojave Desert are classic basin and range topography formed by a series of small mountain ranges, generally oriented north-south, separating valley basins (Fig. 2.2). Extensive alluvial fans, or bajadas, form along the slopes of these mountains as erosional debris flows down steep arroyos on the rocky hillsides. These bajadas extend to the valley basins below where finer sediments collect to form sand plains. The basin centers often contain dry lake beds, or *playas*. Playas, which are usually former Pleistocene lakebeds, receive water runoff in wet years and may contain standing water for brief periods of time (see Chapter 8). The large volumes of water that have evaporated from these basins over thousands of years have often left behind concentrated salt, which turn the soils white.

Over most of its area, the Mojave Desert is geographically separated from the Great Basin to the north and Sonoran Desert to the south by mountain ranges. The western boundary is formed by the southern Sierra Nevada and Tehachapi Mountains. The southwestern border is formed by the San Gabriel and San Bernardino Mountains. These zones of uplift have been created by the active San Andreas and Garlock earthquake faults. The dominant geographic feature in southwestern corner of the Mojave is a broad, flat, high-elevation plateau known as the Antelope Valley. In the late Pleistocene, Lake Thompson rose to 2,300 feet above sea level and covered about 200 mi^2 of the Antelope Valley. The lake slowly dried out following the Pleistocene and the old lakebed today forms a complex of playas including Rogers, Rosamond, and Buckhorn Dry Lakes today. This flat terrain of the Antelope Valley, together with its close proximity to Los Angeles, led to its rapid urbanization in the 1900s. The cities of Palmdale and Lancaster quickly

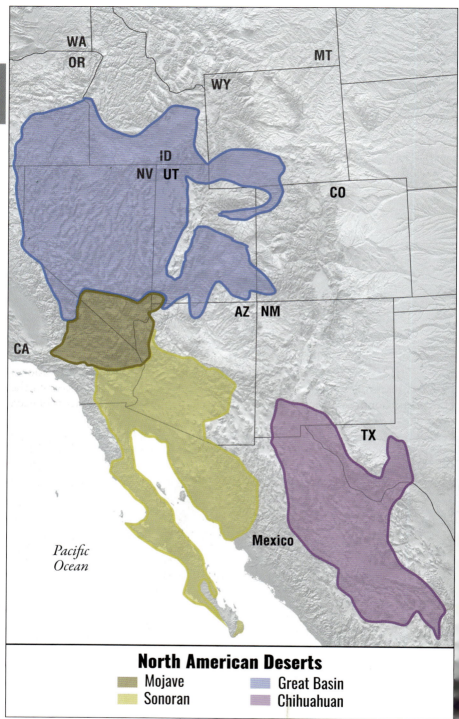

Fig. 2.1. North American Desert Regions.

Fig. 2.2. Looking across the southern Mojave Desert from the Granite Mountains. Photo by Michael Kauffmann.

sprung up. Edwards Air Force Base lies at the northern margin of the Antelope Valley and utilizes the flat area of Rodgers Dry Lake as a landing facility for military aircraft and even the Space Shuttle in the past.

Moving eastward from the Antelope Valley, the southern boundary of the Mojave Desert roughly bisects Joshua Tree National Park within the Little San Bernardino Mountains at around 2,500 feet. The presence of Joshua tree (*Yucca brevifolia*), a diagnostic Mojave species, is indicative of the transition to the Mojave Desert (Fig. 2.3). To the east of Joshua Tree National Park, where sharp elevational gradients disappear along broad sloping valleys, an exact boundary between the Mojave and Sonoran deserts becomes difficult to define as floral elements of each intermix.

Fig. 2.3. Joshua trees in Death Valley National Park. Photo by Robert Childs.

Fig. 2.4. The Providence Mountains, Mojave National Preserve. Photo by Michael Kauffmann.

The topographic relief of the Mojave Desert increases in the central and eastern portions in California. Here there are more than 20 north-south trending mountain ranges, separated by basins with elevations ranging from 2,500-4,000 feet (Figs. 2.4, 2.5). There is broad elevational variation in these small ranges. From southeast to northwest, with maximum elevations in parenthesis, ranges include the Granite Mountains (4,062 feet), Providence Mountains (7,045 feet), Mid Hills (6,409 feet), New York Mountains (7,532 feet), Ivanpah Range (6,035 feet), Clark Mountain Range (7,929 feet), and the Kingston Range (7,323 feet). The Spring Mountains and Sheep Range extend to the north in Nevada with Charleston Peak (11,916 feet), west of Las Vegas, being the highest point in the Mojave Desert (Fig. 2.6). The higher elevations support extensive pinyon-juniper woodlands and sagebrush steppe habitats that are Great Basin communities within the boundaries of the Mojave Desert (see Chapter 11).

Areas of striking basin and range topography are present in the northern Mojave Desert to the east of the Sierra Nevada. In the Owens Valley, bounded to the west by the Sierra Nevada and to the east by the White and Inyo mountains, the Mojave Desert reaches its northern limit around Owens Lake. Here, a gradual transition to the Great Basin occurs with increasing elevation. Interestingly, the lower slopes of the Inyo Mountains to the east support Mojave Desert plant communities while

Fig. 2.5. New York Mountains hold some of the most unique plant assemblages in the Mojave due to the high elevations and proximity to Arizona's Sonoran Desert. Photo by Michael Kauffmann.

the lower slopes of the Sierra Nevada on the west side of the valley are dominated by Great Basin plant communities.

The Panamint Mountains run north-south for approximately 100 miles to the east of the Inyo Mountains, separating Panamint Valley from Death Valley. Telescope Peak (11,049 feet) is the highest peak. (Fig. 2.7). The Badwater Basin, on the floor of Death Valley, is the lowest point in North America at 282 feet below sea level (Fig. 2.8). Only Laguna de Carbón in Argentina has a lower elevation in the Western Hemisphere. The eastern boundary of Death Valley, along the California-Nevada border, is defined by the north-south trending Amargosa Range—which includes the Grapevine and Funeral Mountains. The Amargosa Range, as with other internal Mojave mountains, extends to relatively high elevations with Grapevine Peak (8,738 feet) being the high point. Several well-known Death Valley sites, including Zabriskie Point and Dante's View, are located in the Amargosa Range

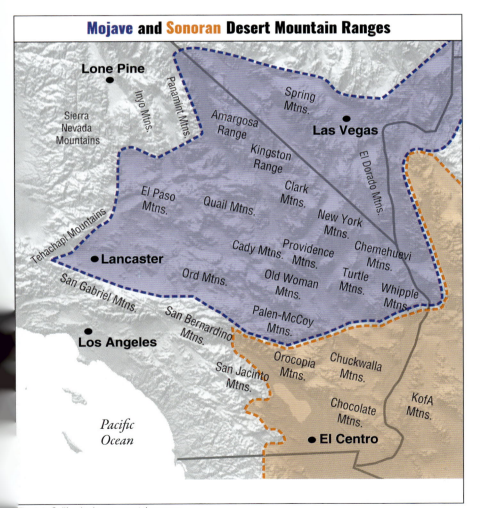

Fig. 2.6. California desert mountain ranges.

Fig. 2.7. Telescope Peak from Badwater, Death Valley National Park. Photo by Stan Shebs.

Fig. 2.8. Badwater, Death Valley National Park. Photo by Stan Shebs.

Fig. 2.9. Zabriskie Point, Death Valley National Park. Photo by Scott Harding.

(Fig. 2.9). East of these mountains lies the Amargosa Desert of western Nevada, a portion of the Mojave Desert region, with elevations between 2,600–2,750 feet in the valley bottoms.

Several large dune fields are found within the Mojave Desert. The Eureka Dunes, in the northwestern portion of Death Valley National Park, are small in area but up to 680 feet tall—making them among the tallest dunes in North America. Several other dune complexes are present in and around Death Valley, most notably those at Stovepipe Wells. The extensive Kelso Dunes extend over 45 mi^2 to the north of the Granite Mountains in the eastern Mojave Desert (Fig. 2.11). These dunes have a base elevation of about 3,100 feet and reach 550 feet in height (see Chapter 9).

Most storm runoff remains trapped within the Mojave Desert and adjacent areas of the southern Great Basin in California. Although extensive systems of lakes and rivers existed within the Mojave during glacial periods of the Pleistocene (Fig. 2.11), there is little surface water in rivers or on lakebeds today. The Owens River watershed today terminates at Owens Lake, but once fed a chain of lakes all the way into Death Valley. The Mojave River begins on the northern slopes of the San Bernardino Mountains and provides intermittent flow for about 110 miles into the desert before it disappears into Soda Lake near Baker. The Mojave River is unique because, over most of its length, water flows below ground under sand and, instead of flowing west to the ocean as with typical California rivers, flows north into the Mojave. The Amargosa River has its origin near Pahute Mesa above Beatty in southern Nevada. Except for limited surface flows, it remains underground for about 185 miles into the eastern Mojave Desert where it curls back north into the Badwater Basin in Death Valley. Aquifers associated with the Armagosa River provide water for numerous freshwater springs—most notably at Ash Meadows in Nevada (Fig. 2.11; see Chapter 7).

As uplift of the Transverse Ranges of Southern California proceeded rapidly in the late Tertiary Period and into the Pleistocene, stream drainages westward from

Fig. 2.10. Kelso Dunes, Mojave National Preserve. Photo by Michael Kauffmann.

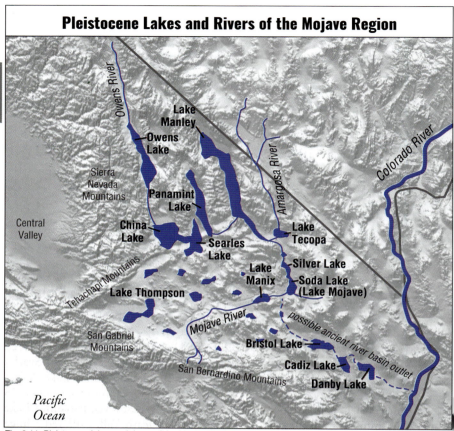

Fig. 2.11. Pleistocene lakes and rivers of the Mojave Region. Adapted from the U.S. Geological Survey.

Fig. 2.12. Southern Saline Valley, Death Valley N. P., in the winter of 2008-2009. Photo by Michael Kauffmann.

the Mojave became blocked. The combination of drainage barriers and increased rainfall with the onset of cooler glacial conditions created an endorheic basin, or an area that retains water and allows no outflow to the ocean. Thus, for example, the Mojave River which carries runoff from the San Gabriel and San Bernardino Mountains, once forming large lakes in low-lying basins in the Mojave Desert. The two largest of these were Lake Manix, east of Barstow, and Mojave Lake around Baker. The dry remnants of these lake basins are seen today in Troy Lake and Coyote Lake for the former, and Silver Lake and Soda Lake for the later (Fig. 2.11).

Afton Canyon, at the eastern end of the Mojave River, was carved about 18,000 years ago as Lake Manix filled to capacity and sent its overflow eastward to create a new channel for the Mojave River. The Mojave River drainage system is also believed to have spilled past the present site of Ludlow into the basins of Bristol Lake, Cadiz Lake, and Danby Lake (Fig. 2.11). From here it continued its flow eastward, connecting with the Colorado River drainage somewhere near the present site of Blythe. Around 10,000–8,000 years ago these lakes went dry, forming the playas that we see today. In years of exceptional rainfall, however, shallow, temporary lakes form for weeks or even months (Fig. 2.12).

Many other ancient lakes were cyclically present in the Mojave region during the cool glacial periods of the Pleistocene. Each of the major valleys east of the Sierra Nevada (Owens, Panamint, Saline, and Death valleys) were sites of large lakes (Fig. 2.11). The Owens River, once fed by glacial runoff from the Sierra Nevada with ten times more water than today, formed Owens Lake with a depth of 250 feet. Overflow from Owens Lake continued south to China Lake and on to Searles Lake, with the latter reaching a depth of about 640 feet. Panamint Lake, fed at times of greatest runoff from Searles Lake as well as local mountains, reached 55 by ten miles in size, with a depth of 950 feet. At its highest level, Panamint Lake spilled over into Death Valley across Wingate Pass. Death Valley offered a huge basin for lake formation but no outlet because of its low elevation. At its peak

development, about 15,000 years ago, Lake Manley in Death Valley reached 90 miles in length and 900 feet in depth. Other inputs into Lake Manley included the Amargosa River, draining areas of southwestern Nevada, and a continuation of the Mojave River northward from Lake Mojave.

Sonoran Desert

The region of the Sonoran Desert in California forms a relatively small portion of the larger Sonoran Desert which extends across the southwestern United States and northwestern Mexico (Fig. 2.1). This California portion is distinguished not just by its political geography but also by a winter rainfall regime. This is in contrast to the summer and winter, or biseasonal, rainfall regime that characterizes other areas of the Sonoran Desert. Many books identify this California portion of the Sonoran Desert as the Colorado Desert, named after the Colorado River that forms its eastern margin. This terminology, however, invariably causes confusion with the state of Colorado, although this area received the name before the state of Colorado was created. Herein we refer to this area as California's Sonoran Desert.

The California's Sonoran Desert encompasses approximately 15,400 mi^2 which is about ⅓ the area of the Mojave Desert. It is bounded to the west by the San Bernardino Mountains of the Transverse Ranges and the San Jacinto and Santa Rosa Mountains of the Peninsular Ranges. These high peaks create a rain shadow, with the Coachella Valley lying in their lee. To the north, the Little San Bernardino, Chocolate, and Chuckwalla mountains provide a transition to the higher elevation Mojave Desert (Fig. 2.6). Although most of these ranges are relatively low, the peaks of the Little San Bernardino Mountains reach to 4,000–5,000 feet in elevation, with a high point at Quail Mountain (5,813 feet).

The Coachella Valley drops gradually in elevation from about 2,200 feet at its western margin to below sea level as it reaches the Cahuilla Basin. The largest portion of our Sonoran Desert is formed by the Cahuilla Basin—a closed basin lying largely below sea level and including the Salton Sea. The basin is considered a portion of the historic Colorado River delta region. Over the last thousand years the Colorado River has meandered west and filled the basin at least three times, forming a freshwater lake called Lake Cahuilla. Each time, the Colorado River eventually returned to its present channel to the east, leaving the lake to evaporate. The only major geologic lakebed in the lower Sonoran Desert area of California is that of ancient Lake Cahuilla, a portion of which is now covered by the modern Salton Sea. Unlike the ancient lakes of the Mojave and Great Basin deserts, whose development is strongly associated with wetter pluvial periods during the Pleistocene, Lake Cahuilla has had a history of existence associated more with Colorado River floods than with glacial cycles. The latest filling of this lakebed is thought to have occurred between about 900–1400 C.E.

The present Salton Sea was formed in 1905 when massive flooding caused the Colorado River to break through an irrigation canal and flow into the Cahuilla Basin over a period of 18 months. The Salton Sea is maintained today largely by agricultural runoff from the Imperial, Coachella, and Mexicali valleys. The surface of the sea lies 227 feet below sea level, making it the second lowest point in North America. With an area of about 340 mi^2, the Salton Sea is the largest lake in Cali-

Fig. 2.13. Anza-Borrego Desert State Park. California State Park photo.

fornia. Its maximum depth, however, is less than 50 feet. The area below sea level in the Cahuilla Basin includes not only the Salton Sea but also major portions of the irrigated agricultural lands of the Coachella and Imperial valleys on the northwest and southeast sides of the Salton Sea, respectively. Groundwater aquifers form freshwater and semi-alkaline marshlands.

Today, two major aqueducts cross the valley. The Coachella Canal, a branch of the All-American Canal built between 1938 and 1948, provides irrigation to hundreds of thousands of acres from the Colorado River. The Colorado River Aqueduct crosses the northeast end of the valley along the base of the Little San Bernardino Mountains and provides drinking water to Los Angeles and San Diego.

The southeastern corner of the Cahuilla Basin contains the Algodones Dunes, the largest dune system in the United States, which extend south into Mexico and east into Arizona. These dunes, discussed in Chapter 9, are formed from wind-blown sands from the shores of the old Lake Cahuilla. The prevailing west and northwest winds have transported the sand eastward to their present location.

Great Basin

The Great Basin forms a large geomorphic region that extends from east of the Sierra Nevada across Nevada and western Utah to the edge of the Rocky Mountains and north to the Columbia Plateau to include southeastern Oregon and southern Idaho (Fig. 2.1). While the entire Great Basin covers a large area, only two small portions reach into California. The relevant area of Great Basin to this book is east of the Sierra Nevada and north of the Mojave Desert, comprising the northern Owens Valley and higher elevations of the White, Inyo, Panamint, and adjacent mountain ranges (Fig. 2.7, 2.14). The second Great Basin region is largely formed by the Modoc Plateau of northeastern California, a sparsely populated area of high desert plains and volcanic uplands with sagebrush steppe and pinyon-juniper woodlands.

Basin and range topography links all ranges within the Great Basin where geologic faults have caused uplift of north-south trending mountains and down-dropped valleys—producing a distinctive pattern of alternating mountain ranges and valleys. This pattern is a result of crustal extension within this area of the North American Plate, caused in part by a reaction to pressures from the Pacific Plate colliding with the North American Plate along the San Andreas Fault. In the Basin and Range Province, the Earth's crust has been stretched to double its original width, making it some of the thinnest anywhere in the world.

The Great Basin is a cold desert because of its latitude, continental position, and high elevations—with most valley basins around 4,000–6,500 feet. Annual precipitation ranges between 7–12 inches and largely falls as winter snow. The topography of the region is such that this low rainfall is not sufficient to produce major rivers and drainage is endorheic, or internal. A group of large, pluvial lakes occurred widely across the Great Basin during the Pleistocene. Today, the Great Salt Lake is a remnant of Lake Bonneville, a giant lake of the Pleistocene.

One of the ecological factors linking broad areas of the Great Basin are characteristic plant communities, most notably sagebrush steppe, shadscale scrub, and pinyon-juniper woodlands (Fig. 2.15). Many of the dominant species in these communities have broad ranges that extend across the entire region. These species generally exhibit a distinctly different floristic relationship compared to those of the warm desert floras that characterize the Mojave and Sonoran deserts. Most Great Basin species have ancestries originating in cold, temperate regions and are thus adapted to survive winters with cold temperatures. This contrasts the warm desert floras whose ancestry developed in mild, sub-tropical climate regimes.

As mentioned above, the boundary between the Mojave Desert and Great Basin is seen in the Owens Valley just south of Owens Lake. Here communities of creosote bush are gradually replaced by Great Basin communities of shadscale and sagebrush steppe on the valley floor. Although the Mojave Desert is mapped as a warm desert, separate and distinct from the Great Basin, the higher mountain ranges of the eastern and northern Mojave Desert and the desert slopes of the San Gabriel and San Bernardino mountains hold relic Great Basin communities including pinyon-juniper woodland and Great Basin sagebrush. These ecological communities are discussed in some detail in Chapter 11.

Climate Regimes

The California's deserts are characterized by a Mediterranean-type climate. This is distinct from climates in the greater Sonoran Desert to the east of the Colorado River and south into Mexico. Although rainfall is highly variable from year to year across California's deserts, it is most common in December and January (Fig. 2.16). Occasional thunderstorms may enter California's deserts from the east in late summer when the sub-tropical high-pressure centers weaken, but these are infrequent events. However, the ratio of winter to summer rainfall shifts moving

Fig. 2.14. White Mountain Peak, view northwest across upper Cottonwood Basin. At 14,246 feet, White Mountain Peak is the third highest mountain in California. Photo by Jim Morefield.

Fig. 2.15. Pinyon-Juniper woodlands in the Granite Mountains, Mojave National Preserve, looking west toward the distant San Bernardino Mountains. Photo by Michael Kauffmann.

Temperature and Precipitation Graphs

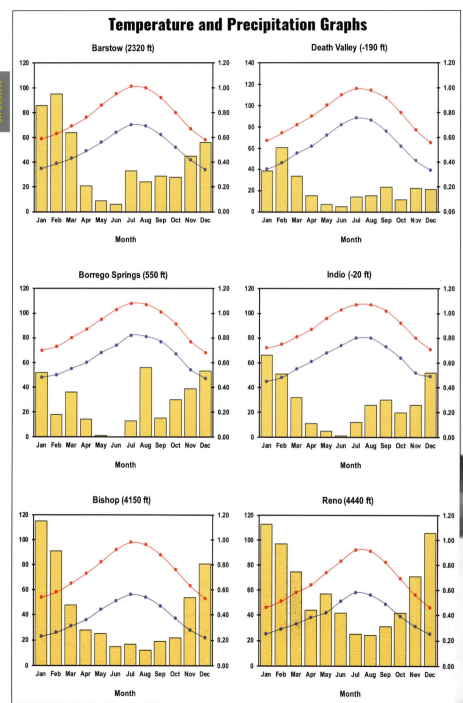

Fig. 2.16. Long-term mean monthly rainfall and high and low mean monthly temperatures for the Mojave Desert (Barstow and Death Valley), Sonoran Desert (Borrego Springs and Indio), and Great Basin (Bishop and Reno). Left y-axis is temperature in Fahrenheit while the right is inches of rain.

eastward. Approaching the Colorado River, the frequency of summer rains with localized thunderstorms increases. Las Vegas, Nevada, in the eastern Mojave Desert, receives half of its mean annual rainfall in summer, although summer rains are highly variable between years. Most of the Sonoran Desert in Arizona and Baja California receives two seasonal peaks of rainfall, centered on December-January and August-September.

Death Valley, in the Mojave Desert, is the driest location in California, with a mean annual rainfall of only 2.4 inches (Fig. 2.16). Most of the Mojave Desert basins receive at least 4 inches of annual rainfall, as at Needles, Trona, and Dagget. Rainfall levels are at or above 8 inches annually at the western margin of the Mojave Desert at Palmdale and higher elevations like Mitchell Caverns in the eastern Mojave. The lower Sonoran Desert areas of the Coachella Valley and Cahuilla Basin typically receive less than 4 inches of annual rainfall. There is a sharp rainfall gradient driving east along Interstate 10 from Los Angeles to Palm Springs. Banning, which forms the transition to the lower desert to the east, receives about 19 inches of annual rainfall while Palm Springs, only a few miles away but in the rain shadow of the San Jacinto Mountains, receives just 5.4 inches. Most of the Great Basin in California is similarly dry. Independence and Bishop in the Owens Valley lie in the rain shadow of the Sierra Nevada and receive only slightly more than 5 inches of mean annual precipitation. Further north, Reno, Nevada receives just over 7 inches on average.

Temperatures in California's Mojave and Sonoran deserts become warm in summer, reaching at or above 110°F (Fig. 2.15). Death Valley commonly exceeds this for many days in a row, with mean maximum July temperature of 116°F. The valley regularly experiences summer temperatures above 120°F, making it famous, or perhaps infamous, as one of the hottest sites in the world. The highest recorded temperature in Death Valley was 134°F on July 10, 1913, However, that measurement is in question as an expert on extreme weather data concluded it was not possible from a meteorological perspective. The highest measured temperature with modern instrumentation is 130°F, recorded in August 2020 and again in June 2021. It is reasonable to assume new records will be set in the coming years. During the 1913 heat wave, Death Valley experienced five consecutive days of 129°F or above. The summer of 1917 had 43 consecutive days where temperatures exceeded 120°F. The summer of 2001 set another heat record with 154 consecutive days reaching a maximum temperature of 100°F or above.

Typical July maximum temperatures over most of the Mojave Desert are 104–106°F, with Needles slightly higher at a mean of 109°F. Palmdale and Victorville, in the western Mojave Desert, are somewhat less extreme in summer with mean maximum July temperatures of about 98°F. Summer temperatures above 120°F occur in the lower Sonoran Desert, but mean July maximum temperatures in the Coachella Valley and Salton Sea Basin are typically 106–108°F. Great Basin summer temperatures are also high, but cooler than those of the warm desert areas because of their higher elevations. Bishop and Independence in the Owens Valley have a mean maximum July temperature of 98°F, while Reno experiences a mean of 92°F.

California desert winter minimum temperatures are variable depending on the elevation and distance from the coast. Considering that we typically think of deserts as being warm, these winter minimums are surprisingly cold. Mean January minimum temperatures are below 40°F at most sites. Freezing nighttime temperatures in winter are common in many areas of the Mojave Desert, and snow is not unusual. Victorville has a mean January minimum temperature of only 30°F, while other Mojave cities experience mean lows of 32–42°F. Mean January low temperatures in the Coachella Valley and the Salton Sea Basin are slightly warmer, with a range of 36–42°F.

There is a sharp distinction of winter low temperatures that separate the Great Basin from those of the Mojave and Sonoran deserts. Bishop, in the western Great Basin at 4,150 feet, has a mean January minimum temperature of 22°F, producing hard frosts (Fig. 2.17). Minimum nightly temperatures remain below freezing for five months in winter. Reno, located at 4,440 feet, has a similar mean winter low temperature of 21°F. It is these cold winter temperatures that have a profound impact on regional floras and provide a strong selective force against the survival by species of sub-tropical ancestry. Although subfreezing temperatures are unusual in low desert areas like Death Valley and most of the Sonoran Desert, rare events with extreme frost occur with temperatures as low as 15–20°F. In 1913, the same year that record the record high temperature in Death Valley, a January temperature at the park headquarters at Furnace Creek fell to 15°F. A record frost event in 1937 produced a low temperature of 13°F in Indio in the Sonoran Desert. These infrequent cold temperature events are notable for causing major dieback of sensitive desert species with sub-tropical ancestry.

Fig. 2.17. Joshua trees in the snow, Joshua Tree National Park. National Park Service photo.

Mean maximum temperatures in January are relatively cool in the Mojave Desert, with most stations in the range of 58–64 °F, with Death Valley warmer at 66 °F. The winter maximum temperatures are consistently colder than the summer minimum temperatures. January maximum temperatures are higher in the low elevations of the Sonoran Desert where they reach 68–71 °F. As would be expected, January maximum temperatures are quite cold in the Great Basin. Bishop winter temperatures reach a mean daily maximum of 53 °F and Reno is colder at 45 °F.

Plant Diversity and Endemism

Figures for the plant species richness of the California desert regions vary depending on how such figures are calculated. *The Jepson Desert Manual* (University of California Press 2002), the most recent floristic treatment of the Mojave, Sonoran, and Great Basin deserts within California, includes 2,162 native vascular plant species. This is more than one-third of the total native species present in the state but includes many species that only barely enter our desert regions. In addition, there are 232 taxa listed as naturalized invasives, making for a total flora of 2,394 species. Many of these invasive species have had, and are continuing to have, significant ecological impacts on desert community structure and ecosystem processes, as discussed in more detail in Chapter 12.

The six largest families in the California deserts make up more than one-quarter of the native flora. These are:

- Asteraceae (sunflower family)   220 species
- Fabaceae (legume family)   98 species
- Poaceae (grass family)   93 species
- Polemoniaceae (phlox family)   78 species
- Polygonaceae (buckwheat family)   77 species
- Hydrophyllaceae (phacelia family) 75 species

Other families with more than 50 species include the Brassicaceae (mustard family) and Plantaginaceae (penstemon family), as defined to include many of genera traditionally included in the Scrophulariaceae). The Asteraceae, Poaceae, Fabaceae, and Brassicaceae are all widespread and important desert families in Old World aridlands as well as New World deserts. Three important families for our desert region (Polemoniaceae, Hydrophyllaceae, and Boraginaceae) have their centers of evolution in western North America.

There are five genera with 25 or more species present naturally in the desert region of California. The largest of these is *Eriogonum* (Polygonaceae) with 49 species, followed by *Astragalus* (Fabaceae) with 38 species, *Phacelia* (Hydrophyllaceae) with 34 species, *Penstemon* (Plantaginaceae) with 28 species, and *Cryptantha* (Boraginaceae) with 26 species.

The California floristic region is widely recognized as a hotspot for biodiversity because of its rich flora and large number of endemic species. However, our desert regions are excluded from the California Floristic Province because of the affinities to other desert areas to the east. In considering the desert areas of the state alone, the level of endemism, based on occurrence only within the political boundaries of California, is quite low compared to endemism in the other parts of the state.

However, this lower level of endemism occurs not because of low species diversity but rather because our desert regions extend beyond the state borders into Nevada, Utah, Arizona, or Mexico. Endemism is quite high for the desert areas over their full range of geographic occurrence.

Again, because desert environments extend beyond the political boundaries of California, there are fewer than 50 plant species with ranges entirely restricted to California's deserts. The majority of these are species confined to wetter areas in the mountains of the eastern and northern Mojave Desert, most notably the ranges around Death Valley, mountains in the eastern Mojave Desert, and the Little San Bernardino Mountains of the southwestern Mojave Desert. These endemics occur because of both geographic isolation and speciation. In the past, some of these species once occurred more widely in wetter periods of the Pleistocene but are, today, confined to favorable moist habitats or limestone soils. The Death Valley region is home to three endemic genera that occur nowhere else. These are *Gilmania* (Polygonaceae; Fig. 2.18), *Swallenia* (Poaceae; Fig. 2.19), and *Holmgrenanthe* (Plantaginaceae; Fig. 2.20). The final group of endemic and near-endemic species from the California deserts is composed of Great Basin plants restricted to the Inyo and White Mountains, which extend into Nevada. This group includes the distinctive shrubby buckwheat genus *Dedeckera* (Polygonaceae; Fig. 2.21), a monotypic endemic. Many of the other endemic species from this region occur in subalpine and alpine habitats. While lying within the boundaries of the desert regions, these high elevation habitats are not typical of desert conditions.

Fig. 2.18. *Gilmania luteola*, Polygonaceae, golden carpet. Photo by Matt Berger.

Fig. 2.20. *Holmgrenanthe petrophila*, Plantaginaceae, rocklady. Photo by Matt Berger.

Fig. 2.19. *Swallenia alexandrae*, Poaceae, Eureka Valley dune grass. Photo by Jim Morefield.

Fig. 2.21. *Dedeckera eurekensis*, Polygonaceae, July gold. Photo by Matt Berger.

Chapter 3
Ecological Strategies of Desert Plants

California barrel cactus (*Ferocactus cylindraceus*).
Photo by Matt Berger.

Introduction

One of the most interesting aspects of desert plants is the complex nature of the adaptations that allow them to not only survive, but to reproduce and maintain populations under the extreme conditions of desert life. These adaptations include a variety of morphological features, physiological mechanisms, and seasonal pattern of growth that closely follows the availability of soil moisture.

Plant Growth Forms

One of the unusual features of deserts is the remarkable diversity of plant growth forms that compete, side by side, in these arid landscapes. Most biomes have a single plant growth form and dominant species that conform to that form. Chaparral has evergreen shrubs, conifer forests have needle-leaf evergreen trees, forests of the eastern United States have broad-leaved winter-deciduous trees, and grasslands have graminoids. These individual growth forms are well adapted for their respective biomes. Deserts are strikingly different. Here, no single growth form is dominant, suggesting that there are multiple strategies for ecological success (Fig. 3.1).

The most obvious growth is seen with the woody shrubs that are scattered across open areas of desert. The great majority of these shrubs are drought-deciduous species. These are species that form new leaves in the winter or spring as water becomes available and temperatures warm, and then grow rapidly through the late spring until summer drought restricts the availability of water in the soil. These plants then go dormant, dropping their leaves until the process begins again the following year. This drought-deciduous growth strategy is the same as is so successfully exploited in shrubs of sage scrub communities in coastal southern California. A few of these species, as described below, combine short-lived leaves with green stems, utilizing these green stems as the primary organs for photosynthesis once the leaves are shed.

While this drought-deciduous growth form has evolved as a successful strategy in the great majority of woody desert shrubs and subshrubs, there are notable exceptions in species that do not go leafless during dry summers. Most obvious

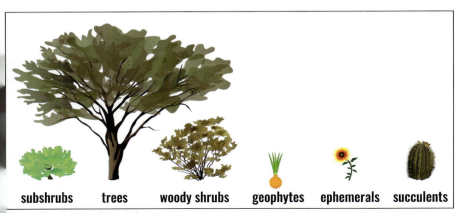

Fig. 3.1. Growth forms of desert plants.

is creosote bush (*Larrea tridentata*), by far the most abundant shrub species in our Mojave and Sonoran desert regions. This evergreen shrub maintains a canopy of leaves throughout the year, with individual leaves having a typical life of 13–15 months (Fig. 3.2).

We think of deserts as being dominated by low woody shrubs, but trees are also present. The tree growth form requires the production of a tall woody stem and so it is not surprising that plants with this growth form require greater water availability than what is present in most desert habitats. For this reason, the relatively small numbers of trees that occur in

Fig. 3.2. Creosote bush leaves. Photo by Matt Berger.

our deserts are either associated with wetland or riparian habitats where water is available, or alternatively have deep root systems that can tap groundwater supplies (Fig. 3.3). These species are termed *phreatophytes*, and include mesquite (*Prosopis glandulosa*), desert ironwood (*Olneya tesota*), palo verde (*Parkinsonia florida*), and desert-willow (*Chilopsis linearis*). The first three are in the legume family (Fabaceae), a group with subtropical ancestry that is most characteristic of summer rainfall deserts. In our summer-dry deserts these species are typically restricted to areas with groundwater, as in our wash woodland habitats (Chapter 6).

Although wetlands and riparian habitats along streams are rare in our deserts, these habitats provide local areas with available soil moisture throughout the year. One example of a specialized habitat with water available near the soil surface are the widespread palm oases defined by the famous California fan palm (*Washingtonia filifera*) in our lower elevation desert areas. Water availability in desert washes

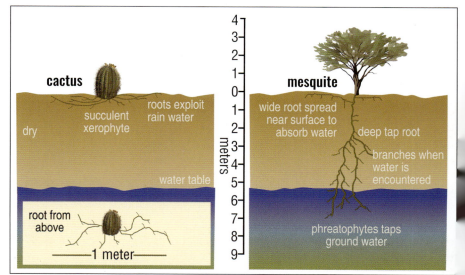

Fig. 3.3. Contrast in rooting architectures of a succulent desert cactus and a woody phreatophyte such as mesquite.

support many of the same riparian tree species that we have in our coastal areas of southern California. Cottonwood, sycamore, ash, and willow species are in this group. In contrast to the subtropical origin of the woody desert legumes, these riparian trees have a temperate climate ancestry. Wetland habitats and riparian trees are discussed in Chapter 7.

Succulent plants comprise another distinctive desert growth form. Most succulents in our deserts are species of cacti, which range from small, globular species to mound-forming opuntias and even giant saguaros. Also in this growth form are large rosettes of agaves with their succulent leaves. The ecological strategies of most desert succulents combine succulent stem or leaf tissues to store water, a thick cuticle to prevent water loss, and crassulacean acid metabolism, described below. The community ecology of cactus scrub habitats and the ecological relationships of individual succulent species are discussed in more detail in Chapter 5.

If we visit our deserts over most months of the year, and put together a list of the plant species we see, we would have a nice enumeration of diverse woody shrubs, subshrubs, a few trees, and a small list of succulents. However, we would be missing the great majority of the diversity. All of the woody and succulent growth forms together combine to define only about one-quarter of the plant species present. The other three-fourths of the plant diversity occurs with annuals and herbaceous perennials that either complete their life cycle and set seed before the end of the growing season, as in the former, or die back to ground level with the onset of drought stress in late spring or summer. Thus, the largest component of the plant biodiversity is cryptic, appearing only for a few months when rainfall conditions favor their germination and growth. The ecological strategies and ecology of desert annuals and herbaceous perennials are described in Chapter 10.

Limiting Environmental Factors

Deserts produce extreme conditions of climatic drought stress due to limited rainfall. California deserts are more extreme than most in this regard as our deserts are heavily influenced by a Mediterranean-type climate regime. This means that summers are generally dry, while rainfall peaks in the winter months, as described in Chapter 2. This rainfall regime contrasts that of most desert regions of the world where rainfall largely occurs in summer and winters are dry.

The environmental challenge in California deserts arises because temperature conditions are often too low for growth in the winter—the time of the year when rainfall is most likely to occur. For much of the Mojave Desert, for example, three-fourths of the annual rainfall has already occurred before temperatures warm sufficiently in the spring to allow new growth. In contrast, the major portions of the Sonoran Desert that lie outside of California experience rainfall that is either centered in the warm summer months or biseasonal with distinct peaks of rainfall in both winter and summer.

When ecologists first began to study deserts a century ago, they logically assumed that the structure and anatomy of desert plants could be viewed as adaptations to limit water loss—that is, to conserve water under the arid conditions present. Many general biology textbooks and popular accounts of the natural history of desert plants continue to focus on this basic principle, categorizing desert species as drought tolerators, as contrasted with the idea of drought evaders or drought avoiders.

As we have come to know more about desert plants over the past few decades, however, a very different view of desert plant structure has developed. While it is true that desert plants clearly show adaptations to help them conserve and use water efficiently, these adaptations generally operate through physiological mechanisms rather than structural or anatomical traits. Instead, we now believe that many of the adaptive traits of leaves and photosynthetic stems in desert plants have evolved to both regulate the energy balance of leaves to reduce heat loads and maximize rates of photosynthesis during those periods when water is available.

Maximizing Rates of Photosynthesis

Plants in any water-limited environment face a dilemma. The uptake of carbon dioxide from the atmosphere can only occur by opening the small pores on the leaves called stomata—which are regulated by special guard cells. However, at the same time that these stomata are open and carbon dioxide diffuses into the leaf tissue for photosynthesis, water vapor diffuses out of the leaf into the air. A plant can reduce water loss by keeping its stomata closed and thereby minimizing water vapor loss. But, during that time, there can be no exchange of carbon dioxide and thus no sugar production—necessary for growth and respiration. Obviously then, stomata must be opened for photosynthesis to occur, but at a significant cost in water loss. The hotter and drier the outside air, the more rapid the rate of water loss.

Despite the temptation to focus on desert plant's *defensive* strategies that minimize water loss, it is important to draw attention to the *offensive* strategies that maximize photosynthesis during those periods of the year when environmental conditions are favorable. For most desert plants, such opportunistic offensive strategies are the key to interpreting many of the morphological adaptations of desert plants.

The leaves of desert plants face many environmental problems simultaneously. They must harvest sunlight and take up carbon dioxide to carry out photosynthesis, regulate leaves to avoid lethal temperatures under hot summer conditions, and manage water relations to allow for maximizing their carbon uptake. All of this occurs in an environment where plant leaves present an inviting target for desert herbivores.

If we look closely at the design and structure of desert plant leaves, we can get clues about the importance of maximizing photosynthesis under conditions when and where water is available. The leaves of most desert species have high stomatal densities on both upper and lower surfaces. This is in stark contrast to the textbook leaf cross-section with stomata only on the lower leaf surface. This occurrence of stomata at high densities, and often in equal numbers on both leaf surfaces, seems at first counter-intuitive. If minimizing the loss of water vapor is the principal strategy of a desert leaf, one would first expect to find low densities of stomata and a restriction of stomata to the lower shaded leaf surface. These morphologies would reduce water loss.

However, under conditions where water and light are not limiting photosynthesis, measured per unit of leaf surface, can be substantially increased by having stomata on both surfaces to double the surface area available for gas exchange. In contrast, plants in communities where canopies are closed (i.e., where combined leaf surface area covers more than canopy area), and light does not readily reach lower leaf surfaces, have stomata only on their lower leaf surface. This is the case in chaparral, oak woodland, and coniferous forest habitats of California. Plants in alpine fellfields, where plant canopies are relatively open and growth is limited to a short summer season, share the desert plant structure of having stomata on both upper and lower leaf surfaces.

If you cut a cross-section of a desert leaf and examine it under a microscope, you will see multiple palisade layers of tiny green cells, rich in chlorophyll, below both leaf surfaces. The multiple layers, and tight packing of these small cells, allow a high density of chloroplasts (the cell organelles where photosynthesis takes place) per unit of leaf area. So long as sunlight is not limiting, leaves with these structures are capable of high rates of photosynthesis. Combining what we see with the high density and position of stomata on both leaf surfaces, and the structure of the chlorophyll-rich palisade cell layers, it seems clear that the structure of the typical desert leaf has evolved to maximize rates of carbon uptake and thus photosynthesis as well (Fig. 3.4).

As soils dry, and shoots are under greater water stress, photosynthetic rates of desert species are reduced but remain comparatively high compared with species from many other ecosystems. At levels of water stress where the leaves of most non-desert plants would die or experience little or no photosynthesis, the leaves of many desert plants still experience substantial rates of carbon uptake. This ability reflects a second important adaptation of desert plants. Desert leaves maintain active photosynthesis and growth at much greater water stress levels than typical non-desert plants using physiological and biochemical adaptations at the cellular level.

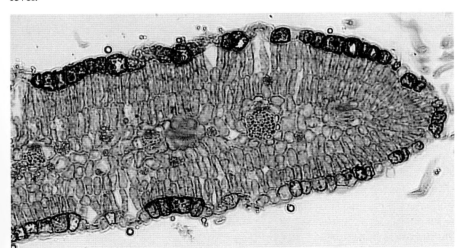

Fig. 3.4. Leaf cross-section of *Larrea tridentata* showing stomata (in red) on both upper and lower surface. Photo by Berkshire Community College Bioscience Image Library, public domain.

Leaf Energy Balance

The combined stresses of high summer air temperatures and low water availability have led to a variety of important morphological and physiological traits in the leaves of desert plants. These traits include size, leaf angle of orientation, and leaf surface reflectance—all maintaining a favorable energy balance under conditions of intense solar radiation (Fig. 3.5).

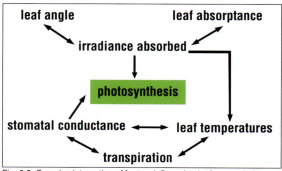

Fig. 3.5. Complex interaction of factors influencing leaf energy balance.

Energy balance for the leaves of desert plants create two problems. The first relates to high temperatures. Although some species are more heat tolerant than others, leaf temperatures above about 120° F may be lethal to plant tissues. Although such temperatures are rare, even in the desert, intense solar radiation can potentially heat leaves to levels well above air temperatures and thus to potentially lethal levels.

The second problem comes from what is called *photoinhibition*. This is a condition in the photosynthetic machinery within plant leaves where much more solar radiation is received than the plant can use. This interferes with the fundamental processes of photosynthesis. Photoinhibition is not caused by high light *per se* but by the absorption of too much light energy. While short-term photoinhibition is reversible, long-term exposure to intense light can permanently damage leaf tissues.

How, then, do traits of desert leaves help to minimize these problems? Let us first consider leaf size. Leaves and leaflets of desert plants are generally smaller than those of species growing in wetter habitats—particularly in terms of their widths which are often less than ¼ inch. This is not an adaptation to reduce the total area of leaves on a plant, as there is generally no difference in total leaf area between plants with many small narrow leaves and those with fewer broad leaves. The value of small leaves is that narrow leaves closely track outside air temperatures by the simple process of convective heat transfer with surrounding air (Fig. 3.6). This is a mechanism that requires no energy or water use. Broad leaves, in contrast, cannot cool efficiently through convection and easily reach lethal tissue temperatures under hot summer conditions without substantial amounts of water loss through *transpiration*—a process that lowers leaf temperatures by evaporative cooling.

Does this mean that desert plants cannot have broad leaves? The answer is no, but broad leaves only exist if the plant has a means to keep its leaves from reaching lethal temperatures in summer. This is possible if a plant is dormant and loses its leaves in the hot summer season or has a root system that can access a permanent supply of groundwater so that moisture is available for transpiration to cool the

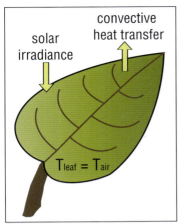

Fig. 3.6. Small leaves closely track outside air temperatures by the simple process of convective heat transfer to the surrounding air.

leaves. There are a few desert species with broad leaves growing in washes with subsurface water which are able to cool their leaves as much as 10–15° F below air temperatures in summer by high rates of transpiration. Good examples are some of the desert vines, as with *Cucurbita* species (Chapter 6). These species make little or no attempt to limit their water use and maintain high rates of photosynthesis with their broad leaves under hot summer conditions so long as they have access to water.

A second means by which desert plants influence the energy balance of their leaves comes with leaf orientation. Many desert leaves have a favored direction of placement, often meaning that they are oriented vertically. Such a position allows the leaves to maximize the amount of direct solar radiation they receive in the morning and afternoon hours when temperatures are cooler, and to minimize the direct solar radiation they receive at midday. By orienting the leaf vertically, chlorophyll and stomata are effectively hidden on both upper and lower leaf surfaces. This reduces solar irradiance during peak, mid-day exposure and maximizes it when the light angle is less direct. This strategy, again, increases the daily amount of photosynthesis in a counter-intuitive way.

Some desert plants show a fixed branch and leaf orientation that maximizes solar irradiance over the growing season and thus net photosynthesis. One such species is creosote bush which orients the display of its foliage toward the southeast (or equator) with steeply inclined branches. This orientation minimizes self-shading of leaves in the morning hours and maximizes the daily amount of photosynthesis by the entire leaf canopy. A related species, growing in the Monte Desert of Argentina, uses the same strategy but instead orients foliage north toward the equator. Directionality is also seen in many cactus species, with our barrel cactus (*Ferocactus cylindraceus*) serving as a good example. The succulent stems of these cacti lean toward the south, maximizing solar radiation on the growing tip and reproductive area of the cactus, and minimizing radiation to the sides of the stem.

Interestingly, several desert annuals exhibit a form of solar leaf tracking, with movement that allows them to orient perpendicular to direct sunlight at all times throughout the day (Fig. 3.7). This trait maximizes interception of solar radiation, and thus total daily net photosynthesis. Other desert annuals use a variant of this solar tracking: orienting perpendicular to the sun in the

Fig. 3.7. Solar tracking by leaves of the desert annual *Eremalche rotundifolia* (Malvaceae).

morning and afternoon hours when solar intensity is lower, and orienting edge-on to the sun under intense midday conditions.

One additional way in which the leaves of desert plants reduce the amount of solar radiation they receive is through leaf surface hairs, scales, or waxes that increase the reflectance of solar radiation. Pronounced grey or white leaves reflect more light than green or greenish leaves and thus have reduced levels of light energy reaching the leaf structures. One of the best regional examples is seen with brittlebush (*Encelia farinosa*). In the spring, when soil water is available, brittlebush produces relative broad and thin leaves with a modest coverage of hairs (pubescence) on their surface. As drought stress gradually increases, brittlebush forms smaller and thicker leaves with a dense covering of silvery hairs. Looking in cross-section, the mass of hairs on both the upper and lower leaf surfaces may be greater than the thickness of the leaf itself. These reflective hairs cut up to half of the solar radiation that would otherwise be absorbed by the leaf surface (Fig. 3.7). The result is a cooler leaf with a reduced loss of water through transpiration, but at a cost of reduced rates of photosynthesis.

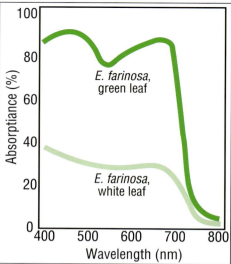

Fig. 3.7. Comparative absorptance of solar energy by green (spring) and white (summer) leaves of *Encelia farinosa*.

Stems as Photosynthetic Organs

Although leaves are the typical photosynthetic organs for plants, many woody desert shrubs and subshrubs utilize green stems as an important, or even primary, photosynthetic organs. These species commonly have small ephemeral leaves, often scale-like, that are present for just a few days or weeks in spring. This functionally leafless trait, with stems as the photosynthetic organs, occurs widely in desert plants. It is notably common in semi-woody members of the legume and sunflower families (Fig. 3.8).

A desert shrub that has both drought-deciduous leaves and photosynthetic stems has an excellent overall strategy for annual carbon gain. Because of the anatomical design, small leaves are well suited to intercept solar radiation and take up CO_2, while maintaining temperatures close to that of the air. However, thin leaves are more prone to herbivory or damage by wind than are stems which are mechanically strengthened. Photosynthetic green stems are generally better at water conservation than leaves and therefore are good choices for persistent photosynthetic organs during drought months. While a mix of leaves and photosynthetic green stems are best seen in subshrubs, as described in Chapter 4, there are many woody shrubs with small and ephemeral leaves that likewise rely heavily on stem photosyn-

Fig. 3.8. Photosynthetic stems of smoke tree (*Psorothamnus spinosus*). Photo by Michael Kauffmann.

thesis. Good examples include several woody legumes and species of the gymnosperm, *Ephedra*.

Being leafless with green stems is often explained as a strategy to reduce transpiration by eliminating leaf surface area, and thus a morphologic adaptation for water conservation. This hypothesis is clearly not true for many leafless species, which have green stems that display as much, or more, total photosynthetic surface area than leaf plants. Although one might assume that a green stem should lose relatively little water because it is essentially leafless, some desert plant stems have moderate rates of water loss through transpiration and even rates per unit surface area similar to those of leaves on the same plant. Consequently, many of these shrubs, with their large total stem surface area, also have relatively high requirements for water. This may explain why many of these stem photosynthetic species in our deserts either inhabit washes and other drainage channels or have deep roots to tap ephemeral pools of water (see Chapter 6).

Succulence and Crassulacean Acid Metabolism

A classic image of a desert landscape often includes a large cactus, such as a giant saguaro (*Carnegeia gigantea*), as a representative desert plant. And rightly so, as cacti are widely successful in our deserts and demonstrate a variety of highly evolved morphological and physiological adaptations to life in desert environments. The thick succulent stems of cacti provide a large volume of tissue for water storage and a thick outer layer of cuticle cells at the outer stem surface that effectively prevents water loss. If you were to weigh, then oven-dry, and reweigh the tissues of a large cactus, you would typically find that as much as 95% of the fresh weight was stored water. This is sufficient water storage to allow some cacti to endure several years of drought without available water uptake. While the water storage tissues are stems in most cacti, other succulents such as agaves can store large volumes of water in leaf tissues.

Beyond this morphological adaptation for water storage, cacti, agaves, and many other succulent desert plants have evolved a special physiological adaptation called crassulacean acid metabolism, or CAM. The name *crassulacean* refers to the succulent plant family (Crassulaceae) in which this metabolic system was first described. With CAM, there is a surprising reversal of the diurnal cycle of the opening of stomata. Instead of opening stomata during the day as in typical plant species, when temperatures are high and relative humidity low, CAM plants open their stomata at night when temperatures are lower, humidity is higher, and thus reduce water loss (Fig. 3.9). While carbon dioxide is absorbed by special enzymes under these dark conditions, there is obviously no light present to complete the process of photosynthesis. CAM plants get around this problem by converting the absorbed carbon each night to organic acids that are stored in special cell structures called vacuoles. The following day these organic acids are broken down and quickly reabsorbed by the traditional photosynthetic enzymes used in all green plants and converted to sugar by photosynthesis. With this stored pool of carbon from the night before, there is no need for stomata to open during the day. Thus, this metabolic system makes CAM succulents exceptionally efficient in their use of water for growth. Simply stated, they can grow more with less water than other species. This is obviously a desirable trait for a desert plant.

The biogeography of plants with CAM metabolism shows interesting patterns of adaptation. While cacti and agaves do not occur in the deserts of Africa and Asia, there are remarkable examples of parallel evolution with succulent species of *Euphorbia* and *Aloe* in these far away regions. Thick cuticle, surface spines, succulent water storage tissues, and CAM metabolism have all arisen half a world away. It might be surprising, however, to learn that CAM metabolism is widely present in wet tropical rainforests. In this case, CAM plants are largely epiphytic species of bromeliads, orchids, and cacti that live high up in the canopy in an environment of high light intensities and little soil for water storage. Overall, at least 40 different plant families have evolved succulent species with CAM metabolism.

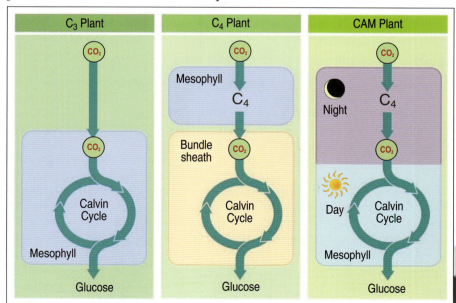

Fig. 3.9. Comparative pathways of carbon fixation in C_3, C_4, and CAM metabolism.

C_4 Metabolism

There is another metabolic system present in a number of plant families that provides an important physiological mode of adaptation to desert environmental conditions. This system is called C_4 metabolism, named for the number of carbon atoms in the first molecule formed in the carbon-uptake process. The photosynthetic process, typical of most green plants, is called the C_3 or Calvin cycle after the scientist who first described its biochemistry—it forms a three-carbon compound. In most respects C_4 metabolism is biochemically similar to CAM metabolism. In each metabolic system the same special enzyme, called PEP carboxylase, is used to fix carbon and convert it to organic acids. This fixed carbon is then released and refixed again using the Calvin cycle enzymes. However, unlike CAM plants where these two processes of carbon fixation occur in the same cells but at different times of the day, C_4 plants have the two processes of photosynthesis occurring in the same daylight hours but in different cell types (Fig. 3.9).

C_4 metabolism provides two types of advantages for desert plants. The first is that the highly efficient manner of carbon uptake by the initial C_4 enzymes is not inhibited by high temperatures. Plants with more typical C_3 metabolism have an optimal temperature for photosynthesis, but these rates decline at higher temperatures as the Calvin cycle enzymes become less efficient and release carbon dioxide during photorespiration. C_4 plants avoid loss of carbon in photorespiration and can maintain high rates of photosynthesis at high temperatures. Corn and sugarcane are familiar examples of plants with C_4 metabolism, and there are examples in summer-active perennial grasses in the California deserts.

A second potential advantage of C_4 metabolism comes from the highly efficient fixation of carbon by the C_4 enzymes. With this efficiency, C_4 plants open their stomata only a small amount and still achieve the same amount of carbon dioxide uptake present in typical plants without this metabolic system. Under these conditions, C_4 plants exhibit high rates of efficiency in water use to aid their success in desert environments—although they lose some of their potential for high rates of photosynthesis by achieving high water use efficiency through this type of stomatal control.

In an evolutionary context, we know that C_4 metabolism has evolved in at least 40 different plant families. In our deserts we commonly see it in three groups. These are summer-active perennial grasses, saltbush members of the chenopod family (Chenopodiaceae) typically growing in saline environments (Chapter 8), and a small but diverse group of annual species adapted to germinating and growing under hot summer conditions (see Chapter 10). It is interesting to note that globally the greatest ecological success of C_4 species is not in deserts, but rather in subtropical and tropical grasslands where C_4 species of grasses (Poaceae) and sedges (Cyperaceae) are often dominant. These two families have evolved distinctive lineages characterized by exhibiting either C_4 or C_3 metabolism.

Chapter 4
Creosote Bush Scrub and Joshua Tree Woodlands

Creosote bush (*Larrea tridentata*) in Greenwater Valley along Jubilee Pass Road, Death Valley National Park, Inyo County, California. Photo by Tim Messick.

Introduction

The most widespread and dominant plant community across both the Mojave and Sonoran deserts is creosote bush scrub. This community, in varied forms, covers perhaps 70 percent of the total area of both deserts—occupying a broad range of habitats and geomorphic substrates. On broad alluvial plains this community may include high densities of creosote bush with a relatively low diversity of other woody plants (introductory image). Moving up onto bajada slopes and rocky sediments, there is typically an increased diversity of associated woody shrubs and succulents and reduced dominance by creosote bush. The upper elevations of creosote bush scrub, around the periphery of the Mojave Desert at elevations of 3,500–5,200 feet, are characterized as Joshua tree woodland because of the presence of Joshua trees (*Yucca brevifolia*). In many respects, the associated plants of the Joshua tree woodlands in this elevational belt match the flora of typical creosote bush scrub (Fig. 4.1). However, creosote bush drops out of Joshua tree woodlands at higher elevations with colder winter temperatures.

Creosote bush (*Larrea tridentata*) is a remarkable species in many respects. To begin with, no other desert shrub even comes close to rivaling it in sheer ecological success. Creosote bush not only dominates broad areas of the Mojave and Sonoran deserts, but the Chihuahuan Desert as well. This success is particularly surprising when we consider that it is a relatively recent immigrant to our deserts from South America, with no evidence from fossil or pollen records before about 22,000 years ago. There are four other species of *Larrea*, all occurring in arid regions of South American, with ranges centered in the Monte Desert of Argentina. One of these species, *Larrea divaricata*, is almost morphologically identical to our species and would likely be considered the same species were it not for the thousands of miles separating the populations. Interestingly, while *L. divaricata* is ecologically successful in the Monte Desert, it is often outcompeted by another similar species, *Larrea cuneifolia*, which occurs over a broader amplitude of ecological habitats. We have no idea how creosote bush was able to disperse and become established in North America, or why it has become so remarkably successful in only a few tens of thousands of years.

As described in Chapter 3, creosote bush is an evergreen shrub (Fig. 4.2). Being evergreen is unusual for desert shrubs in California—with the vast majority being drought deciduous and losing their leaves as water availability

Fig. 4.1. Creosote bush scrub with scattered Joshua trees near Darwin, California. Photo by Matt Berger.

Fig. 4.2. *Larrea tridentata*. Zygophyllaceae, creosote bush. Photo by Robert Gustafson.

declines in the summer. The ability to maintain leaves through such stressful summer conditions requires a number of ecophysiological adaptations. Foremost of these is the ability to maintain metabolic activity under conditions of extreme water stress.

The individual leaves of creosote bush consist of two wedge-shaped leaflets up to ½ inch in length. This small size is effective in allowing them to maintain leaf temperatures close to air temperatures through convective heat transfer. Since the leaves are evergreen and experience temperature as high as 120°F during the extremes of summer, they avoid utilizing evaporative cooling to keep from reaching lethal temperatures. The foliage of creosote bush shows an interesting pattern where branch clusters are arrayed facing leaves to the southeast, with an inclination of 35–60 degrees from horizontal. This orientation minimizes self-shading during the morning hours and thereby maximizes the total amount of solar radiation received over the course of a day

There is indirect evidence that genetic individuals of creosote bush may be extremely long-lived. As creosote shrubs grow and expand outward from their center, young stems develop at the periphery at the same time that the central portions of the plants die. In old plants this continued growth pattern forms rings of living tissue—all genetically identical—around an open center. A very large clone of this type, in the Mojave Desert near Lucerne Valley, is named King Clone because of its size (Fig. 4.3). It has an average diameter of 45 feet and reaches up to 67 feet in diameter at its widest point. If one plots a regression of the size of this ring against known rates of growth for creosote bush in historical time, a questionable statistical approach, King Clone is estimated to be almost 12,000 years old. It would thus be the oldest living organism in the world.

Fig. 4.3. King Clone near Victorville, California is a clonal ring of *Larrea tridentata*. Photo by Grant Klokeid, public domain. Inset of King Clone from Google Earth imagery.

Whatever the age of these Methuselahs of the creosote bush world, there is no question that individual shrubs commonly live for at least decades and often centuries. Long-lived shrubs like this play a keystone role in desert ecology as they serve as a site where windblown dust and organic matter collect. This collection of debris, around the base of creosote and other long-lived shrubs, builds up mounds of what are called *fertile islands* in the desert (Fig. 4.4). These are the critical habitats for many desert annuals which require more nutrition than that available in open sandy areas. The mature shrubs and their fertile islands also serve as nurse plants that aid in the establishment of many desert perennials.

Native Americans use an extract of creosote bush as a sunscreen and potent antioxidant for the treatment of blood poisoning and liver diseases. Stores selling herbal remedies often carry "chaparral tea" which is composed entirely of leaves of creosote bush. Leaf resins of the plant contain a smorgasbord of chemical compounds that serve to deter herbivores.

Fig. 4.4. *Larrea tridentata* with fertile island accumulation of organic matter at Kelso Dunes, Mojave National Preserve. Photo by Michael Kauffmann.

Joshua Tree and Other Yuccas

There are four species of yucca in our desert regions. The most famous, and indeed well-known around the world, is the Joshua tree (*Yucca brevifolia*). Joshua tree is a true arboreal species that commonly attains a height of 30 feet or more, with some individuals larger with massive, branched crowns (Fig. 4.5). Its presence, in what is otherwise typical creosote bush scrub, leads to such stands being called Joshua tree woodlands (Fig. 4.6). The species occurs widely in a ring of higher elevation stands

Fig. 4.5. *Yucca brevifolia*, Asparagaceae, Joshua tree in the Mojave National Preserve. Photo by Julie Evans.

of creosote bush scrub around the Mojave Desert, although present at elevations as low as 2,000 feet in the western extent. It reaches elevations above 6,000 feet in the southern Inyo Range to the north of Death Valley. Two varieties of Joshua tree are recognized by botanists. The variety *brevifolia* is distributed in the western and northern Mojave Desert from north of Death Valley south to Joshua Tree National Park, with a western limit of distribution in the Tehachapi Mountains near Tejon

Fig. 4.6. Joshua tree woodland. Photo by Robert Childs.

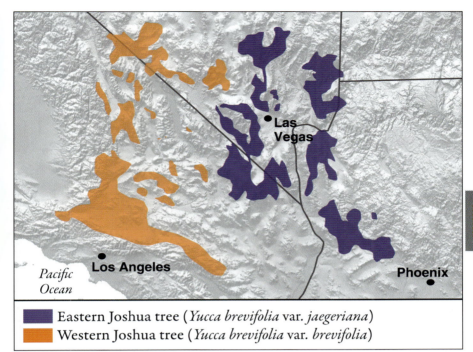

Fig. 4.7. Distribution of *Yucca brevifolia* var. *brevifolia* and var. *jaegeriana*.

Pass. It is taller, branches higher on the trunk, and has longer leaves than the variety *jaegeriana* which is distributed in the northeastern Mojave Desert from the Mojave National Preserve eastward into Nevada and northern Arizona (Fig. 4.7).

Joshua trees are slow growing, typically adding only a few inches of height annually. The rigid, narrow leaves are 8–14 inches in length, and clustered at the growing tips of branches. Older dead leaves retain their stiffness and are bent downward, playing a role in preventing rodents from climbing up the stems and feeding on the fruits. From March–May dense clusters of cream-colored flowers are produced at the branch tips, followed by the production of large, three-chambered fruits with developing seeds (Fig. 4.8). These Joshua tree fruits are spongy rather than fleshy as in other yucca species—suggesting that this species forms its own distinct group within the genus.

Fig. 4.8. *Yucca brevifolia*. Photo by Matt Berger.

Although there is no absolute means of aging Joshua trees because, as monocots, they lack tree rings, it has been suggested that typical life spans are 150 years and that larger individuals may live to 300 years. Some suggest that the largest Joshua trees may reach an age of 1,000 years, which is highly speculative at best. Today, there is considerable concern about the future survival of Joshua trees due to accelerated climate change. Drought and associated fires burning through invasive annual grasses have had major impacts on many populations—killing hundreds of thousands of individual Joshua trees (see Chapter 12).

Mojave yucca (*Yucca schidigera*) is an important species of dry rocky flats in creosote bush scrub, Joshua tree woodland, and blackbrush scrub in the southern and eastern Mojave Desert at elevations up to about 5,000 feet. Its range also extends west across the Peninsular Range of Southern California and reaches the coast at Torrey Pines State Park north of San Diego. This species is recognized by a conspicuous above-ground stem thatched with dead leaves and forming a rosette of stiff spine-tipped leaves up to 4 feet in length (Fig. 4.9). While single-trunked plants are typical, clumped clusters of trunks are also found. Overall, the plants are commonly 4–8 feet in height but can reach as tall as 15 feet. The narrow leaves are distinctive not only for their length but their yellow-green color, white base, and margin of peeling fibers. Like Joshua tree, Mojave yucca reproduces vegetatively from underground rhizomes. Clusters of cream-colored flowers are produced in April and May on leafless stalks 2–4 feet in length. Individual plants do not flower every year, with flowering intervals of about three years common.

The third yucca species is bananna yucca (*Yucca baccata*), which is found in Joshua tree woodlands and lower pinyon-juniper woodlands of the eastern Mojave Desert where it may co-occur with Mojave yucca. Nevertheless, banana yucca is much more a species of the biseasonal rainfall areas of Arizona and southern Utah than the winter rainfall areas of California. In morphology this species lacks the trunk of Mojave yucca and forms a basal rosette of stiff leaves 1–3 feet in length, often with multiple rosettes in a clumped group (Fig. 4.10). While banana yucca

Fig. 4.9. *Yucca schidigera*, Asparagaceae, Mojave yucca. Photo by Michael Kauffmann.

Fig. 4.10. *Yucca baccata*, Asparagaceae, Spanish bayonet. Photo by Stan Shebs.

shares the characteristic of stringy fibers along the leaf margins that is found in other yuccas, its leaves have a prominent pale blue-green color that is generally distinct from the yellow-green hue of Mojave yucca. Flowers in banana yucca are produced on short stalks. Although cream-colored on the inside, the flowers are reddish-brown on their outer surface.

Our fourth species is chaparral yucca (*Hesperoyucca whipplei*) which extends into the western margins of the California desert but is more characteristic of chaparral and coastal shrublands of southern California (Fig. 4.13). Chaparral yucca has several traits that distinguish it from other yucca species and have led to it being segregated into a separate genus. These traits include a dry fruit, an unusual structure of the flower stigma, and a monocarpic growth habit like that of most agaves—where the vegetative rosette dies as the tall flowering stalk matures.

Joshua trees, along with other species of *Yucca*, have a remarkable pollination system that involves a mutualistic relationship with species of yucca moths (*Tegeticula* spp.). The female yucca moth gathers pollen from yucca flowers using her specially adapted mouthparts. Once she has collected enough sticky pollen, she forms it into a ball which she presses against the stigma of every yucca flower she visits, pollinating these flowers. At the same time, she injects her eggs into the female tissue of the yucca flower. As the fruits of the yucca mature, they produce numerous large seeds and, at the same time, host the developing larvae of the yucca moth. The food sources of these developing larvae are the seeds of the yucca, but the larvae consume only a portion of the seeds. When the larvae are mature, they excavate an exit hole from the fruit, drop to the ground, form a cocoon, and emerge the following year. The undamaged seeds mature and are shed—and under appropriate conditions—germinate and produce yucca seedlings. Neither the yuccas nor the moths could survive without this mutualistic relationship.

The mature yucca capsules have high caloric content, with Joshua tree and Spanish bayonet being the preferred species. Traditional uses of these fruits include grinding them into flower or drying them and eating them whole. Fibers from the leaves of yuccas are woven into baskets and formed into sandals. When the roots are mashed, they releases a soapy compounds called saponins that can be used for bathing.

Fig. 4.11. *Hesperoyucca whipplei*, Asparagaceae, chaparral yucca. Photo by Naomi Fraga.

Sunflower Family (Asteraceae) Shrubs

The most diverse and ecologically significant family of woody and semi-woody shrubs in creosote bush scrub is the sunflower family (Asteraceae). This group collectively includes many of the most familiar shrubs encountered on a desert hike—whether on bajada slopes or broad, sandy alluvial plains. Globally, the Asteraceae is second only to the Orchidaceae in number of species. Unlike the orchids, which are largely tropical and subtropical in distribution, many Asteraceae are well-adapted to arid conditions.

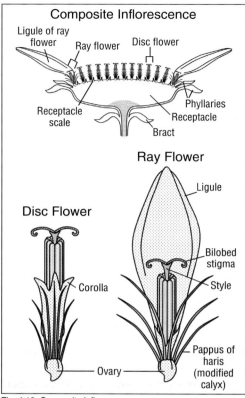

Fig. 4.12. Composite inflorescence.

Members of the Asteraceae are challenging to identify until one becomes familiar with flower structures. For that reason, a quick training is useful. The essential feature defining the Asteraceae is the presence of composite flower heads that typically include numerous tiny flowers joined in what, at first, resembles a single large flower—as seen in a familiar sunflower (Fig. 4.12). The typical composite flower head is composed of two types of flowers, although either one of these types may be absent in some genera.

The outer whorl of flowers in a typical composite head has three petals fused to form what appears to be a single large petal, while the other two petals are absent. These fused petals of the *ray* flowers, or *ligule*s, are the attractive structures for pollinators. Ray flowers are almost always only female. The inner groups of flowers are called *discoid* and consist of five tiny petals fused into a tube with radial symmetry and only their tips separated. Disk flowers typically include both male and female parts. The flower heads, which are found in the majority of species with both disk and ray flowers, are called *radiate* heads. *Discoid* heads are composed of only disk flowers and, although they lack the showy ligules, can nevertheless be colorful and effective at attracting pollinators. There are a few genera of Asteraceae where disk flowers are entirely absent. In these, all five petals fuse to form single *ligule* as a variant of typical ray flowers. In these cases, with dandelions being a familiar example, the ligulate flowers are all bisexual with both male and female organs. The presence of either radiate or discoid flower structures is a key trait in identifying members of this family.

The individual flowers within the heads of Asteraceae lack typical sepals. Instead, the organs that would give rise to sepals have been modified to scales, hairs, or bristles called the *pappus*. This pappus attaches to the single-seeded ovary and serves as a dispersal organ that readily floats through the air—or is hooked and readily attaches to the fur of animals. The plumed white parachutes of dandelions, and many bristly stickers that attach to hikers' socks, are examples of a specialized pappus. The efficiency of these structures in dispersal makes members of the Asteraceae effective colonizers of open habitats. All of this description of the flower structure of Asteraceae will be relevant again in Chapter 10, which describes desert spring annuals.

In describing the important woody shrub species of creosote bush scrub, it is appropriate to begin with bursage (*Ambrosia dumosa*). Next to creosote bush itself, it is the most abundant desert shrub species across both of our desert regions. Bursage is a low compact shrub up to 2 feet in height, with white downy branches and pubescent leaves pinnately divided twice, or even three times, into short, rounded lobes (Fig. 4.13). In summer these leaves may be so dry that it is difficult to tell whether they are alive or dead, but plants are typically drought-deciduous. Although separate male and female flowers occur on the same plant, they are arrayed in separate discoid heads. The female heads consist of only a single flower that matures to form a spiny bur that is easily caught in animal fur and dispersed. Growing together with the larger creosote bush, these species dominate the plant cover of outwash plains and lower bajada slopes over vast areas of the desert as a relatively monotonous and low-diversity shrubland. When compared to creosote bush, bursage has a lower stature and darker foliage (Fig. 4.14). There are studies indicating that creosote bush produces a chemical that inhibits the growth of bursage. Other research has suggested that bursage roots produce a chemical that causes individual plants to space themselves to reduce competition for water resources.

Fig. 4.13. *Ambrosia dumosa*, Asteraceae, bursage. Photo by Matt Berger.

Fig. 4.14. Creosote bush scrub with *Larrea tridentata* and *Ambrosia dumosa* in Mojave Trails National Monument. Photo by Julie Evens.

Next in importance in creosote scrub, because of its abundance and wide distribution, is brittlebush (*Encelia farinosa*). It is a familiar and conspicuous shrub that colors broad areas of the desert plains in the spring with its large, radiate yellow flowers. It is easily recognized as a tall shrub up to 5 feet in height, often with multiple main stems, displaying large lemon-yellow sunflowers (Fig. 4.15). As described in Chapter 3, brittlebush is a classic species for describing seasonal leaf dimorphism. The early spring leaves of brittlebush are broad and thin with a light white pubescence. As the season progresses and water stress increases, the newly produced leaves become smaller, thicker, and have an increased density of hairs on their surface. Leaves are ultimately shed under conditions of summer drought stress. A unique character of brittlebush, in comparison to its related species, is that several flower heads are born on each stem. Other *Encelia* species have just a single flower head per stem. Brittlebush frequently forms hybrids with button encelia (see below), as well as with California encelia (*Encelia californica*), in sage scrub habitats of coastal Southern California. Although it avoids higher elevations above about 3,000 feet, the range of brittlebush extends from creosote bush scrub in Death Valley across the Mojave Desert and all through the Sonoran Desert into Mexico. Over this range it shows a preference for rocky well-drained soils on south-facing slopes (Fig. 4.16).

Button encelia (*Encelia frutescens*) is a shrub of similar size and growth form to brittlebush It is easily distinguished from brittlebush when flowering because its yellow flower heads are discoid (lack ray flowers) and produce only a single flower head per stem (Fig. 4.19). It has dark green, ovate leaves with stiff hairs on the surface and young stems with white pubescence. It is moderately common in sandy washes and bajadas slopes of creosote bush scrub below about 2,500 feet in the southern Mojave Desert and throughout the Sonoran Desert. While button encelia is a drought-deciduous shrub with spring flowering in most of our desert areas, it responds to summer rains in the eastern Sonoran Desert along the Colorado River by blooming in August or September.

Fig. 4.15. *Encelia farinosa*, Asteraceae, brittlebush. Photo by Stan Shebs.

Fig. 4.16. *Encelia farinosa*, Palm Canyon trail, Coachella Valley. Photo by Robert Gustafson.

Fig. 4.17. *Encelia frutescens*, Asteraceae, button encelia. Photo by Matt Berger.

Fig. 4.18. *Encelia actoni*, Asteraceae, Acton brittlebush. Photo by Matt Berger.

Fig. 4.19. *Bahiopsis parishii*, Asteraceae, desert sunflower. Photo by Robert Gustafson.

There are two more species of encelia with more restricted ranges. Acton encelia (*Encelia actoni*) occurs in scattered areas of the western Sonoran Desert; creosote bush scrub and upland communities of the Mojave Desert; and arid areas of the southern San Joaquin Valley (Fig. 4.20). The ovate leaves are 1–1½ inches in length and covered by a fine grayish-white mat of hairs. The large radiate yellow flower heads resemble those of brittlebush but are born singly on flowering stems. Virgin River encelia (*Encelia virgenensis*) is similar in appearance to Acton encelia but has slightly smaller leaves with scattered long stiff hairs rather than a dense mat of only fine hairs and smaller ray flowers. It is largely restricted to bajadas slopes and sandy plains of the eastern Mojave Desert. All species of encelia are good colonizers of disturbed soils and thus are commonly found along roadsides and after fires.

Desert sunflower (*Bahiopsis parishii*), or Parish's golden-eye, is a widespread and common low shrub that occurs in rocky washes and at the base of canyon walls of the eastern Mojave and lower Sonoran deserts. Although seldom reaching more than 2 feet in height, it can reach 4–6 feet in diameter. It is easily recognized in spring by its broad triangular leaves and large yellow radiate flower heads (Fig. 4.19). A related species is Death Valley golden-eye (*Bahiopsis reticulata*) which is characteristic of arid bajadas in the eastern Mojave Desert. Although similar in size and general appearance, desert sunflower is distinguished from Death Valley golden-eye by a more rounded leaf shape and by prominently raised veins on the lower leaf surface. These two species were formerly placed in the genus *Viguiera*.

Another diverse group in the Asteraceae includes ten species of goldenbush (*Ericameria*) that extend into creosote bush scrub in our desert regions. Most of these are all small shrubs, generally 2–3 feet in height, but there are both taller and smaller subshrubs represented in the group as well. The genus is characterized by resinous and often glandular leaves that range from wedge-shaped, to linear or threadlike, and round in cross-section. The common name refers to the abundant gold-colored radiate flower heads that cover the canopy of goldenbush in spring.

There are two shrub species of goldenbush that are relatively common in creosote bush scrub habitats, extending upward into the lower margins of pinyon-juniper woodland. The largest of these is interior goldenbush (*Ericameria linearifolia*), which can reach to a height 5 feet (Fig. 4.20). The species name comes from the elongate linear leaves that reach 2 inches in length and are distinctly sticky to the touch. Interior goldenbush extends widely across the Mojave Desert and western Sonoran Desert where it is common in creosote bush scrub and lower elevation pinyon-juniper woodlands. It often occurs among granitic boulders and on rocky flood plains along arroyos. Cooper goldenbush (*Ericameria cooperi*) is a smaller shrub up to about 2 feet in height, with shorter linear leaves and less prominent ray flowers (Fig. 4.21). It ranges from the Little San Bernardino Mountains northward across the Mojave Desert where it is most commonly encountered on rocky slopes, gravelly washes, and bajadas in creosote bush scrub or Joshua tree woodlands. A related species, black-stem goldenbush (*Ericameria paniculata*), is common colonizer of desert washes and is described in Chapter 6. Higher elevation species typical of Great Basin habitats are described in Chapter 11.

There are two additional species of goldenbush whose primary range lies in Mediterranean-type shrublands of southern California, but which extend into the western margin of the Sonoran Desert. These are pine-bush (*Ericameria pinifolia*) with long thread-like leaves and Palmer goldenbush (*Ericameria palmeri*) with elongate linear leaves. Both of these goldenbush species are tall shrubs that can reach up to 5 feet or more in height.

Fig. 4.20. *Ericameria linearifolia*, Asteraceae, interior goldenbush. Photo by Stan Shebs.

Fig. 4.21. *Ericameria cooperi*, Asteraceae, Cooper's Goldenbush. Photo by Matt Berger.

Fig. 4.22. *Peucephyllum schottii*, Asteraceae, pygmy cedar. Photo by Matt Berger.

Fig. 4.23. *Tetradymia stenolepis*, Asteraceae, Mojave cottonthorn. Photo by Matt Berger.

Pygmy-cedar (*Peucephyllum schottii*) is a large woody shrub widely distributed throughout both our Mojave and Sonoran desert areas. It prefers rocky bajadas slopes, especially areas with boulders, in creosote bush scrub at elevations below 3,000 feet. The dark green, needle-like leaves—clustered near the ends of its branches—are shiny with resin glands giving pygmy-cedar an appearance like a conifer and hence its common name (Fig. 4.22). Its generic name is taken from the Greek for "fir leaf." Each flower head contains about 15–20 yellow disk flowers. Historical photography studies indicate that shrubs of pygmy-cedar reach ages over 100 years.

The genus *Tetradymia*, known as horsebrush or cottonthorn, includes seven species of woody desert shrubs in California—all with compact yellow to cream-colored discoid heads with a dense woolly pappus present in most species. One of these, Mojave cottonthorn (*Tetradymia stenolepis*), is widespread across the Mojave Desert on rocky bajadas in creosote bush scrub and Joshua tree woodlands (Fig. 4.23). It is a spiny shrub up to 4 feet in height. Several other horsebrush species characteristic of pinyon-juniper-woodlands and sagebrush scrub of higher elevation Great Basin communities are described in Chapter 11.

Sunflower Family (Asteraceae) Subshrubs

Communities of creosote bush scrub and Joshua tree woodlands typically include a number of prominent members of the sunflower family that are called subshrubs. These subshrubs lack perennial woody tissues except near their base, a character that separates them from woody shrubs While most of these are relatively small plants, several can nevertheless attain heights up to 5 feet despite the absence of a perennial woody canopy.

Broom snakeweed (*Gutierrezia sarothrae*) and sticky snakeweed (*Gutierrezia microcephala*) are ecologically widespread species of rounded subshrubs 1–2 feet in height . They are characterized by highly branched, thin stems with a resinous texture and aromatic smell. Both species have linear to thread-like leaves. Broom snakeweed has an extremely wide range across the western United States in both grasslands and desert habitats and is most common in our desert region in higher elevation pinyon-juniper communities (Fig. 4.24). Its abundance is often related to overgrazing or other disturbances. Sticky snakeweed is found in creosote bush scrub and Joshua tree woodlands throughout the Mojave and Sonoran deserts. Both species have small flower heads scattered in clusters over the tips of the branches. Sticky snakeweed has particularly small radiate heads with just 1–2 ray flowers and 1–2 disk flowers, while broom snakeweed has heads with up to 16 individual flowers. The foliage of snakeweeds contains chemical compounds called saponins that make leaves poisonous to livestock. Areas with high densities of snakeweed generally indicate heavy grazing by cattle that has eliminated other competing species. The common name comes from the reported use of a poultice to treat rattlesnake bites on sheep. Another common name for these species is matchweed, in reference to the highly flammable nature of the foliage.

Fig. 4.24. *Gutierrezia sarothrae*, Asteraceae, broom snakeweed. Photo by Matt Berger.

Fig. 4.25. *Acamptopappus sphaerocephalus*, Asteraceae, goldenhead. Photo by Stan Shebs.

Goldenhead (*Acamptopappus sphaerocephalus*) is a rounded subshrub reaching to about 3 feet in height (Fig. 4.25). It is common on gravelly slopes and washes in creosote bush scrub and Joshua tree woodlands over most of the Mojave Desert and northern Sonoran Desert. It has small linear leaves ¼–¾ inch in length. The discoid flower heads consisting of as many as 25 yellow disk flowers with ray flowers absent, are borne singly at the ends of each branchlet. There is a second species in this genus, Shockley gold-

Fig. 4.26. *Xylorhiza tortifolia*, Asteraceae, Mojave aster. Photo by Stan Shebs.

enhead (*Acamptopappus shockleyi*), which is a smaller subshrub, no more than 18 inches in height. It occurs on flats and washes at elevations up to 6,000 feet in the eastern Mojave Desert and north to the Inyo and White mountains. It differs in having larger radiate flower heads that include both ray and disk flowers.

Mojave aster (*Xylorhiza tortifolia*) is woody only at its base and reaches no more than 2 feet in height. It is common on bajadas slopes and sandy washes throughout the Mojave Desert—except the western margin where it is much less frequent and reaches into the northern Sonoran Desert. The linear leaves of Mojave aster, 1–4 inches in length, have a surface covered by soft hairs, a toothed margin, and white midveins. In spring the canopy of Mojave aster is covered by large pale lavender to blue radiate flower heads up to 2 inches in diameter (Fig. 4.26). Two other rare species of *Xylorhiza* form larger shrubs up to 5 feet in height in the Sonoran Desert. Mecca woody-aster (*Xylorhiza cognata*) is known only from a few canyons in and around the Mecca Hills, while Orcutt's woody-aster (*Xylorhiza orcuttii*) is known from sandy washes and canyons in scattered areas of Anza-Borrego Desert State Park and the Salton Sea basin. Both of these have a CNPS Rare Plant Rank 1B: plants rare, threatened, or endangered in California and elsewhere.

Fig. 4.27. *Porophyllum gracile*, Asteraceae, odora. Photo by Stan Shebs.

Odora (*Porophyllum gracile*), sometimes called slender pore leaf, is a small subshrub growing up to 30 inches in height in creosote bush scrub on rocky bajadas slopes and sandy washes in both our desert regions—and also into coastal shrublands of Orange and San Diego counties (Fig. 4.27). The narrowly linear leaves of odora are dotted with dark glands that give the foliage a distinctly unpleasant smell when crushed. The dense discoid flower heads have compact clusters of white to pale purple disk flowers.

There are three related subshrubs that are likewise characterized by a pungent and unpleasant odor generated from oil glands on the leaves. The first two are Cooper dyssodia (*Adenophyllum cooperi*) and San Felipe dyssodia (*Adenophyllum porophylloides*). Both have woody bases to their stems and reach to about 2 feet in height, and in spring exhibit colorful yellow to orange-red heads composed of both ray and disk flowers—although the former are few in number and occasionally absent. Cooper dyssodia is found in sandy washes and dry bajadas slopes of creosote bush scrub and Joshua tree woodlands of the central and eastern Mojave Desert, and characterized by simple, coarsely toothed leaves (Fig. 4.28). It is a good colonizer and often appears on roadsides. San Felipe dyssodia occurs on dry rock slopes of the southern Mojave and Sonoran deserts and has leaves that are deeply, pinnately divided into linear lobes.

Fig. 4.28. *Adenophyllum cooperi*, Asteraceae, Cooper dyssodia. Photo by Matt Berger.

A related plant is five-needle prickly-leaf (*Thymophylla pentachaeta*), a low subshrub reaching only 12 inches in height with many slender leafy stems (Fig. 4.29). It is found on dry slopes of creosote bush scrub and Joshua tree woodlands, as well as disturbed roadsides, of the eastern Mojave Desert. Its opposite glandular leaves are dark green in color and pinnately divided into threadlike, spine-tipped lobes. The radiate flower heads of five-needle prickly-leaf are only ½ inch in diameter, with a whorl of 13 showy yellow ray flowers. Older books placed all three of these species in the genus *Dyssodia*.

Fig. 4.29. *Thymophylla pentachaeta*, Asteraceae, five-needle prickly-leaf. Photo by Robert Gustafson.

Barely woody enough to be considered a subshrub is Fremont's chaff–bush (*Amphipappus fremontii*), with a spreading crown reaching to about 2 feet in height growing on rocky flats and bajadas slopes of the eastern and northern Mojave Desert. It has densely branched crown with many thin stiff branches and ovate leaves up to 1 inch in length (Fig. 4.30). Flowering stems display clusters of broad heads, with individual heads quite small and having the odd trait of just one or two ray flowers and 3–7 disk flowers. These heads are similar to those described above for sticky snakeweed, but the oval leaves of Fremont's chaff–bush are quite different from the linear to thread-like leaves of sticky snakeweed.

Fig. 4.30. *Amphipappus fremontii*, Asteraceae, Fremont's chaff-bush. Photo by Stan Shebs.

Arrow-leaf (*Pleurocoronis pluriseta*) is a low rounded subshrub 1–2 feet in height that is widely distributed on rocky soils of creosote bush scrub in both deserts (Fig. 4.31). The flower heads of arrow-leaf are discoid, with whitish flowers. The lower leaves are oppositely arranged and diamond-shaped with a few distinct teeth, while the upper stem leaves become more linear in form with on pairs of small teeth and alternate on the stems.

Fig. 4.31. *Pleurocoronis pluriseta*, Asteraceae, arrow-leaf. Photo by Stan Shebs. Inset by Mat Berger.

Desert Sages (Lamiaceae)

A commonly encountered and easily recognized group of drought-deciduous shrubs species of sage (*Salvia*) and the related bladder sage (*Scutellaria*). These members of the mint family are characterized by aromatic foliage and oppositely-arranged leaves. In most, but not all, species the young stems are distinctly square in cross-section. In addition to eight woody sage species in our deserts, we have two annual sages, thistle sage (*Salvia carduacea*) and chia (*Salvia columbariae*), which are discussed in Chapter 10. Another important member of the Lamiaceae is desert lavender (*Condea emoryi*), a wash plant described in Chapter 6.

There are four sage species that have ranges entirely, or largely limited to, the Mojave Desert. The most widespread Mojave Desert species are purple desert sage (*Salvia dorrii*) and Mojave sage (*Salvia mojavensis*). Purple desert sage typically has a rounded to trailing growth form reaching up to 2 feet in height, with distinct blue-gray, spoon-shaped, and densely-white-scaly foliage (Fig. 4.32). It is found at elevations above about 3,000 feet on bajada slopes and alluvial pediments in upland areas of the Mojave Desert. Its blue flowers occur in three to four whorls on each flowering stem. Mojave sage has a more upright form of growth, reaching 2–3 feet in height, and occurs widely across the Mojave Desert at elevations up to about 5,000 feet. Its foliage has only simple hairs and is much greener than those of purple desert sage. The leaves have a finely wrinkled or puckered surface. The flowers of Mojave sage are lavender, with only a single whorl present on each flowering stem.

Fig. 4.32. *Salvia dorrii*, Lamiaceae, purple desert sage. Photo by Robert Gustafson.

The most unusual of the Mojave Desert sages is Death Valley sage (*Salvia funerea*), a local endemic with a range restricted to limestone soils of Death Valley in the Amargosa and Panamint Mountains. The characteristic feature of Death Valley sage is the white appearance of its densely-branched canopy, with both leaves and stems covered by layer of woolly white hairs (Fig. 4.33). In addition, the leaves lack a significant petiole and have sharp spines around their margins. Mountain desert sage (*Salvia pachyphylla*) is a prostrate shrub found in the eastern Mojave Desert and higher desert slopes of the Transverse and Peninsular ranges at elevations of 4,000 feet and above. It often, but not invariably, grows as a mat—rooting at its nodes. The ovate leaves are

Fig. 4.33. *Salvia funerea*. Lamiaceae, Death Valley sage. Photo by Stan Shebs.

generally 1 inch or more in length, with minute hairs on both upper and lower surfaces.

There are three shrubby sage species with relatively local patterns of distribution in the Sonoran Desert. Desert sage (*Salvia eremostachya*) is an erect shrub with a range largely limited to the Santa Rosa Mountains on the western margin of the desert. A related rare species is Orocopia sage (*Salvia greatae*) which is restricted to the Orocopia and Chocolate Mountains near the Salton Sea (Fig. 4.34). It has a CNPS Rare Plant Rank 1B: plants rare, threatened, or endangered in California and elsewhere. Desert sage and Orocopia sage, both with bluish to lavender colored flowers, are easily separated by their leaf morphology. Desert sage has lance-shaped leaved edged with small, rounded teeth, while Orocopia sage has ovate leaves with sharp spines along their margins. The third species is brittle sage (*Salvia vaseyi*) which occurs on the desert slopes of the Peninsular Ranges—on the western margins of the desert. Brittle sage, more a subshrub than a truly woody shrub, has oblong to ovate leaves at the base of tall wand-like branches with white flowers above. The leaves are densely covered with fine hairs, giving them a white to gray-green color.

Fig. 4.34. *Salvia greatae*, Lamiaceae, Orocopia sage. Photo by Robert Gustafson.

Bladder sage (*Scutellaria mexicana*) appears much like a sage species but with a flower structure that separates it into a different genus. Additionally, bladder sage does not exhibit the square stems of most members of the mint family. While the foliage is strongly aromatic it lacks the minty smell of the true sages. Bladder sage is found commonly on sandy to gravelly slopes and washes in creosote bush scrub and Joshua tree woodlands throughout the Mojave Desert and mountain slopes of the Sonoran Desert. Although it may reach to 4 feet in height, the canopy structure of bladder sage is open, with a distinctive pattern of stems diverging at right angles from larger branches (Fig. 4.35). The small, ovate leaves have short petioles or even appear to be sessile on the stems. The large flowers, sparsely arrayed, have a white to light purple upper lip and purple lower lip. Bladder sage however, is most distinctive in the late spring when its developing fruits form in flated bag-like structures—an inch in diameter—which resemble papery bladders. These structures have led to another common name, paper-bag bush.

Fig. 4.35. *Scutellaria mexicana*, Lamiaceae, bladder sage. Photo by Stan Shebs.

Spiny Boxthorns (Solanaceae)

A distinctive group of spiny shrubs in our deserts are the boxthorns in the genus *Lycium* within the tomato family. The boxthorns comprise a group of about 90 species distributed across arid and subtropical habitats on each of the major continents of the world—with about 20 species in North America. Seven of these occur in our California deserts. The boxthorns are typically woody shrubs with a rigid structure of divaricately branched spiny stems. This means that smaller branches diverge at right angles from the larger branches—making the shrub canopy undesirable to most grazers. Boxthorn leaves, with a few exceptions as described below, are small and fleshy and drought-deciduous, losing their leaves in summer and regrowing them the following spring. Although bitter in taste, boxthorn berries provide an important food for wildlife and humans alike.

The separation of boxthorn species is quite difficult as the identification keys of floras typically requires one to have both fresh flowers and fruits at the same time. The most widespread and commonly encountered species of these is Anderson boxthorn (*Lycium andersonii*), which occurs widely across our desert areas on gravelly or rocky slopes flats and slopes, with habitats ranging from creosote bush scrub up into pinyon-juniper woodlands. It is also found in scattered locations in the arid areas of the southern San Joaquin Valley and desert slopes of the Transverse Ranges and extends eastward in the Great Basin. Anderson boxthorn is commonly 3–5 feet in height but can reach as tall as 8 feet (Fig. 4.36). It has small fleshy leaves usually less than ½ inch in length that are hairless, and thus generally pale greenish in color.

Fig. 4.36. *Lycum andersonii*, Solanaceae, Anderson boxthorn. Photo by Robert Gustafson.

Also common in creosote bush scrub, and widely distributed, is rabbit thorn or pale wolfberry (*Lycium pallidum*)—another spiny shrub of similar size to Anderson boxthorn. It occurs at low to moderate elevations across the western and northern Mojave Desert and south into the northern margin of the Sonoran Desert. It also extends far eastward into the Great Basin and Chihuahuan deserts. The semi-evergreen leaves of rabbit thorn, 1–2 inches in length, are clustered around short spines that have a waxy covering that gives them a pale gray-green color. The ¾ inch bell-shaped flowers, lavender to white in color, droop from short stalks in spring. The significance of rabbit thorn to Native Americans in the American Southwest is suggested by stands of rabbit thorn frequently associated with ancient Anasazi ruins in the Four Corners area of the Southwestern United States. Apparently, the soil floors of abandoned pueblo sites are a favorable habitat for seeds that were dropped by the Anasazi when gathering the fruits.

A third common species of *Lycium* is peach thorn (*Lycium cooperi*) which is widely distributed across the Mojave Desert and into the northern margins of the Sonoran Desert on rocky soils of bajadas slopes, flats, arroyos, and canyon bottoms (Fig. 4.37). It is found in creosote bush scrub, Joshua tree woodlands, and up into lower elevations of pinyon-juniper woodland. Distinctive characters of peach thorn, separating it from our other species, is the egg-shaped form of the green fruits, compared to red or purple with a spherical shape in most species.

Fig. 4.37. *Lycium cooperi*, Solanaceae, peach boxthorn. Photo by Robert Gustafson.

There are two species of boxthorn that are largely restricted to the lower Sonoran Desert. Desert thorn (*Lycium brevipes*) is an interesting coastal-desert disjunct—with most of its range in the western half of the Sonoran Desert and scattered coastal populations at sites such as San Clemente and Santa Catalina islands and the Palos Verdes Peninsula (Fig. 4.38). Fremont desert thorn (*Lycium fremontii*) is found on flats and alkaline soils of the Salton Sea basin and Colorado River corridor (Fig. 4.39). It has elongate floral tubes, violet flower color, and finely pubescent leaves. Parish's boxthorn (*Lycium parishii*) is a relatively rare species found on sandy to rocky slopes and canyons of the western Sonoran Desert (CNPS Rare Plant Rank 1B: plants rare, threatened, or endangered in California and elsewhere). Torrey wolfberry (*Lycium torreyi*) is a species found along washes and streambanks of the southern Mojave and Sonoran deserts.

Fig. 4.38. *Lycium brevipes*, Solanaceae, desert boxthorn. Photo by Robert Gustafson.

Fig. 4.39. *Lycium fremontii*, Solanaceae, Fremont desert boxthorn. Photo by Robert Gustafson.

Legume (Fabaceae) Shrubs and Subshrubs

The legume family, or Fabaceae, forms an important group of desert plants which exhibit a wide range of growth forms. One important group are those with ephemeral annual or herbaceous perennial life histories, many of which are described in Chapter 10. Another group includes woody shrubs and trees typical of desert washes or wash woodlands described in Chapter 6, some of which are also be found in sandy soils of creosote bush scrub and Joshua tree woodlands.

There are several shrubby legumes that are widespread components of creosote bush scrub. These include five species of indigo bush in the genus *Psorothamnus*. A sixth species in this genus with an arboreal form of growth, smoke tree (*Psorothamnus spinosus*), is described in Chapter 6. All shrubby species of indigo bush are intricately branched with most having spinescent branches. They are also characterized by glandular foliage with a distinctive odor that is quite persistent on one's hand if you crush the foliage. The name indigo bush comes from its traditional use as a blue dye that is extracted from the plants. Two other related genera of legumes, *Amorpha* and *Dalea*, are also called indigo bush. The latter are herbaceous desert species which are described in Chapter 6.

Three species of indigo bush are largely restricted to the Mojave Desert in their California distribution. Mojave indigo bush (*Psorothamnus arborescens*) and Fremont indigo bush (*Psorothamnus fremontii*) are closely related. Both are shrubs reaching to 3 feet in height and possess blue-purple flowers that are pea-like in appearance and extend in a cluster 2 inches or more in length. Both are found in creosote bush scrub, Joshua tree woodland, and occasionally in higher elevation Great Basin communities. Mojave indigo bush is gray-green in color with a light covering of hairs with fruits that possess scattered, large glands over their surface (Fig. 4.40). Fremont indigo bush has silvery foliage and stems due to long straight hairs that cover their surface. Its fruits differ in having many small glands arranged in rows. Although Fremont indigo bush has its primary range of occurrence in the eastern Mojave Desert, it has a variety that extends into lower elevations of the eastern Sonoran Desert.

Nevada indigo bush (*Psorothamnus polydenius*) is a widely branched shrub that reaches 5 feet in height. It occurs in creosote bush scrub and Joshua tree woodlands of the eastern Mojave Desert, often in sandy washes and dune habitats. Its stems are only mildly hairy and spotted with large glands—giving it an alternate common name of spotted indigo bush (Fig. 4.41). The flowers of Nevada indigo bush are pale rose to lavender and are restricted to short tight clusters.

Scott indigo bush (*Psorothamnus schottii*) and Emory indigo bush (*Psorothamnus emoryi*) are the two legume shrubs with a Sonoran Desert distribution. Scott indigo bush has the distinctive feature of simple linear leaves lacking in leaflets (Fig. 4.42). Only smoke tree shares this trait among California species of *Psorothamnus*. It occurs as a large woody shrub 4–6 feet in height on bajadas slopes and sandy washes in creosote bush scrub at low elevations in the Sonoran Desert. Scott indigo bush has gray-green foliage that is either hairless or with scattered long hairs. In contrast, Emory indigo bush has leaves and stems that are whitish due to a thick matt of hairs that cover their surface. It favors desert flats, sandy washes, and dunes in creosote bush scrub at lower elevations of the Sonoran Desert and into the southern Mojave Desert. It generally forms a broad shrub no more than 3 feet in height but twice as wide with purple flowers dotted with white. In addition to the scent present in all of the species of indigo bush, the foliage of Emory indigo bush will stain one's hands a saffron color.

Although not a legume or a shrub, this is an appropriate time to mention Thurber's pilostyles (*Pilostyles thurberi*, Apodanthaceae), an unusual parasitic plant which is only know in California. As a parasite on indigo bush, particularly Emory indigo bush in areas of the Salton Sea basin, Apodanthaceae is a small tropical family of specialized parasitic plants that attach themselves to legumes. The entire vegetative tissues of *Pilostyles* are filamentous structures that grow within the stems. Flower buds develop internally and eventually break through the stems to appear in the open air (Fig. 4.43). Otherwise, this plant is entirely invisible. Individual flowers are either male or female and it is expected that each sex occurs on a different plant. Virtually nothing is known about the manner of pollination or dispersal of these strange little parasites.

Another semi-woody legume in our deserts is desert rock pea (*Acmispon rigida*), a species formerly known as *Lotus rigidus*. The California species formerly in the genus *Lotus* have now been transferred to *Acmispon* and *Hosackia*—formerly ranked as subgenera. Desert rock pea is common in desert flats and washes of creosote bush scrub, Joshua tree woodland, and lower elevations of pinyon-juniper woodlands in both of our desert regions. This is a low sprawling subshrub about 2 feet in height, with small leaves with 3–5 pinnately arrayed leaflets (Fig. 4.44). Large yellow pea-like flowers about ¾ inch in length are clustered in groups of 2–3 at the ends of long stems.

Fig. 4.40. *Psorothamnus arborescens*, Fabaceae, California indigo bush. Photo by Matt Berger.

Fig. 4.41. *Psorothamnus polydenius*, Fabaceae, Nevada indigo bush. Photo by Stan Shebs.

Fig. 4.43. *Pilostyles thurberi*, Apodanthaceae, Thurber's pilostyles. Photo by Robert Gustafson.

Fig. 4.42. *Psorothamnus schottii*, Fabaceae, Scott indigo bush. Photo by Matt Berger.

Fig. 4.44. *Acmispon rigida*, Fabaceae, desert rock pea. Photo by Matt Berger.

Chenopods (Chenopodiaceae)

Woody species of the Chenopodiaceae are common in cold desert regions and often associated with alkaline soils. Species of saltbush (*Atriplex*) form a widespread group of chenopods typically associated with alkaline soils and saline habitats. However, two species of saltbush may occur in creosote bush scrub and Joshua tree woodlands. These are allscale (*Atriplex polycarpa*) and desert holly (*Atriplex hymenelytra*), which are described in Chapter 8. Several other genera of woody chenopods frequently occur in creosote bush scrub and Joshua tree woodland.

Winterfat (*Krascheninnikovia lanata*) is a widespread and common shrub in a range of habitats above about 2,000 feet from creosote bush scrub and Joshua tree woodlands up to higher elevations in pinyon-juniper woodlands, blackbrush scrub, and shadscale scrub. (Chapter 11). Winterfat has an erect growth form 1–3 feet in height with of narrow leaves up to 2 inches in length arrayed in bundles along upright stems (Fig. 4.45). A distinctive feature of winter fat are the densely covered white star-shaped hairs that turn rust-colored with age. Like many other members of the chenopod family, male and female flowers are borne separately but, with winterfat, this happens on separate portions of the branches rather than on separate plants. The male flowers are arrayed in spike-like clusters at the top of the stems while female flowers are clustered in the leaf axils below. Because the leaves are palatable to grazing animals, winter fat is an important browse in winter.

Fig. 4.45. *Krascheninnikovia lanata*, Chenopodiaceae, winterfat. Photo by Matt Berger.

Fig. 4.46. *Grayia spinosa*, Chenopodiaceae, hopsage. Photo by Robert Gustafson.

Another common chenopod ranging across Mojave creosote bush scrub and Joshua tree woodlands up into pinyon-juniper woodland and shadscale scrub is hopsage (*Grayia spinosa*). Although it may be found in a diversity of communities over a broad elevational range, from 1,800–9,000 feet, it favors areas with alkaline soils. Hopsage is a woody shrub up to 3 feet in height with distinctive, gray-striped bark and small twigs that harden into spines (Fig. 4.46). The leaves, described as mealy to slightly succulent in texture, are ½–1½ inch in length and oblanceolate— meaning that they are elongate ovals with the widest portion near the tip. Male and female flowers occur on separate plants.

Blazing Star/Sandpaper Plant Family (Loasaceae)

Our desert regions are home to a group of small shrubs in the blazing star family, or Loasaceae. A family trait is the presence of well-developed, stiff hairs along the stem and leaf surfaces. These hairs allow stems to readily stick to clothing, giving rise to the name velcro plants. Three of our species share the common name, sandpaper plant. This name comes from the numerous, stiff and barbed hairs that cover the leaf surface—giving them a texture like that of sandpaper.

Thurber sandpaper plant (*Petalonyx thurberi*) is a low rounded shrub up to 3 feet in height that is widely distributed in open sandy or gravelly flats of creosote bush scrub and sandy washes at elevations up to about 3,900 feet over both of our desert regions. The triangular- to diamond-shaped leaves are up to 1 inch in length but may be linear on the upper portion of branches (Fig. 4.47). They lack a distinct petiole and have a dull, gray-green appearance. The white- to yellowish-flowers are arrayed in dense spikes at the end of short branches. Death Valley sandpaper plant (*Petalonyx thurberi* subsp. *gilmanii*) is a species with a range limited to sandy washes and dunes in the area of Death Valley. It differs from the typical subspecies in having relatively soft hairs on the leaves and stems with a felt-like texture. It has a CNPS Rare Plant Rank 1B: plants rare, threatened, or endangered in California and elsewhere.

Shiny-leaf sandpaper plant (*Petalonyx nitidus*) is a low subshrub, generally no more than 18 inches in

Fig. 4.47. *Petalonyx thurberi*, Loasaceae, shiny-leaf sandpaper plant. Photo by Robert Gustafson.

Fig. 4.48. *Petalonyx nitidus*, Loasaceae, shiny-leaf sandpaper plant. Photo by Stan Shebs.

height, that is found at elevations above 3,200 feet in creosote bush scrub, Joshua tree woodlands, and pinyon-juniper woodlands in the mountains of the eastern and northern Mojave Desert. It differs from the larger Thurber sandpaper plant in having larger shiny ovate leaves with prominent petioles (Fig. 4.48). Another less common species of sandpaper plant occurs in our deserts. Linear-leaf sandpaper plant (*Petalonyx linearis*) is found in sandy washes and open sandy to gravelly flats of creosote bush scrub at elevations below about 3,200 feet in the Sonoran Desert and southeastern Mojave Desert. It is a shrub reaching 3 feet in height, with narrow typically linear leaves whose margins lack the stiff hairs of the main leaf surface It has a CNPS Rare Plant Rank 2B: plants rare, threatened, or endangered in California and elsewhere.

Rock nettle (*Eucnide urens*) is a close relative of sandpaper plant, but one with a much more sinister characteristic of its hairs. This subshrub ranges from 1–3 feet in height with gray-green ovate leaves (Fig. 4.49). The stiff hairs on the foliage of rock nettle are hollow and positioned above a glandular sack of toxic chemicals. Although unrelated to stinging nettle, the mechanism is much the same. Brushing the leaves or stems of rock nettle pushed the hollow hairs into the chemical sack, producing a painful skin blister. Although stinging hairs occur in several plant families and in other members of the Loasaceae, this is the only member of our flora with this trait. Rock nettle is most common at lower elevations of the eastern and northern Mojave Desert on cliff faces and washes with available moisture.

Fig. 4.49. *Eucnide urens*, Loasaceae, rock nettle. Photo by Robert Gustafson.

Rose Family (Rosaceae)

Although a large and important family in California, species of Rosaceae are not common in the arid conditions of the Mojave and Sonoran Deserts. However, several woody shrub species are present and form important community elements of the higher elevation pinyon-juniper woodlands of the eastern Mojave Desert, as described in Chapter 11. Three woody species of *Prunus* occur in our warm desert region with largely non-overlapping ranges. These all share the trait of being large woody shrubs with rigid branches that become spinescent with age, and winter deciduous leaves.

Desert peach (*Prunus andersonii*) is found in creosote bush scrub and pinyon-juniper woodlands at elevations of about 3,000–8,500 feet in the mountains of the northern Mojave Desert as well as the eastern Sierra Nevada and Great Basin. It is a woody shrub reaching to 6 feet in height, with oval clustered leaves with finely toothed margins and pinkish-red flowers (Fig. 4.50). Desert apricot (*Prunus fremontii*) is restricted to creosote bush scrub and pinyon-juniper woodlands of the western Sonoran Desert and adjacent Peninsular Ranges at elevations up to about 4,000 feet. It is a heavily branched shrub up to 12 feet in height, with rounded leaves with finely saw-toothed edges and reddish to salmon-colored flowers (Fig. 4.51). Desert apricot has a small range, extending from California only into northern Baja California.

Fig. 4.50. *Prunus andersonii*, Rosaceae, desert peach. Photo by Robert Gustafson.

The third species, desert almond (*Prunus fasciculata*), favors open wash habitats within creosote bush scrub, Joshua tree woodland, and pinyon-juniper woodlands of the Mojave Desert and western and northern margins of the Sonoran Desert at elevations of about 2,300–7,200 feet. It reaches 4–6 feet in height, with small narrow leaves and white flowers, and is described and pictured in Chapter 6.

Fig. 4.51. *Prunus fremontii*, Rosaceae, desert apricot. Photo by Robert Gustafson.

Hibiscus Family (Malvaceae)

Apricot mallow (*Sphaeralcea ambigua*) is a perennial subshrub widely distributed on sandy flats and bajadas slopes in creosote bush scrub and Joshua tree woodlands of both of our desert regions. Like other Malvaceae, apricot mallow has characteristic broad, three-lobed leaves with scalloped margins and wand-like clusters of showy orange-red flowers (Fig. 4.52). The flower structure is typical of the hibiscus family with multiple stamens fused into a tube surrounding the stigma. The foliage and stems are densely covered by cream-colored star-shaped (*stellate*) hairs. Although only woody at its base, apricot mallow can reach anywhere from 1–4 feet in height. It is widespread in cultivation.

Pink velvet mallow (*Horsfordia alata*) is another subshrub in the mallow family that is recognized by large pink flowers borne singly from the leaf axils. It is characterized by the presence of dense, stiff, stellate hairs on the stems and broad, ovate leaves (Fig. 5.53). Although only woody at the base, it reaches to 5–10 feet in height. It has a relatively restricted range in creosote bush scrub and washes of the lower Sonoran Desert. A closely related species present in the same habitat and range is the somewhat less woody *Horsfordia newberryi* with yellow flowers.

Fig. 4.52. *Sphaeralcea ambigua*, Malvaceae, apricot mallow. Photo by Robert Gustafson.

Fig. 4.53. *Horsfordia alata*, Malvaceae, pink velvet mallow. Photo by Joey Santore.

Mustard Family (Brassicaceae)

The mustard family is generally characterized as herbaceous and several members of this family are described in Chapter 10. There are three species, however, that are subshrubs. Two of these are prince's plume (*Stanleya pinnata*) and Panamint plume (*Stanleya elata*)—both exhibiting tall flowering shoots that reach 5 feet or more in height. The effect of the flowering is enhanced by long stamens that extend well beyond the length of the petals in individual flowers. Prince's plume, with lower stem leaves having entire or toothed margins, is a widespread species found in washes from low elevations to pinyon-juniper woodlands across the Mojave Desert and the Great Basin (Fig. 4.54). Panamint plume, with deeply lobed lower stem leaves, has a more restricted range in washes and rocky slopes within Joshua tree woodlands and pinyon-juniper woodlands of the northern Mojave Desert and White mountains. Both species favor soils with high selenium contents and concentrate this element in their tissues, making them toxic to grazing animals.

Fig. 4.54. *Stanleya pinnata*, Brassicaceae, Prince's pluma. Photo by Stan Shebs.

The third species of woody Brassicaceae is desert peppergrass (*Lepidium fremontii*), a densely branched semi-woody species that reaches up to 3–4 feet in height. While inconspicuous when dormant, desert peppergrass is highly conspicuous in the spring with masses of small white flowers produced in branched leafy clusters (Fig. 4.55). One indication of its position in the mustard family is gained by crushing the leaves which give off a smell of cabbage or broccoli. Desert peppergrass is found widely on sandy flats and rocky slopes of creosote bush scrub and Joshua tree woodlands across both of our desert regions.

Fig. 4.55. *Lepidium fremontii*, Brassicaceae, desert peppergrass. Photos by Joey Santore.

A Mix of Other Shrubs and Subshrubs

There are several additional important woody shrub species in scattered families that are common in creosote bush scrub and Joshua tree woodlands. Turpentine broom (*Thamnosma montana*) is a low shrub with distinctive yellow-green bark dotted with glands and spine-tipped stems (Fig. 4.56). It is widely distributed across both our desert regions in creosote bush scrub, and occasionally higher elevation communities. The leaves are small and ephemeral, giving the upright stems a broom-like appearance and making stem photosynthesis the primary mode of carbon fixation. Turpentine bush may, at first, seem as if it is a miniature species of *Ephedra*, but the aromatic scent of the stems will clearly identify it. The foliage has a smell like turpentine, and this trait with its branch structure, gave rise to its common name. Extracts of the foliage are traditionally used as a blood purifier and for treatment of gonorrhea. Turpentine broom is our only desert member of the citrus family or Rutaceae—largely a tropical group.

Two of our usual desert shrubs are pima rhatany (*Krameria erecta*) and white rhatany (*Krameria bicolor*). These members of the small family Krameriaceae is comprised of only a single genus with unusual ecological and morphological traits. These species were formerly known as *Krameria parviflora* and *K. grayi*, respectively. Both of our species of rhatany are highly branched shrubs reaching up to 3 feet in height. Pima rhatany is characterized by gray-green erect branches—the source of its species name—and blunt-tipped stems (Fig. 4.57). White rhatany is named for the whitish reflective hairs that cover its leaves and young stems. It is also distinguished from pima rhatany by its spreading, rather than erect, branch structure and spine-tipped stems.

Fig. 4.56. *Thamnosma montana*, Rutaceae, turpentine broom. Photo by Robert Gustafson.

Fig. 4.57. *Krameria erecta*, Krameriaceae, pima rhatany. Photo by Robert Gustafson.

Fig. 4.58. *Fagonia laevis*, Zygophyllaceae, California fagonia. Photo by Stan Shebs.

Fig. 4.59. *Crossosoma bigelovii*, Crossosomataceae, Bigelow crossosoma. Photo by Matt Berger.

The floral structure of the rhatanies is quite odd and hard to discern at first glance. What appear to be the five petals of the deep purple to rose-colored flowers—arranged with bilateral symmetry much like that of legume flowers—are actually sepals. The petals of rhatany have been reduced to three small upright flags positioned above the center of the flower and two glands along the ovary. These glands secrete an oil that is collected by pollinating bees. An unexpected aspect of their ecology is that rhatany species are root parasites, at least when young, tapping into the root systems of associated perennials like creosote bush. Rhatany species are hemiparasites as they retain chlorophyll and active photosynthesis in their leaves and young stems. Rhatany leaves are small and scattered on the stems of both species, making stem photosynthesis an important aspect of their carbon budget. While the range of white rhatany overlaps with that of pima rhatany across the lower elevation Mojave and Sonoran deserts and on to Texas, it prefers creosote bush scrub on lower bajadas slopes and sandy flats.

The Zygophyllaceae, the same family as creosote bush, is home to California fagonia (*Fagonia laevis*) a small shrub up to three feet in height that is widespread at elevations below 2,000 feet, most notably in the Sonoran Desert area. The intricate branching architecture and semi-succulent stems, along with purple flowers in spring, make this species easy to recognize (Fig. 4.58). A second species, sticky fagonia (*Fagonia pachyacantha*), is a prostrate perennial with glandular hairs on the semi-succulent stems. It is restricted to the lower elevation Sonoran Desert in California.

Bigelow crossosoma (*Crossosoma bigelovii*) is a large shrub, 3–5 feet in height, that occurs is scattered locations of creosote bush scrub across the lower elevations of the Mojave and Sonoran deserts. It is characterized by intricately divided thorn-tipped branches with clusters of small drought-deciduous gray-green leaves (Fig. 4.59). Each inflorescence consists of a single white to purple-tinged flower up to a ½ inch in diameter and with a prominently constricted base. This species is a member of the small family Crossosomataceae which consists of just four genera and seven species. The only other member of this genus is California crosossoma (*Crossosoma californica*) which occurs on the southern California Channel Islands and one site on the Palos Verdes Peninsula.

An interesting desert shrub species that most people know by name but have not seen growing in its natural habitat is jojoba (*Simmondsia chinensis*)—a robust evergreen shrub that reaches as much as 6 feet or more in height (Fig. 4.60). Jojoba

Fig. 4.60. *Simmondsia chinensis* (female plant), Buxaceae, jojoba. Photo by Robert Gustafson.

Fig. 4.61. *Eriogonum fasciculatum* var. *polifolium*, Polygonaceae, desert buckwheat. Photo by Robert Gustafson.

Fig. 4.62. *Peritoma arborea*, Capparidaceae, bladderpod. Photo by Robert Gustafson.

is locally common on dry bajadas slopes of creosote bush scrub and Joshua tree woodlands of the Sonoran Desert and extends its range into Baja California and western Arizona. Jojoba is easily recognized by its simple gray-green leaves, 1–2 inches in length, that are arrayed in opposite pairs along the stems. Jojoba has separate male and female plants, and it is the female plants that produce a thick-walled capsule that contains jojoba oil—which is more precisely a liquid wax. Jojoba oil is widely used in cosmetics, shampoos, and body oils.

California buckwheat (*Eriogonum fasciculatum*), a familiar plant in the sage scrub of southern California, has a variety that occurs commonly and abundantly in creosote bush scrub and Joshua tree woodlands—and less so in pinyon-juniper woodland of the Mojave Desert and western Sonoran Desert. Desert populations of California buckwheat are low, spreading shrubs 2–3 feet in height, much like the coastal populations. The desert form is the variety *polifolium*, which differs from the coastal variety in having leaves with hairs on their upper surface (Fig. 4.61).

Bladderpod (*Peritoma arborea*) is an erect, highly branched shrub up to 6 feet in height with distinctive evergreen leaves having three equal-sized leaflets and a pungent and somewhat unpleasant smell (Fig. 4.62). The compounds producing these smells are mustard oils which are characteristic of the caper family (Capparidaceae) in which bladderpod is placed. The name bladderpod comes from the inflated capsules, 1–2 inches in length, which surround the developing seeds. The distribution pattern of bladderpod is unusual as it is common in sage scrub communities along the coast of southern California and shows up again in creosote bush scrub and Joshua tree woodland in the western portions of the Mojave and Sonoran Deserts.

Spiny menodora (*Menodora spinescens*) is a low shrubby member of the olive family, or Oleaceae, that might be viewed—at first impression—as a small version of a buckthorn (*Lycium*). It is a low shrub 1–3 feet in height with intricate stout branches that become very spiny with age. It has clusters of small fleshy leaves that are absent much of the year, and green stems that exhibit at least low rates of stem

Fig. 4.63. *Menodora spinescens*, Oleaceae, spiny menodora. Photo by Robert Gustafson.

photosynthesis (Fig. 4.63). Spiny menodora is a species of the higher elevations of the eastern Mojave Desert, occurring in Joshua tree woodlands, mixed scrub, blackbrush scrub, and shadscale scrub.

Desert Gymnosperms

An unusual group of woody plants in our desert region are the species of *Ephedra*. *Ephedra* species are an ancient group but widespread in arid regions around the world—particularly in cold desert and arid mountain systems. While most species are woody shrubs, the group also includes woody vines and small trees. What makes this group so unusual is that they are not flowering plants but instead gymnosperms, with their closest relatives being the conifers. An interesting adaptive trait of ephedras is that they have evolved an efficient water transport system in their xylem consisting of vessel elements (open tubes) and these structures are key to their ecological success in arid regions. This water transport system is much like the vessels present in flowering plants but has evolved totally independently. In contrast, conifers have a water transport system using fiber tracheids, a much less efficient structure of living cells.

Euro-American settlers of the western United States brewed a medicinal tea from *Ephedra*, giving rise to the name Mormon-tea. The basis for the effects of the tea lies with ephedrine and pseudoephedrine, which are alkaloids present in *Ephedra*. These compounds have stimulant and decongestant qualities and are related chemically to amphetamines. Although extracts of these compounds were once widely used in dietary supplements and as an appetite suppressant, these uses are restricted in over-the-counter sales because of adverse effects from high doses.

Fig. 4.64. *Ephedra californica* (male), Ephedraceae, California ephedra. Photo by Christian Schwarz.

Fig. 4.65. *Ephedra funerea*, Ephedraceae, Death Valley ephedra. Photo by Morgan Stickrod.

Our seven native species of *Ephedra* in California are all woody shrubs that have a broom-like appearance—with jointed stems and leaves reduced to triangular scales at the nodes. As gymnosperms, there are no flowers. The cones are borne in the axils of the nodes, which occur on separate male and female plants. It is difficult, at first, to separate our species of ephedra, but with practice they can be distinguished. The first trait to look for is the number of scale-leaves and or cones at each node. Four of our species have these arrayed in groups of three. The most common of these is California ephedra or desert tea (*Ephedra californica*), which is a wide-ranging species found in broad washes below about 3,600 feet throughout both the Mojave and Sonoran Deserts—as well as extending to scattered areas of Mediterranean-type shrublands in southern California (FIg. 4.64). The young stems of California ephedra are yellow-green and the leaf bases are deciduous, and thus shed when the leaves senesce. Similar in appearance is Death Valley ephedra (*Ephedra funerea*), which likewise occurs in creosote bush scrub but is largely restricted to the eastern and northern Mojave Desert at elevations up to about 5,000 feet (Fig. 4.65). It differs from California ephedra in having a symmetrical rounded canopy shape, gray-green young stems, and persistent leaf bases that form a black, thickened collar where they were positioned on the nodes. Both California ephedra and Death Valley ephedra have stems which are blunt rather than sharp at the branch tips. This character separates them from the third species, longleaf ephedra (*Ephedra trifurca*), with rigid spine-like tips to the stems. It has a broad range extending to the Chihuahuan Desert but is relatively uncommon in California where it is largely restricted to sandy soils and low dunes in the southeastern Sonoran Desert (Fig. 4.66). A fourth species with scale-leaves in groups of three is *Ephedra torreyana*, a species that barely enters California at higher elevations in the eastern Mojave.

The second group of ephedra species is formed of those with pairs of leaves at each node. The first of these is boundary ephedra (*Ephedra aspera*), which has a scattered occurrence on rocky slopes and sandy flats of creosote bush scrub and Joshua tree woodlands in both desert areas (Fig. 4.67). It has dark green young stems, and persistent leaves that are not shed with drought. Earlier treatments described another species, *Ephedra fasciculata*, as distinct but this is now included within the concept of boundary ephedra. The remaining two species have pairs of leaves that are deciduous, although the leaf base may be persistent. Nevada ephedra (*Ephedra nevadensis*) is a common and widespread species in creosote bush scrub and Joshua tree woodlands across the Mojave and northern Sonoran deserts, extending into arid sites in the Sierra Nevada (Fig. 4.68). It is characterized by pale

Fig. 4.66. *Ephedra trifurca*, Ephedraceae, longleaf ephedra. Photo by Matt Berger. Inset by Jim Andre.

Fig. 4.67. *Ephedra aspera*, Ephedraceae, boundary ephedra. Photo by Matt Berger. Inset by Jon Rebman.

or gray-green young stems and has branches diverge at almost right angles from the major stems. Green ephedra (*Ephedra viridis*) occurs in the upper elevations of creosote bush scrub in the Mojave Desert but is more characteristic of pinyon-juniper woodlands of the desert mountains and Great Basin. Green ephedra has bright green to yellow-green young twigs and deciduous leaves with persistent gray leaf bases.

Fig. 4.68. *Ephedra nevadensis*, Ephedraceae, Nevada ephedra. Photo by Matt Berger. Inset by Tim Messick.

Chapter 5
Cactus and Succulent Scrub

California barrel cactus (*Ferocactus cylindraceus*) and teddy bear cholla (*Cylindropuntia bigelovii*) along the Banner Grade, California. Photo by Morgan Stickrod.

Introduction

Dry desert slopes and rocky upper bajadas of the Sonoran Desert often nurture a diverse assemblage of cacti and other succulent plants. While creosote bush is generally present in such stands, the dominance of cacti makes these areas distinct. Such stands are common on the desert slopes of the San Jacinto, Santa Rosa, and Laguna mountains, as well as along the south-facing slopes of the Little San Bernardino, Chocolate, and Chuckwalla mountains. Cactus species are certainly widespread in the Mojave Desert, but generally lack the abundance in individual stands that is common in the lower elevations of the Sonoran Desert.

Rocky bajadas and pediment slopes share the characteristic of coarse, well-drained and shallow soils. This favors the survival and ecological success of succulent plant species (Fig. 5.1). Succulents with shallow root systems have the ability to quickly exploit even light rains. Rocky soils not only promote rapid infiltration by rainwater but also provide favorable microclimate conditions for water absorption by root masses that form under and around the rocks themselves. Similar to the phenomenon in a home garden where large masses of roots form under rocks, one can observe this in desert plant roots entwined around rocks by excavating a small area after spring rains. Fine-textured soils which retain moisture do not favor succulents because they are susceptible to soil fungal pathogens.

Fig. 5.1. Cactus scrub in the Granite Mountains, highlighted by silver cholla. Photo by Michael Kauffmann.

Cacti (Cactaceae)

Cacti represent an iconic component of California's desert landscapes as well as more broadly across many semi-arid and arid regions in both North and South America. The cactus family is a species-rich group containing about 125 genera and 1,800 species. Although the cactus flora of California is large, it is less diverse than the Sonoran Desert area of Arizona and far less rich than the Chihuahuan Desert of Mexico.

Most of the dominant succulent species in cactus scrub communities in California are in the once-much-larger genus *Opuntia*. The opuntioid cacti of North and South America include about 200 species with diverse appearances. This has led plant taxonomists to divide the genus into distinctive groups now recognized as new genera. Our 22 species in California, including two stabilized hybrids, fall into three groups. The first of these are chollas, placed in *Cylindropuntia*, and include species with a rounded cross-section and a distinctive papery sheath around the spines. A second group, with a rounded cross-sections of the stems but lacking the papery sheath around the spines, forms the genus *Grusonia*. The prickly-pears, with flattened stems and a papery sheath around the spines, remain as the genus *Opuntia*. Regardless of the classification, all of our species of opuntia (in the broad sense) share the trait of primary spines with a barbed tip, which easily hooks into flesh. If one carefully grips the lower end of a major opuntia spine away from the tip and pulls gently, it will detach a papery layer that covers each spine.

Brushing a prickly-pear or cholla cactus will often result in the painful attachment of numerous spines, often with a stem joint attached. These spines are best removed from the skin by sliding a comb beneath the joint and flicking the joint away quickly. The spines themselves deter herbivores, but the combined presence of hooked spines and easily detachable joints provides an example of the evolution of an animal dispersal system. These detachable joints, most notably in cholla species, provide an effective means of vegetative reproduction that is important for ecological success and geographic distribution.

Beyond the problems of the major barbed spines, another unpleasant lesson is avoided by carefully noting the tiny hair-like spines at the base of the primary spines in prickly-pear species. These spines, called glochids, are barely visible to the naked eye. When a prickly-pear joint (fruit) is handled, the glochids readily embed themselves and defiantly resist removal. Unlike the primary spines, which clearly deter herbivores and aid in dispersal of cholla joints, it is unclear what role the glochids play.

Perhaps the best known of the cactus species in the cactus scrub community is the teddy-bear cholla (*Cylindropuntia bigelovii*). This is a relatively tall cactus, 3–6 feet in height, with a primary stem (Fig. 5.2). Despite the implication of its common name, which suggests a softness of form, the hooked spines grab any object that comes close. Teddy bear cholla form large, nearly-pure stands—as seen in Joshua Tree National Park—through vegetative reproduction via the easy separation of individual joints which become rooted when they fall to the ground.

A second common cactus is silver, or golden, cholla (*Cylindropuntia echinocarpa,* formerly known as *Opuntia echinocarpa,* Fig. 5.3). This species reaches 3–5 feet in height and gets its name from its silvery or golden spines. At first glance silver cholla is similar to a related buckhorn cactus (*Cylindropuntia acanthocarpa*) and the two may occur together. One way to separate them is to look at the shape of the tubercles, or raised mounds along the stem. In silver cholla the tubercles are never more than about twice are as long as they are broad, while in buckhorn cholla the tubercles are more elongate and their length is at least three times their width (Fig. 5.4). Another difference is that silver cholla has a distinctive main trunk that extends for a third to half of the height of the plant, while buckhorn cholla has a short trunk that forms no more than a fifth of the plant height, with branched stems above this point. In the springtime when the cacti are flowering, there is an easier way to separate the species. Silver cholla has greenish flowers while those of buckhorn cholla are typically reddish-purple to yellow

Another distinctive cholla of cactus scrub communities is the pencil cactus (*Cylindropuntia ramosissima*), named for its elongate pencil-shaped joints (Fig. 5.5). A second common name is diamond cholla, a name that refers to the hexagonal shape of the small tubercles along the stem. This is a shrubby cactus reaching heights of 2–4 feet, with its slender stems covered with prominent spines 1–2 inches or more in length. The length and major barbs on these spines make this a species that deserves space while walking by. Although more characteristic of our lower Sonoran Desert, these three cholla species extend broadly into the lower elevations of the Mojave Desert.

Prickly-pear cacti, that remain in the genus *Opuntia,* are dominant species under

Fig. 5.2. *Cylindropuntia bigelovii*, Cactaceae, teddy bear cholla. Photo by Robert Gustafson.

Fig. 5.3. *Cylindropuntia echinocarpa*, Cactaceae, silver cholla. Photo by Morgan Stickrod.

Fig. 5.4. *Cylindropuntia acanthocarpa*, Cactaceae, buckhorn cholla. Photo by Stan Shebs.

proper conditions in the Sonoran Desert areas of Arizona and Baja California with biseasonal rainfall—but are less evident in the California deserts. One common prickly-pear species with a wide elevational and geographic range across our desert region is beavertail cactus (*Opuntia basilaris*). It occurs in sites from the lower Sonoran Desert through the Mojave Desert to desert mountains as high as 7,000 feet. This is a small species, generally no more than about 20 inches in height, with oval pads of a distinctive blue-green or purplish color (Fig. 5.6). Large spines are generally absent but the usual potent glochids, characteristic of prickly-pear species, are certainly present. While the small size of the beavertail cactus makes it easy to overlook in summer, its large magenta flowers standout at some distance in the spring. Although the plants are relatively small, repeat photographs of desert sites where these occur suggest that individuals can live for 60 years or more.

Fig. 5.5. *Cylindropuntia ramosissima*, Cactaceae, pencil cholla. Photo by Robert Gustafson.

Fig. 5.6. *Opuntia basilaris*, Cactaceae, beavertail cactus. Photo by Robert Gustafson.

Mojave prickly-pear (*Opuntia polyacantha* var. *erinacea*) occurs widely across the Mojave Desert in cactus scrub, Joshua tree woodlands, and pinyon-juniper woodlands. This is a low, clumped prickly-pear that reaches up to 18 inches in height and 2–3 feet in diameter (Fig. 5.7). It has small densely-spined elliptical pads 2–8 inches in length. The flowers vary from yellow to pink-magenta in color.

Fig. 5.7. *Opuntia polyacantha*, Cactaceae, Mojave prickly-pear. Photo by Matt Berger.

Several additional prickly-pear species occur in the Peninsular Ranges and at higher elevations in the eastern Mojave Desert in pinyon-juniper woodland or higher Joshua tree woodland. The most distinctive of these is pancake prickly-pear (*Opuntia chlorotica*). This is an upright species with a distinct trunk and reaches 4–6 feet in height (Fig. 5.8). The name of this species comes from the round joints 6–8 inches in diameter and resemble pancakes or plates. There are two other *Opuntia* species common along the coast of southern California that do not range into the desert.

The third group of opuntia-like cacti is the genus *Grusonia* with two species in California. Matted cholla (*Grusonia parishii*) is restricted to sandy plains at elevations of 3,000–5,000 feet in the eastern Mojave Desert and northern Sonoran

Fig. 5.8. *Opuntia chlorotica*, Cactaceae, pancake prickly-pear. National Park Service photo by Lian Law.

Desert. This is a low mat-forming species no more than 6 inches in height and covered by spiny tubercles. But individual patches may extend to diameters up to 6 feet (Fig. 5.9). It is easy to miss in drier times of the year because of its low stature and dehydrated, seemingly dead, appearance in summer. With rain, however, it quickly grows new joints with prominent reddish spines that reach 1–1.5 inches in length. Unlike most opuntia species, the spines of matted cholla are distinctly flattened rather than round in cross-section. The broad mats of this cholla and its long sharp spines give it a second common name, the horse-crippler cholla. It has a CNPS Rare Plant Rank of 2B (rare, threatened, or endangered in California; common elsewhere). A second rare species, *Grusonia pulchella*, occurs in dune habitats of the northern Mojave Desert and southern Great Basin. It has a CNPS Rare Plant Rank: 2B (rare, threatened, or endangered in California; common elsewhere).

Fig. 5.9. *Grusonia parishii*, Cactaceae, matted cholla. Photo by Matt Berger.

California barrel cactus (*Ferocactus cylindraceus*) is arguably the most charismatic of our desert cacti (Fig. 5.10). The cylindrical stem is a foot or more in diameter and 3–10 feet in height when mature. Its coarse flattened spines, reddish or yellowish in color and curved but not hooked, cover the stem. As mentioned in Chapter 3, most California barrel cactus exhibit a prominent tilt toward the south. This is thought to minimize the absorption of midday sun on the stem as well as to aid in the rapid development of flowers in the spring. A showy whorl of yellow flowers covers the top of the stem in March and April. Although most characteristic of cactus scrub communities of the lower Sonoran Desert, a cold tolerant variety of California barrel cactus is widespread in the eastern Mojave Desert. Seedlings of barrel cactus are difficult to find and long-term studies have shown that seedling establishment of this, and many other cacti, is restricted to years with exceptional amounts of rainfall, conditions that may only occur once or less per decade.

Fig. 5.10. *Ferocactus cylindraceus*, Cactaceae, California barrel cactus. Photo by Morgan Stickrod.

Cotton-top cactus (*Echinocactus polycephalus*) resembles a colony of small barrel cacti, with clumps of 10–30 globose stems up to 1–2 feet in height and 12 inches in diameter (Fig. 5.11). Cotton-top typically occurs on rocky ridges and slopes in creosote bush scrub habitat at elevations of 2,000–5,000 feet across the Mojave and higher elevations areas of the northern Sonoran Desert. At each areole there are 3–4 large central spines 2–3 inches in length that are red to gray and prominently flattened, as well as 6–8 similar but smaller spines. The common name cotton-top cactus comes from the dense woolly covering of the fruits.

The hedgehog cactus (*Echinocereus engelmannii*) is a widespread species of cactus scrub occurring from the lower Sonoran Desert through the Mojave Desert up into pinyon-juniper woodlands. This is another clumping cactus with a cluster of cylindrical stems 8–12 inches in height with an overall diameter of 2–3 feet (Fig. 5.12). The stems display a loose covering of large multi-hued spines 1–2.5 inches in length. The showy magenta flowers are 2–3 inches in diameter and are produced singly at the tops of the stems. Although the developing fruits are protected by spines, these fall away as the fruit matures—making them available to birds and rodents which consume the fruits and disperse the seeds.

Fig. 5.11. *Echinocactus polycephalus*, Cactaceae, cotton-top cactus. Photo by Matt Berger.

A closely related species is the Mojave mound cactus (*Echinocereus mojavensis*). It is found across the Mojave Desert and eastward as far as Texas. Although individual stems are cylindrical and smaller than those of the hedgehog cactus, they cluster to form large mounds up to 6 feet across with hundreds of individual heads (Fig. 5.13). Beyond this difference in growth form, Mojave mound cactus is distinguished by a central spine that is not flattened compared to the prominently flattened spine in hedgehog cactus. Another interesting trait of Mojave mound cactus is the reddish flowers remain open at night, while hedgehog cactus close at night. It is not clear what the selective advantage of this trait may have, but it likely relates to the respective pollinators.

Fig. 5.12. *Echinocereus engelmannii*, Cactaceae, hedgehog cactus. Photo by Stan Shebs.

Fig. 5.13. *Echinocereus mojavensis*, Cactaceae, Mojave mound cactus. Photo by Jim Morefield.

Fig. 5.14. *Coryphantha vivipara*, Cactaceae, pincushion cactus. Photo by Matt Berger.

Fig. 5.15. *Sclerocactus polyancistrus*, Cactaceae, pineapple cactus. Photo by Joey Santore.

The pincushion or beehive cactus (*Coryphantha vivipara*) has a small cylindrical stem 3–6 inches in height occurring singly or as small clumps (Fig. 5.14). The stem surface is nearly covered by clusters of fine white spines. There are three varieties of this species, with two of these specialists on limestone substrates in the eastern Mojave Desert.

The Mojave Desert is home to two genera of small globular cacti superficially resembling *Echinocereus* but with hooked, rather than straight, spines (Fig. 5.15). One of these is seen with *Sclerocactus polyancistrus*, a pineapple-shaped cactus 12–16 inches in height and densely covered with gray, white, and red spines. It is found in scattered populations on limestone soils of creosote bush scrub and pinyon-juniper woodlands of the central and eastern Mojave Desert. It displays large purple flowers in spring, which turn red and then pink after a few days. Although pineapple cactus generally grows poorly in cultivation, widespread collecting has made significant impacts on its numbers.

The other group of smaller fishhook cacti form the genus *Mammillaria*. This group includes more than 150 species in North America, three of which occur in the California desert. These are all small globular cacti generally no more than 2–6 inches in height and covered by dense masses of spines with prominent hooks at their ends. It is these spines that have given rise to their common name. The most widespread fishhook cactus is *Mammillaria tetrancistra*—a small species with a solitary stem 3–6 inches tall and 1.5–2.5 inches in diameter (Fig. 5.16). It occurs across the lower Sonoran Desert of California and up into the lowest margin of the Mojave Desert. Interestingly, this species is characterized by a large, corky protuberance on each of its seeds, a structure that is absent in our other species of fishhook cacti. This may well be involved in dispersal by ants or other organisms.

A second species of fishhook cactus is *Mammillaria dioica*. It has unusual reproductive morphology as suggested by its species name. Populations occur with indi-

Fig. 5.16. *Mammillaria tetrancistra*, Cactaceae, fishhook cactus. Photo by Matt Berger.

Fig. 5.17. *Mammillaria dioica*, Cactaceae, fishhook cactus. Photo by Robert Gustafson.

viduals having normal bisexual flowers, while other individuals display only female flowers. It is distributed along the western margin of the Sonoran Desert east of the Peninsular Ranges and then in coastal sage scrub and maritime succulent scrub along the coast of southern California from Del Mar south into northwestern Baja California—where it is often abundant. Of the three species, this is the only one that can form multi-stemmed clumps, although solitary stems are also found (Fig. 5.17). The third fishhook cactus, *Mammillaria grahamii*) is a relatively uncommon and known only from southeastern San Bernardino County in California. It has a CNPS Rare Plant Rank: 2B, rare, threatened, or endangered in California; common elsewhere.

Saguaro (*Carnegeia gigantea*) is arguably the most famous cactus in the world—as well as an iconic image of the desert southwest—with its massive form and upraised branches that give it an almost human form (Fig. 5.18). While it is common in the desert uplands of Arizona and adjacent parts of northern Mexico, it is relatively uncommon in California. It has a CNPS Rare Plant Rank: 2B, rare, threatened, or endangered in California; common elsewhere. Saguaros are found infrequently on gravelly slopes and flats of creosote bush scrub to about 1,500 feet near the Colorado River and in the Whipple Mountains of southeastern San Bernardino County.

Fig. 5.18. *Carnegiea gigantea*, Cactaceae, saguaro. Photo by Matt Berger.

Agaves, Nolinas, and Yuccas

The family level of classification for agaves, nolinas, and yuccas has a history of taxonomic disagreement. Yuccas have been included within a broad concept of the lily family (Liliaceae) while agaves and nolinas were once placed in separate small families. The current agreement is to place all three groups within a broad concept of the asparagus family, the Asparagaceae, with agaves and yuccas together in one subfamily and nolinas in another. In terms of physiological adaptations, agaves typically exhibit CAM metabolism (see Chapter 3) while nolinas and yuccas do not.

Although the genus *Agave* is a large group of some 250–300 species that range across arid North America, Central America, and the Caribbean, just two species of agave occur in the desert regions of California. Many more agave species are found to the south in Baja California and southeast and east in other portions of the Sonoran Desert with biseasonal or summer rainfall regimes. Like the cacti,

Fig. 5.19. *Agave deserti*, Asparagaceae, desert agave. Photos by Matt Berger.

Fig. 5.20. Clonal growth ring of *Agave deserti*. Photo by Matt Berger.

agaves have succulent storage tissues and utilize Crassulacean acid metabolism. A difference between the groups, however, is that leaves are the primary organs for water storage—although the fibrous leaf structure of agaves holds only moderate amounts of water compared to the succulent stems of most cacti.

Our most widespread species is desert agave (*Agave deserti*), which occurs widely on rocky slopes across our Sonoran Desert region. The gray-green leaves of this species—with margins displaying widely spaced sharp spines—are arrayed in a rosette 2–3 feet in diameter (Fig. 5.19). Flowering rosettes quickly produce a tall stalk 8–15 feet in height, topped with a branched structure of pale-yellow flowers. Field studies suggest that plants begin flowering after about 20 years, although this period may vary depending on resource availability. The metabolic cost of forming the flowering stalk depletes the resources from the rosette, which dies following flowering. Vegetative offshoots from the base of the plant form new daughter rosettes and maintain the survival of the genetic individual. Continued vegetative reproduction from such offshoots leads to clonal rings representing a slow outward movement of daughter rosettes (Fig. 5.20). Although at least some plants within a population flower and set seed every other year, seedling establishment is rare—occurring at intervals of as much as two decades or more when conditions are favorable.

The second species in California is Utah agave (*Agave utahensis*), which has a limited distribution in Joshua tree woodlands and shadscale scrub in the mountains of the eastern Mojave Desert where it replaces desert agave. It has smaller rosettes than desert agave and branched stems (Fig. 5.21). Where the two species overlap in the Ivanpah Mountains, Utah agave is restricted to limestone soils, while desert agave grows on granites. Shaw's agave (*Agave shawii*) is common in the desert and maritime succulent scrub of northern Baja California, but only enters California at a few coastal sites in San Diego County.

The genus *Nolina* comprises about 25 species that extend from Texas and Oklahoma west to southern California and south into Mexico. Close relatives include several other genera with ranges centered in arid areas of Mexico—which are often widely planted in aridland gardens in southern California including *Dasylirion, Beaucarnia,* and *Calibanus. Nolina* and these three genera share several distinctive characteristics. First, all are *dioecious*, meaning they have separate male and female individuals. In addition, they have long inflorescences with tiny white flowers and produce indehiscent fruits with ovoid seeds—in contrast to the capsules of agaves that split open at maturity and have flattened seeds

We have four species of *Nolina* in southern California. Two of these are restricted to coastal foothill areas and Mediterranean-type shrublands and not discussed here. Bigelow's nolina (*Nolina bigelovii*) occurs in creosote bush scrub habitats of the central and eastern Mojave Desert and in lower elevation areas of the Sonoran Desert in southeastern California. Mature plants develop a woody trunk up to ten feet in height, with a rosette of narrow leaves 2–3 feet or more in length (Fig. 5.22). These long, linear leaves give young plants, that have not yet developed a trunk, the appearance of a large bunchgrass—giving rise to the common name beargrass. Distinctive features of the leaves of Bigelow's nolina are the dull blue-green to gray-green color of the leaves and the curled fibers that occur along the margins of mature leaves. Traditional uses include roasting and eating the flowering stalks.

Parry's nolina (*Nolina parryi*) ranges from desert edge chaparral and sage scrub to Joshua tree and pinyon-juniper woodlands of the Mojave Desert and higher areas of the Sonoran Desert in California and Baja California. Parry's nolina is generally similar in appearance to Bigelow's nolina with 3–6-foot trunks and rosettes of long linear leaves. It is distinguished by its greener leaves with margins that are sharp to the touch because of tiny teeth along their edge (Fig. 5.23 and Fig. 5.24). Parry's nolina inflorescence has a broader diameter and retains the papery bracts—while these are shed with maturity in Bigelow's nolina. Both species may occur with single stems or branch to form clusters of woody trunks.

Yuccas are a common and important member of the agave subfamily within the

Fig. 5.21. *Agave utahensis*, Asparagaceae, Utah agave. Photos by Matt Berger.

Fig. 5.22. *Nolina bigelovii*, Asparagaceae, Bigelow's Nolina. Photo by Stan Shebs.

Fig. 5.23. *Nolina parryi*, Asparagaceae, Parry's nolina. National Park Service photo by Rob Hannawacker.

Fig. 5.24. *Nolina parryi* in the Kingston Range of the eastern Mojave Desert. Photo by Stan Shebs.

Asparagaceae, with approximately 50 species that range from the Prairie Provinces of Canada to the Gulf Coast of the United States and south to Mexico, Guatemala, and the Caribbean. While not true succulents in the sense of having stems or leaves that store large amounts of water and not exhibiting CAM metabolism (see Chapter 3), yuccas share many of the habitat preferences of cacti and are widespread in cactus scrub communities. Our desert yucca species are discussed in Chapter 4.

Chapter 6
Wash Woodlands and Arroyos

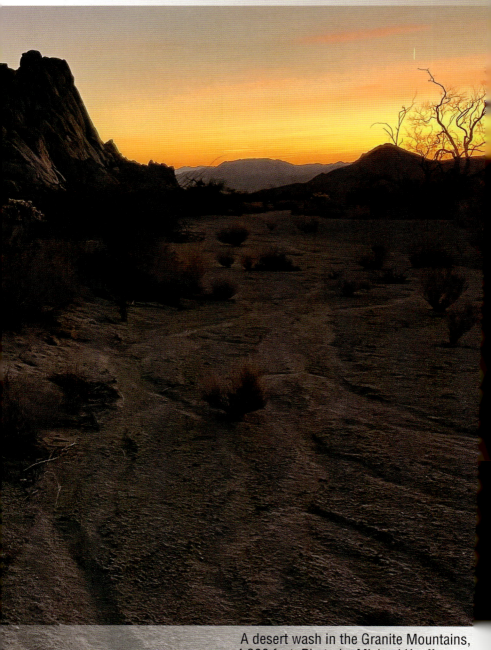

A desert wash in the Granite Mountains, 4,300 feet. Photo by Michael Kauffmann.

Introduction

When it precipitates in the desert, shallow soils cannot absorb the rainfall and the water flows down relatively unvegetated slopes towards natural watercourses known as arroyos. Runoff first collects in steep arroyos, then carves dynamic channels as it descends the bajada, or a broad slope of alluvial material at the foot of a mountain, on its way to washes in the valley bottoms (Introductory image). The concentration of rainfall in washes allows water to infiltrate the soil and creates both local soil moisture and broad pools of groundwater in topographic basins (Fig. 6.1). The principle of water availability in groundwater catchments beneath desert washes was discovered thousands of years ago in the Middle East, where vibrant agricultural civilizations developed in arid regions with only a few inches of annual rainfall.

While arroyos and broad washes are common landscape features across our desert regions, the species composition of wash woodland plant communities differs between the Mojave and Sonoran deserts. Higher elevations of the Mojave Desert experience cold winter temperatures, which inhibit the survival of species with subtropical ancestry that thrive in the lower Sonoran Desert. Because of seasonal low temperature extremes, Mojave Desert wash woodland communities lack many of the iconic desert trees and other subtropical floristic elements that are widespread in our lower Sonoran Desert.

Before describing the common wash woodland species in detail, it is useful to note that many of these are members of the legume family. Interestingly, although California's foothills and coastal flora contain many herbaceous members of the legume family—with related genera and species in our deserts—our woody legumes are primarily Sonoran Desert species with subtropical or tropical ancestry and a sensitivity to low temperatures.

Fig. 6.1. Flash flooding in 2015 near the north entrance of Joshua Tree National Park. National Park Service photo by Brad Sutton.

Wash Woodlands

Wash woodland communities primarily occur in the Sonoran Desert in California. They are open woodlands of small desert trees growing along the margins of arroyos, in sandy washes, or on coarse-textured bajadas (Fig. 6.2). The key to the occurrence of this community is the presence of a permanent or semi-permanent groundwater aquifer that can be tapped by deep roots. Most of the wash woodland species in California, as described below, are more typical of the Sonoran Desert of Arizona or Baja California where there is a biseasonal pattern of rainfall and thus seasonal water availability. In Arizona and Baja California, summer monsoons allow these desert trees to grow in areas without permanent groundwater pools. In California, where summer monsoons are rare, these species only survive where their roots can tap permanent or ephemeral groundwater and thus minimize water stress during the arid summer months. California's dry summers make it hard for seedlings of these drought sensitive species to establish. It is only in rare years with heavy rainfall that seedlings can extend their root systems deep enough to survive their first summer. As described in Chapter 3, plants with roots that tap groundwater are known as phreatophytes.

In addition to being drought sensitive, many wash woodland species of subtropical origin are sensitive to cold winter conditions. This cold sensitivity restricts many species from extending their ranges into the higher areas of the Mojave Desert where hard frosts occur every winter. Very low temperatures occasionally penetrate into the Sonoran Desert area of California and impact the range of the more sensitive species.

In California, detailed ecological studies of large woody wash-woodland species have identified three groups with different adaptations in growth form and leaf phenology to manage summer drought. The first group is winter deciduous: they lose their leaves for about three months from December to early March. The second group includes species with photosynthetic stems and scale-like or short-lived leaves. The final group comprises shrub species which are drought-deciduous: they lose their leaves and go largely dormant under summer drought conditions. Many drought-deciduous species also depend heavily on stem photosynthesis.

Fig. 6.2. Smoke trees in a broad wash east of Eagle Mountain, Riverside County. Photo by Julie Evens.

Winter Deciduous Trees and Shrubs

Despite their arboreal structure, desert wash woodlands are considered pioneer communities that, over decades or centuries, give way to other plant communities as sediments accumulate and river channels move. This dynamic nature of riparian habitats is seen in the alluvial floodplain terraces above stream and river channels that support a different community from the riparian woodlands described in Chapter 7. Like the riparian trees, these species have a phenology with leaf loss in the winter season—the time of the year when our rainfall is most likely to occur. This behavior is different from the drought-deciduous behavior described in other chapters where desert species are responding to California's characteristic summer drought.

The most widespread wash woodland tree is honey mesquite (*Prosopis glandulosa* var. *torreyana*; Fig. 6.3). Although most common in the Sonoran Desert areas of California, honey mesquite extends its range across lower elevations of the Mojave Desert as far north as Death Valley and over huge areas of desert and semi-desert in the southwestern United States and adjacent Mexico. It is a classic phreatophyte with roots that tap groundwater pools as deep as 30 feet or more below the soil surface. In semi-arid grasslands of the southwestern United States with summer rainfall, however, it behaves less like an obligate phreatophyte and readily invades desert grasslands. It must be remembered, however, that plant roots do not grow through dry soil actively seeking out groundwater. Roots will only follow moist fracture zones in soil profiles. Honey mesquite is quite variable in growth form. It may take on the morphology of a large tree up to 30 feet tall in wash habitats, or may form a broad shrub 20–30 feet in diameter with multiple stems, particularly on dune habitats (Fig. 6.4).

Each pinnate leaf of honey mesquite is divided into two clustered sets of oblong-linear leaflets, with paired straight spines at each node. All leaves senesce and are lost in early December. The plants are leafless for about three months until early March, when a cohort of new leaves are formed. Leaf production is not continuous but is constrained to a limited period of weeks and is followed by flowering and pod production in spring. Surprisingly, a second, smaller cohort of leaves and flowers is produced in August under the hottest conditions of the summer. It may seem strange that the honey mesquite shouldlose its leaves during the winter months —when rainfall is most likely to occur—and form new leaves in the heat of the summer even when it doesn't rain. The reason for this appears to be that the timing of leaf loss and growth arose as adaptations in regions

Fig. 6.3. *Prosopis glandulosa* var. *torreyana*, Fabaceae, honey mesquite. Photo by Robert Gustafson.

Fig. 6.4. *Prosopis glandulosa* var. *torreyana* at Edwards Air Force Base. Photo by Phil Rundel.

with dry winters and summer rainfall. Honey mesquite in California still retains ancestral traits that are better suited to conditions present in the rest of its range. As a phreatophyte tapping groundwater for its growth, there is little limitation of water resources for spring and summer growth, and cool winter conditions limit potential photosynthesis. Thus, there have not been sufficient evolutionary pressures on honey mesquite in the winter rainfall regime of California to evolve away from this winter deciduous habit.

Honey mesquite possesses nitrogen-fixing root nodules and, with the help of symbiotic bacteria, fixes nitrogen into its root tissues. This is an important aspect of its ecological success. Being a phreatophyte and using deep roots to tap groundwater allows mesquite to decouple itself from the limiting factor of water availability. Once water is no longer limiting, nitrogen availability takes over as limiting for growth. With nitrogen-fixing root nodules, however, this limiting factor is also removed—allowing for remarkable rates of productivity by mesquite trees. As mesquite roots die and decompose, they release nitrate—a form of inorganic nitrogen available for plant uptake—which greatly improves soil fertility. Nitrate, which is water soluble, normally leaches out of soils, but dry conditions allow for the buildup of soil nitrate. For this reason, many mesquite stands have been cleared for agriculture in areas where irrigation water can be supplied.

In many respects, honey mesquite is a keystone desert species. Its broad canopy and high rate of growth provide shade for many animal species. Equally important is its high productivity and ability to fix nitrogen, which allows honey mesquite to produce huge annual crops of protein-rich leaves and pods. These calories provide an important food source for many animal species. Native Americans have long used the pods of the honey mesquite tree for food. Mesquite wood is extremely dense and has been rather overused for fence posts, building materials, and fuel.

Much like creosote bush, which is described in Chapter 4, our North American desert mesquite species probably originated in South America. Argentina's Monte Desert is home to more than 30 species of mesquite and is the likely center of evolution and distribution. In fact, South American ancestry applies not only to creosote bush and mesquite, but to several other lineages of woody desert plants. The manner by which these groups were able to disperse long distances and colonize North American deserts in the geologic past remains unclear.

Catclaw acacia (*Senegalia greggii*) is another woody desert legume and is our only native acacia in California. A common name for this scraggly shrub is wait-a-minute bush—a reference to how easily its curved spines grab clothes and skin alike (Fig. 6.5). Catclaw acacia often forms thickets along washes and narrow stream channels across the Mojave Desert and in the lower Sonoran Desert areas of California. As with honey mesquite, it loses its leaves during the winter months. Yet catclaw no longer falls in the same genera as honey mesquite. Molecular data have recently shown that the traditional genus *Acacia* should be broken up into five separate genera. Species retaining the name *Acacia* descend from an Australian group of species with *phyllodes* (leaf-like flattened stems), while *Senegalia* includes about 200 pantropical species.

Fairyduster (*Calliandra eriophylla*) is another winter deciduous wash plant and legume relative of mesquite and acacia. It is a small shrub that typically grows up to 3 feet in height. This species is restricted to wash channels of the lower elevations of Anza Borrego Desert State Park and eastern Imperial County. As with many wash woodland species, fairyduster is much more widespread in monsoonal

Fig. 6.5. *Senegalia greggii*, Fabaceae, catclaw acacia. Photo by Stan Shebs.

areas of the Sonoran Desert in Arizona and Mexico (Fig. 6.6). No other California shrub species has the clustered long, pink stamens extending well beyond the petals—a trait which gives rise to its common name.

Ironwood (*Olneya tesota*) is a moderate-sized, winter deciduous tree that grows 15–30 feet in height with a spreading crown and thin scaly gray bark (Fig. 6.7). Ironwood is sensitive to cold temperatures and does not extend into the Mojave Desert or higher elevations of the Sonoran Desert in Arizona. It favors broad washes and middle slopes of large alluvial fans, often occurring with blue palo verde (*Parkinsonia florida*). The pinnate gray-green leaves of ironwood are semi-evergreen but are generally shed during the winter months. Ironwood features a pair of sharp, curved spines beneath each leaf all along the major branches and trunk of the tree. Although many desert trees serve an important ecological role as nurse plants—aiding in the establishment of seedlings of other species—ironwood is particularly important in sheltering other species. Ironwood is also a legume with root nodules that fix nitrogen. The name ironwood comes from the extremely high density of its wood, which is so dense that it will sink in water.

Fig. 6.6. *Calliandra eriophylla*, Fabaceae, fairyduster. Photos by Morgan Stickrod.

There are several winter deciduous wash woodland species that are not legumes. Desert-willow (*Chilopsis linearis*) is our only California member of the tropical

Fig. 6.7. (LEFT) *Olneya tesota*, Fabaceae, desert ironwood near Bajada Nature Trail Joshua Tree National Park. National Park Service photo. (RIGHT) Desert ironwood in flower. Photos by Robert Gustafson.

bignonia family, the Bignoniaceae. The growth form of desert-willow ranges from a sprawling shrub to a small tree reaching up to 20 feet in height (Fig. 6.8). The name desert-willow comes from the fact that its long and narrow leaves, 4–6 inches in length, resemble those of a true willow. This species is largely restricted to low-nutrient gravelly washes in Sonoran Desert areas such as in the Coachella Valley and Anza Borrego Desert State Park—although it extends into scattered areas of the lower Mojave Desert. As with the other species described above, desert-willow loses its leaves for three to four months in winter. Large, showy pink- to whitish-flowers are produced each spring and make desert willow an attractive plant for desert gardens. The fruits of desert-willow are elongate pod-like capsules 4–10 inches in length which enclose flat wind-dispersed seeds with silky hairs tufted at each end.

Desert almond (*Prunus fasciculata*) is a higher elevation species with temperate ancestry, rather than subtropical, and winter deciduous phenology. It takes the form of a large woody shrub, up to 6 feet in height, with spinescent branches and clusters of small narrow leaves that are shed in winter (Fig. 6.9). Desert almond is common in rocky washes across higher elevations of the Mojave Desert, though it can be found in lower washes with creosote bush scrub plants up into canyons with pinyon-juniper communities. In spring, dense colonies of tent caterpillars often establish themselves in desert almond foliage.

Fig. 6.8 *Chilopsis linearis*, Bignoniaceae, desert-willow. Photo by Stan Shebs, inset by Robert Gustafson.

Fig. 6.9. *Prunus fasciculata*, Rosaceae, desert almond. National Park Service photo by Robb Hannawacker, inset by Robert Gustafson.

Stem Photosynthetic Trees and Shrubs

The second group of wash woodland plants is comprised of small trees with subtropical ancestry. This group has evolved away from using their leaves for photsynthesis and instead utilize green stems as their primary photosynthetic organs. Smoke tree (*Psorothamnus spinosus*), which is virtually leafless, displays this evolutionary strategy. It is a common and often dominant species in desert washes in the Coachella Valley and Anza Borrego Desert State Park. This small tree, which reaches up to 25 feet in height, exhibits a dense silvery-gray pubescence that covers it spine-tipped branches (Fig. 6.10). The combination of the gray branches and the leaflessness of these trees gives them a decidedly smoky appearance when viewed from a distance—especially with low sun angles near dawn or dusk. Like other legumes, smoke trees have root nodules with symbiotic nitrogen-fixing bacteria; this clearly helps this species to successfully colonize nutrient-poor soils in desert washes. Five species of *Psorothamnus* in addition to smoke tree occur in our California deserts but differ from smoke tree in their adaptive strategies. All of these shrub species are described in Chapter 4, yet none relies on stem photosynthesis to the extent of smoke tree.

The *Parkinsonia* genus which comprise the palo verde trees— whose name refers to their distinctive green bark—are another group of closely related trees that rely on photosynthetic stems yet also form leaves after spring rains. These species keeps their leaves for only for a matter of weeks before shedding them and relying on green stems for photosynthesis over the remainder of the year. *Parkinsonia* is an interesting genus in that it occurs widely in arid and semi-arid regions of both the Americas and Africa. While it might seem that the largest photosynthetic area of these trees must be on their broad, green trunks, the majority of photosynthetic stem surface area is actually in the first- and second-year stems. Palo verde species are not able to fix atmospheric nitrogen, yet they successfully colonize nutrient-poor wash habitats.

Blue palo verde (*Parkinsonia florida*) is a moderate sized tree reaching up to 25 feet in height. It is common in washes in the lower desert areas of California where it often occurs with desert ironwood (Fig. 6.11). Blue palo verde is the characteristic palo verde species of the Coachella Valley

Fig. 6.10. *Psorothamnus spinosus*, Fabaceae, smoke tree. Photos by Stan Shebs.

and Salton Sea basin. A related species is little-leaf palo verde (*Parkinsonia microphylla*) which is a smaller tree, up to 20 feet in height, that is more typical of bajada slopes than washes. In California, little-leaf palo verde is only found along the Colorado River in San Bernardino County and south to Imperial County near the Mexico border. Both species, however, are widespread across the broader Sonoran Desert outside of California. Several characteristics distinguish the two palo verde species from each other. The bark of blue palo verde is a distinctive blue-green, compared to the yellowish-green bark of little-leaf palo verde (Fig. 6.12). In addition, blue palo verde has spines at each node and leaves with clear petioles, while little-leaf palo verde lacks nodal spines and has spine tipped branches with smaller ephemeral leaves that lack a petiole.

Mexican palo verde (*Parkinsonia aculeata*), does not occur naturally in California but has been used widely in landscaping and shows the potential to become an invasive in our wash woodland habitats. Mexican palo verde is a large tree up to 40 feet in height. While it has yellowish-green bark on its upper young branches, it lacks a green trunk like our two native palo verde species. The most distinctive trait is its unusual leaves, which are pinnately divided with an exposed central rachis and almost no foliar area.

There are several low-growing legumes that also represent good examples of stem photosynthetic adaptations to desert life in desert washes. The genus *Hoffmanseggia* comprises 24 species that are split in distribution between the southwestern

Fig. 6.11. *Parkinsonia florida*, Fabaceae, blue palo verde. Photo by Stan Shebs, inset by Robert Gustafson.

Fig. 6.12 *Parkinsonia microphylla*, Fabaceae, little-leaf palo verde. Photos by Stan Shebs.

United States and Mexico, and Chile and Argentina. Although there are many species in the greater Sonoran Desert, only two species occur in California. Rushpea (*Hoffmannseggia microphylla*) inhabits washes and arroyos in the lower Sonoran Desert. The common name of this legume shrub comes from its green, rush-like stems that reach 2–4 feet or more in height (Fig. 6.13). The pinnately divided leaves are short-lived, with a significant amount of the photosynthetic responsibility given to the green stems which can attain high rates of photosynthetic output. *Hoffmannseggia glauca* is a low-growing herbaceous perennial uncommon on alkaline flats at lower elevations.

Fig. 6.13. *Hoffmannseggia microphylla*, Fabaceae, rushpea. Photo by Matt Berger.

Other examples of stem photosynthesis are found in *Senna*, a large legume genus of perhaps 250 species that occurs widely in both North and South America as well as subtropical areas around the world, with two species occurring naturally in California. Spiny senna (*Senna armata*) is a low, stem photosynthetic shrub 2–4 feet in height that occurs widely in sandy washes of both the Mojave and Sonoran deserts in California. Although pinnately compound leaves are produced in the spring, these are typically shed after only a few weeks; the plant therefore resembles a cluster of leafless, greenish stems over most of the year (Fig. 6.14). Coves' senna (*Senna covesii*) is a smaller plant, but has large, more persistent gray leaves covered by dense white hairs. Coves' senna is largely restricted to washes in the Sonoran Desert and has a CNPS Rare Plant Rank 2B: plants rare, threatened, or endangered in California and elsewhere.

Fig. 6.14. *Senna armata*, Fabaceae, spiney senna. Photo by Robert Gustafson.

Drought-deciduous Wash Shrubs

A small number of shrubby wash species exhibit drought-deciduous behavior by shedding their leaves under summer water stress. Desert lavender (*Condea emoryi*) is a large shrub found in rocky washes and channels throughout the Sonoran Desert and lower elevation Mojave Desert up to 3,000 feet elevation, and eastward as far as the Chihuahuan Desert. This erect shrub is generally 4–10 feet in height, with simple ovate leaves covered with a dense, white pubescence (Fig. 6.15). The opposite arrangement of the leaves and the sweet fragrance of the foliage help identify desert lavender as a member of the mint family, Lamiaceae. Like other drought-deciduous shrubs, desert lavender exhibits seasonal leaf dimorphism (see Chapter 3). The first leaves produced in spring are relatively large and thin, with less dense pubescence. As the season progresses and water stress slowly increases, new leaves are increasingly smaller and thicker, with denser pubescence. This seasonal leaf dimorphism allows the plant to produce leaves adapted to the immediate growing conditions at the time they form. While desert lavender in California drops its leaves due to water stress in summer, it is often evergreen over its broader range in Arizona and northwestern Mexico where there is biseasonal or summer rainfall. The attractive foliage and flowers of desert lavender make it a popular plant for aridland gardening and landscaping.

Cyclical Disturbance and Colonization of Wash Woodland and Arroyo Habitats

Fig. 6.15. *Condea emoryi*, Lamiaceae, desert lavender. Photo by Matt Berger.

Desert washes and arroyos experience an irregular yet cyclical disturbance regime with episodic flooding that produces significant sediment movement, channelization, and localized groundwater recharge. The irregularity of disturbances forced woody plant species to evolve and adapt to colonizing open wash and arroyo habitats. Many of the most common colonizing shrub species of wash woodland and arroyo habitats are members of the sunflower family (Asteraceae). Most of these species are not restricted to wash habitats and are also found on upper bajada slopes where runoff creates small channels. Many of these colonizers are also found on disturbed sites and arroyos in the Mediterranean-type shrublands of southern California.

Cheeseweed (*Ambrosia salsola*), named for the cheesy smell emitted from crushed leaves, is perhaps the most prolific wash colonizer. Cheeseweed is a highly branched shrub 2–6 feet in height that occurs widely in washes and on alluvial fans across both our Mojave and Sonoran Desert regions (Fig. 6.16). Cheeseweed is drought-deciduous and relies heavily on photosynthesis in its green stems. Although the shrubs themselves may be spindly, they typically have a deep root system that taps groundwater. Cheeseweed has relatively inconspicuous male and female flowers on separate heads that are wind pollinated. Its seeds are also wind-dispersed, and seedlings are highly stress tolerant. These traits allow cheeseweed to be an active colonizer of dynamic desert washes as well as disturbed sites like abandoned mining towns. As a relative of ragweed, the pollen of cheeseweed can cause hay fever.

Some less widespread species of *Ambrosia* also thrive on the alluvial deposition of sediments on desert floodplains following heavy rains. All of these species have winged burs that disperse the seeds. Burrobush (*Ambrosia monogyra*) is a tall, fall-flowering shrub that occurs throughout washes and arroyos of California's lower Sonoran Desert region and adjacent chaparral (Fig. 6.17). Hollyleaf bursage (*Ambrosia ilicifolia*) is limited to sandy washes and rocky canyons in lower elevations of the Sonoran Desert. It has elongated leathery leaves with toothed margins. Outside California, the Sonoran Desert areas of Arizona and Baja California are home

Fig. 6.16. *Ambrosia salsola*, Asteraceae, cheeseweed in a wash in Death Valley National Park. Photo by Julie Evens, inset by Stan Shebs.

to a diverse assemblage of other low-growing *Ambrosia* species that require regular summer rainfall.

Sweetbush (*Bebbia juncea*) is a commonly encountered shrub in wash habitats below 4,000 feet in both the Mojave and Sonoran Deserts. It is a highly-branched subshrub in the Asteraceae family that reaches up to 4 feet in height. The small linear leaves of sweetbush are oppositely arrayed low on the plant and alternate above; they are only present for a short period of time in the spring and the plant's stems are the primary photosynthetic organ during the remainder of the year. The pale-yellow flower heads of sweetbush are discoid, as there are no outer flowers with petal-like organs (Fig. 6.18). Sweetbush is a nondescript plant for most of the year when neither leaves nor flowers are present, but it is easily recognized by its sweetly aromatic stems from which it gets its name.

Cooper's paper daisy (*Psilostrophe cooperi*) is a semi-woody clumping shrub 2–3 feet in height, and notable for stems and leaves covered by a white woolly mat of hairs. During the spring and early summer flowering season, its clusters of mustard-yellow ray flowers are quite showy (Fig. 6.19). Cooper's paper daisy is found in sandy washes and gravelly slopes within creosote bush scrub and Joshua tree woodland at elevations up to 6,000 feet in the eastern Mojave and

Fig. 6.17. Ambrosia monogyra, Asteraceae, burrobush. Photo by Joey Santore.

northern Sonoran deserts in California and eastward to Utah and New Mexico.

The genus *Brickellia* comprises a large group of semi-woody shrubs in the Asteraceae family, with 13 species present in the margins of our desert regions. All *Brickellia* species have aromatic foliage with glandular hairs; odors range from fragrant to unpleasant. All California *Brickellia* species have discoid heads of whitish flowers, sometimes tinged with a reddish color. Most species are opportunistic in their establishment and growth, colonizing washes and other disturbed sites. Four of our desert *Brickellia* form relatively large shrubs up to 4 feet or more in height. California brickellbush (*Brickellia californica*) is widespread along the western margins of both of our desert regions, as well as throughout southern California coastal shrublands (Fig. 6.20). Desert brickellbush (*Brickellia desertorum*), a closely related species similar in appearance to California brickellbush, is widely distributed in creosote bush scrub in both the Mojave and Sonoran Desert regions. White brickellbush (*Brickellia incana*) has foliage heavily covered in dense white hairs (Fig. 6.21). It

Fig. 6.18. *Bebbia juncea*, Asteraceae, sweetbush. Photo by Jim Morefield.

Fig. 6.19 *Psilostrophe cooperi*, Asteraceae, Photo by Stan Shebs.

Fig. 6.20. Brickellia californica, Asteraceae, California brickellbush. Photo by Robert Gustafson.

Fig. 6.21. *Brickellia incana*, Asteraceae, white brickellbush. Photo by Matt Berger.

Fig. 6.22. *Brickellia atractyloides*, Asteraceae, pungent brickellbush. Photo by Robert Gustafson.

Fig. 6.23. *Baccharis salicifolia*, Asteraceae, mulefat.. Photo by Matt Berger.

occurs on rocky slopes and in sandy or gravelly washes across both desert regions at elevations below 4,000 feet. Pungent brickellbush (*Brickellia atractyloides*)—a smaller shrub with ovate, prominently toothed leaves (Fig. 6.22)—is perhaps the most distinctive species because of its smell.

Five species of *Baccharis*, tall shrubby members of the Asteraceae, are found in desert washes—particularly in the lower Sonoran Desert. *Baccharis* is an unusual genus within its family because it has separate male and female plants. Two of our desert *Baccharis* are tall multi-stemmed shrubs that reach as much as 12 feet in height and may form dense thickets. Mule fat (*Baccharis salicifolia*) is a familiar semi-evergreen species from riparian habitats of the Mediterranean-type shrublands of southern California that extends its range throughout the Sonoran Desert and western Mojave Desert. Mule fat has a willow-like appearance, with multiple vertical branches and narrow evergreen leaves 2–6 inches in length (Fig. 6.23). These leaves are quite sticky to the touch. Willow baccharis (*Baccharis salacina*, formerly *Baccharis emoryi*), is a species that grows in riparian corridors of the Mediterranean-type shrublands and eastward into the Sonoran Desert. It is easily distinguished from mule fat by its smaller wedge-shaped and generally toothed leaves that are no more than 1.5 inches in length.

Two other species of *Baccharis* have a broom-like appearance with clusters of vertical branches that are largely leafless. Broom baccharis (*Baccharis sarothroides*), is a wash species with narrow linear leaves no more than 2 inches in length (Fig. 6.24). It occurs widely across the western Sonoran Desert, as well as extending into coastal areas of southern California. Like the two species above, it reaches 12 feet in height. Somewhat smaller is desert baccharis (*Baccharis sergiloides*), which reaches only about 6 feet in height. It is distinguished by small ovate leaves that are no more than an inch in length and wider near the tip than at their base (Fig. 6.25). Desert baccharis can commonly be found in dry canyon bottoms across both the Mojave and Sonoran Deserts.

Fig. 6.24. *Baccharis sarothroides*, Asteraceae, broom baccharis. Photo by Matt Berger.

Fig. 6.25. *Baccharis sergiloides*, Asteraceae. desert bacharis. Photo by Stan Shebs.

The fifth species of this group is shortleaf baccharis (*Baccharis brachyphylla*), which is woody only at its base and reaches no more than 3 feet in height. It is distinguished by glandular hairs along its stems and small sessile leaves that become scalelike on the upper stems. Shortleaf baccharis occurs in dry washes of the western Sonoran Desert and up into lower elevations of Joshua Tree National Park.

Shrub species of goldenbush are characteristically good colonizers of open sites. Several species were described in Chapter 4 and Great Basin species are described in Chapter 11. Black-banded rabbitbrush (*Ericameria paniculata*) is a large shrub reaching 4–6 feet in height that is a widespread colonizer of open washes, roadsides, and disturbed sites across both desert regions at elevations of 1,300–5,200 feet in elevation (Fig. 6.26). The erect stems and leaves are resinous and often banded with black fungal stripes.

Scale broom (*Lepidospartum squamatum*) is an important pioneer species of Asteraceae that grows in sandy, gravelly soils of alluvial washes and open disturbed

Fig. 6.26. *Ericameria paniculata*, Asteraceae, black-banded rabbitbrush near Van Winkle Mountain. Photo by Julie Evens, inset by James Morefield.

sites in the Mediterranean-type shrublands and the western Mojave Desert of southern California. It is a tall, multi-stemmed shrub reaching 6 feet or more in height (Fig. 6.27). The common name comes from the scale-like leaves and stiff, leggy branches that resemble a broom. Single or small clusters of discoid flower heads occur at the ends of branches. As the fruits mature and the flower parts fall away the flower cluster takes on a cottony look. These traits have led it to be described as a bunch of green cornstalk brooms tied together with yellow flowers on top.

Fig. 6.27. *Lepidospartum squamatum*, Asteraceae, scale broom. Photo by Morgan Stickrod.

Outliers of Subtropical Aridlands

Beleperone (*Justicia californica*) is a scraggly shrub 2–5 feet in height with gray-green photosynthetic stems that is virtually leafless most of the year. It is frequently found growing in sandy washes of our lower desert areas—and widely throughout the Sonoran Desert outside of California with summer rainfall. Both summer drought and cold temperatures can cause beleperone to lose its leaves. A prominent, tubular red flowers appear in spring (Fig. 6.28) and are frequently visited by hummingbirds to harvest the nectar. Beleperone is an outlier of the largely tropical Acanthaceae family, which has extended its range into the low desert region of California. The only other native member of this family in our state is the rare Arizona carlowrightia (*Carlowrightia arizonica*)—a low subshrub similar in vegetative appearance to beleperone. It has broad drought-deciduous leaves, gray-green photosynthetic stems, and unusual large white flowers that seem lily-like with three-petals at first glance but are actually composed of five petals. Arizona carlowrightia is known in California from only a few desert localities in eastern San Diego County. It has a CNPS Rare Plant Rank 2B: plants rare, threatened, or endangered in California and elsewhere.

California trixis (*Trixis californica*) is an erect subshrub reaching 1–3 feet in height with brittle whitish stems. It has large leaves for a desert species, ¾ by 1½ inches in length, that are shed with summer water stress (Fig. 6.29). It is widespread across the greater Sonoran Desert but restricted in California to lower elevation desert washes and sheltered canyons. Cold temperatures keep it out of the Mojave Desert. The bright yellow heads of flowers are unusual and deserve a close examination. While they appear to be radiate or ligulate, a careful look reveals that they are discoid with odd elongated two-lipped discoid flowers. California trixis is one of the few representatives in California of what is otherwise largely a South American group within the Asteraceae.

Fig. 6.28. *Justicia californica*, Acanthaceae, beleperone. Photo by Robert Gustafson.

Fig. 6.29. *Trixis californica*, Asteraceae, California trixis. Photo by Matt Berger.

Although true subtropical thorn scrub does not occur in California deserts, several large spiny shrubs that represent thorn scrub elements of northwestern Mexico often occur in wash woodland habitats of the Sonoran Desert in of California. These large, drought-deciduous, woody shrubs are characterized by branches so spiny that they are difficult to ignore. The four least spiny species are members of the buckthorn family (Rhamnaceae), while the other two species are the only representatives of their tropical families in California.

Graythorn (*Ziziphus obtusifolia*) is a large shrub reaching 8–10 feet in height. Although it is widely distributed across the Sonoran and Chihuahuan Deserts, it is limited in California to wash habitats in the Chuckwalla and Orocopia Mountains north of the Salton Sea. Graythorn branches spread at right angles to the main stems and end with sharp spines (Fig. 6.30). The ovate leaves, with small teeth along their margins, are drought-deciduous and dropped in in summer. The California variety of graythorn features stems covered with persistent whitish-gray hairs, which gives rise to its common name. Although a relatively uncommon species in California, graythorn is an important component of stream channel vegetation in Arizona, where it may form dense thickets. Lotebush or Parry's jujube (*Ziziphus parryi*) is a related species that is limited in distribution to the western margins of the Sonoran Desert. It is mostly found along the arid interior foothills

Fig. 6.30. *Zizyphus obtusifolia*, Rhamnaceae, graythorn. Photo by Robert Gustafson.

Fig. 6.31. *Condalia globosa*, Rhamnaceae, bitter snakewood. Photo by Stan Shebs.

Fig. 6.32. *Colubrina californica*, Rhamnaceae, California colubrina. Photo by Joey Santore.

of the Peninsular Range. Although similar in size and general appearance, it does not overlap in distribution with graythorn. Lotebush is separated from graythorn by larger fruits with prominent beaks.

Bitter snakewood (*Condalia globosa*) is similar in general appearance and size to the two species of *Ziziphus* and shares the trait of sharp spinescent branch tips diverging at right angles from the stem (Fig. 6.31). One trait distinguishing bitter snakeweed is the presence of three to four prominent pairs of veins on the lower leaf surface. Bitter snakewood is relatively uncommon in California, with its range largely restricted to the southeastern margin of the state near the Colorado River. It is widespread and more abundant in the Sonoran Desert outside of California. The Seri Indians of Sonora, Mexico have long used this species for tattooing. The fruits provide a dye and the spiny branch tips serve as a needle.

California colubrina (*Colubrina californica*) is the fourth species of spiny Rhamnaceae. It occurs in scattered desert washes in the low hills to the east and southeast of the Salton Sea basin, as well as scattered locations throughout the broader Sonoran Desert. California colubrina is a densely-branched shrub typically no more than 3–6 feet in height. The small leaves are about ½-1 inch long and have a gray-green color due to fine pubescence on their surface (Fig. 6.32). Like all of the Rhamnaceae wash species, California colubrina is drought-deciduous. The fruits of *Colubrina* are dry capsules containing three seeds, while those of *Ziziphus* and *Condalia* are classified as small drupes, meaning they are fleshy fruits surrounding a hard pit —like apricots and peaches.

Two additional species of large spiny shrubs rely primarily on stem photosynthesis rather than their leaves. Crown-of-thorns (*Koeberlinia spinosa*) is a large, rigidly-branched shrub reaching up to 15 feet in height. Its leaves have been reduced to ephemeral scale-like structures and the green branches substitute as photosynthetic organs (Fig. 6.33). Each sharply spine-tipped branch diverges from larger branches at a right angle, making for an absolutely impenetrable canopy. Crown-of-thorns is the only species that exists in the Koeberliniaceae family. It is widespread across the broader Sonoran Desert but only occurs in five known locations in the Chocolate Mountains in California. It has a CNPS Rare Plant Rank 2B: plants rare, threatened, or endangered in California and elsewhere.

Fig. 6.33. *Koeberlinea spinosa*, Koeberliniaceae, crown-of-thorns. Photo by Robert Gustafson.

Crucifixion thorn (*Castela emoryi*) is the final species of large spiny shrub of subtropical lineage within our desert wash flora. Like other subtropical biogeographic elements of our flora, it has a widespread distribution in the Sonoran Desert but is relatively rare in California. Crucifixion thorn is found in scattered areas to the east and southeast of the Salton Sea basin and north into the southern margin of the Mojave Desert. It is best known from Crucifixion Thorn Natural Area in Imperial County, where some of the largest known populations are found and plants reach up to 15 feet in height. As with crown-of-thorns, the leaves of crucifixion thorn are reduced to ephemeral scales and stout spine-tipped branches serve as primary photosynthetic organs (Fig. 6.34), yet the branching pattern is quite distinct between these two species. Crucifixion thorn has sharper branching angles and a paler green branch color. Crucifixion thorn is the only member of its tropical family, the Simaroubaceae, which occurs naturally in California. It has a CNPS Rare Plant Rank 2B: plants rare, threatened, or endangered in California and elsewhere.

Fig. 6.34. *Castela emory*, Simaroubaceae, crucifixion thorn. Photo by Matt Berger.

The genus *Bursera* forms a group of about 40 species native to subtropical and semi-arid tropical regions of the Americas, with a distribution extending from the southwest United States to northern Argentina. Six of these species occur in the summer rainfall areas of the Sonoran Desert; just one of these species manages to extend its range into California. The elephant tree (*Bursera microphylla*) is a squat, stem-succulent tree reaching up to 15 feet in height found in scattered wash habitats of Anza Borrego Desert State Park (Fig. 6.35). The common name comes from the thick trunk and major branches which contain succulent tissues for the storage of water and resemble an elephant's trunk. While central Baja California and areas of Sonora, Mexico possess other stem-succulent tree species that resemble the elephant tree, this is the only one of this group found in California. In addition to its distinctive swollen trunk and major branches, elephant tree is recognized by its bark that exfoliates in thin sheets and by its reddish, young stems. Peeling back the exfoliating bark reveals a greenish main trunk. These stem tissues maintain low levels of photosynthesis during the dry portions of the year when the plants are leafless, but probably not enough to do more than partially balance the costs of respiration. The drought-deciduous leaves are clustered at the ends of short shoots and contain highly aromatic terpenoids. A puff of these compounds can be seen spraying into the air if one carefully pulls a single leaf from a branch of elephant tree and watches carefully. It has a CNPS Rare Plant Rank 2B: plants rare, threatened, or endangered in California and elsewhere.

    Ocotillo (*Fouquieria splendens*) is an unusual species with a remarkably wide range across the entire Sonoran Desert and into the Chihuahuan Desert. It is one of only a few woody species that naturally occurs in both desert regions. The spiny stems of ocotillo are highly distinctive, giving the appearance of tall wands or carriage whips (Fig. 6.36). Perhaps the most remarkable feature of the ecology of ocotillo is how rapidly it responds to rainfall. For most of the year ocotillo stands leaf-

Fig. 6.35. *Bursera microphylla*, Burseraceae, elephant tree. Photo by Len Mazur, inset by Matt Berger.

less, but following a significant rain event it produces a new cohort of leaves within 24–48 hours. If the rainfall is substantial, these leaves may remain on the plant for months. Under such conditions, showy red flowers are produced. With less rainfall, the leaves have a relatively short life span; they dry out and are shed within a few weeks. Ocotillo demonstrates remarkable flexibility in its ability to produce new leaves. Rather than limit this event to just once a year, ocotillo can leaf out as many as five to six times in a season if rains are scattered. At the other extreme, in a dry year, leaf production may not occur. The stems of ocotillo are green and maintain a small amount of photosynthesis when the plant is leafless. The rate of photosynthesis by these stems is low, and probably serves only to balance some of the metabolic costs of respiration rather than enable new growth.

Ocotillo is a member of an interesting genus of stem succulent plants that form the family Fouquieriaceae. The most famous species of the genus is the boojum tree or cirio (*Fouquieria columnaris*) of Baja California, Mexico whose tall stem can reach 70 feet. The family extends from California, where ocotillo is the only representative, through the warm desert areas of Mexico and south into dry tropical forest areas. An interesting feature of ocotillo and most of its sibling species of *Fouquieria*, is that cut branches will readily root if placed in the ground. This trait is the basis of the widespread custom of making living fences out of these branches in many rural areas of Mexico.

Fig. 6.36. *Fouquieia splendens*, Fouquieriaceae, ocotillo, colonizing washes in Eastern Imperial County. Photo by Julie Evens.

Desert Gourds

There are several members of the Cucurbitaceae or gourd family that are found in desert washes where they can tap underground water. These species have large, fleshy tuber-like roots that store carbohydrates and allow for diurnal water storage. As mentioned in Chapter 3, many of these desert cucurbits have relatively large leaves that operate at leaf temperatures below ambient air temperature in the late spring and early summer. They do this by cooling via high transpiration rates. Coyote melon (*Cucurbita palmata*) is a sprawling vine with rough, stiff-haired stems and leaves palmately divided into five triangular lobes (Fig. 6.37). The mottled bright green- to yellow-fruits are spherical in shape and 3–4 inches in diameter. Closely related and similar in appearance is finger-leaved gourd (*Cucurbita digitata*), with linear leaf lobes that are divided nearly to the petiole. The fruits of both species are generally distasteful to most animal species, but the seeds are nutritious.

Fig. 6.37. *Cucurbita palmata*, Cucurbitaceae, coyote melon. Photo by Stan Shebs.

Another gourd occasionally found scattered in dry washes is desert starvine (*Brandegea bigelovii*). This sprawling vine trails out from a large tuber-like root in huge masses that can overwhelm adjacent shrubs with its fine branches and tendrils. The small, dark green leaves are palmately lobed and covered with white oil glands (Fig. 6.38). Unlike the yellow squash-like flowers of the two *Cucurbita* species, desert starvine has small white flowers and produces prickly fruits containing only a single seed.

Fig. 6.38. *Brandegea bigelovii*, Cucurbitaceae, desert starvine. Photo by Robert Gustafson.

Chapter 7
Desert Wetlands:
Palm Oases, Riparian Woodlands, and Marshes

Crystal Spring in the Ash Meadows National Wildlife Refuge is home to the rare desert pupfish. Photo by Michael Kauffmann.

Introduction

The term *desert wetlands* seems like an oxymoron. How can there be wetlands in a desert ecosystem? Despite the low levels of rainfall in our desert regions, local geological and hydrological conditions can combine to produce areas where artesian springs, or accumulations of water flow from floodplain basins, produce seasonally or permanently saturated soils. Available groundwater makes this precious resource available to relatively shallow-rooted plants that would otherwise not be able to survive desert aridity. There are three main types of wetland habitats seen in our deserts: palm oases, riparian woodlands along desert streams, and local areas of freshwater and semi-alkaline marsh systems.

Palm Oases

The California fan palm (*Washingtonia filifera*) is the only palm native to California. It is thought to be an ancient species with a history dating back to the middle Tertiary when it occurred more broadly across coastal and Mojave Desert areas of the state. Today, the natural range of this species is highly localized at scattered desert sites where permanent water exists relatively close to the soil surface. There are approximately 100 palm oases in California, with populations ranging from only a few to hundreds of mature palms (Fig. 7.1). The largest groups of palm oases occur around the Coachella Valley where geologic conditions along the San Andreas fault promote shallow groundwater tables. From this center of distribution, California fan palm extends to the north to Twentynine Palms and the Cottonwood Mountains and south into northern Baja California where it is replaced by the related Mexican fan palm (*Washingtonia robusta*). Although simi-

Fig. 7.1. Dense grove of *Washingtonia filifera* in Palm Canyon, southeast of Palm Springs. Photo by Stan Shebs.

lar in appearance, the Mexican fan palm has bright green fronds compared to our California species with gray-green fronds, and reaches much greater heights with a narrow tapered trunk. Both are widely cultivated in southern California and other parts of the world.

Mature California fan palms reach to 70 feet in height, and up to 3 feet or more in diameter. However, where the trees have not been trimmed or burned, the diameters seem far greater as the old leaf bases and portions of dried leaves are maintained on the trunk surface (Fig. 7.2). The highly flammable nature of this dead leaf material points to a key aspect of the ecology of these palms. Palm seedlings require full sun for growth and survival but are easily overtopped and shaded where a dense shrub cover is present below the parent palms. Fire, an unexpected element of a desert environment, provides a means of reducing this shrub cover and allowing palm seedlings to become established (Fig. 7.3). Today, the origin of natural fires are summer lightning strikes associated with convective storms moving into the California deserts from Arizona or the Gulf of California. A lightning strike on a mature palm can readily ignite a fire on the dry leaf material along their trunks. The thick and fibrous trunk of the palms makes them relatively impervious to the fire, while the biomass of woody shrubs below is consumed. Indigenous cultural burning practices were historically important in maintaining healthy palm oases systems. Various tribes periodically set fire to oases to increase fruit production, decrease shrub competition, and remove fronds on the oasis floor. The Cahuillas, and likely others, planted palm seeds in promising locations.

Since California fan palms have a relatively long lifespan, extending perhaps to 200 years or more, occasional reproduction of seedlings is sufficient to maintain popula-

Fig. 7.2. *Washingonia filifera*, Arecaceae, California fan palm, in Palm Canyon. Photo by Stan Shebs.

Fig. 7.3. Post-fire palm reproduction in Anza-Borrego Desert State Park. Photo by Matt Berger.

tions. Years with heavy desert rains have been associated with successful seedling establishment by the palms. Coyotes and other vertebrates eat the palm fruits and provide a means of transporting seeds between oasis areas. Although there are exaggerated accounts of fan palms living for thousands of years, there is no scientific basis for such ages. In fact, there is no direct way to date palms as their trunk structure does not produce annual growth rings. The best estimates of maximum age come from measured rates of leaf production along the trunk over several years, extrapolated to the full height of the palm.

There are two primary topographic situations where California fan palm, and its associated oasis community, occurs. One of these is a wash-oasis habitat along canyons or arroyo bottoms where ground water collects. In the Coachella Valley these are often positioned where movements along the San Andreas Fault force deep groundwater to the surface. These habitats are typically heterogeneous in the distribution of subsurface soil moisture and thus promote the localized presence of the palms and other associate species. Often there is a gradient from wetland sites with surface water to the fan palm areas with permanent groundwater pools at shallow soil depths, and then on to more typical wash communities with ephemeral groundwater. The second form of topographic sites are steep hillsides or small hanging canyons where springs or groundwater seeps provide a permanent water supply (Fig. 7.4). While such sites would seem to be unsuited for a long-lived spe-

Fig. 7.4. Palm oases in rocky upland slopes, Anza-Borrego Desert State Park. Photo by Morgan Stickrod.

cies such as the fan palm, comparisons of century-old photographs with present stands of these seep oases suggest that they are stable.

While the palm oases are not typically high in species diversity, there are a number of woody and herbaceous species that are associated with these areas. Quailbush (*Atriplex lentiformis*), or big saltbush, is a large shrub that reaches as much as 8–10 feet in height, but with a sprawling growth form that makes it generally much wider than tall. Rather than being exclusively a desert species, quailbush is common in coastal areas of southern California as well. While it is found in alkaline and saline washes and in mixed salt scrub communities around playas (see Chapter 8), it is widely distributed around the margins of both coastal and desert wetlands. Although it may occasionally occur in sheltered areas at elevations up to 4,500 feet, it is more typical of the lower desert areas below 2,000 feet.

Fig. 7.5. *Pluchea sericea*, Asteraceae, arrow weed. Photo by Stan Shebs.

Arrow weed (*Pluchea sericea*) is a tall willow-like shrub with straight slender branches reaching to 10-12 feet (Fig. 7.5). It occurs along river channels, in palm oases, and other wetland sites throughout the Mojave and Sonoran deserts and is particularly abundant along the flood plain of the Colorado River. Arrow weed's name comes from Native American use of its stems to make arrow shafts.

Desert Riparian Woodlands

Although there are few streams and rivers in the desert, those with permanent surface or shallow subsurface water flows once supported extensive riparian woodlands. The flood plain of the Colorado River continues to support such woodlands (Fig. 7.6), but the Mojave and Amargosa rivers have lost much of the surface flow that they had 10,000 years ago. However, limited areas of active flow-channels with riparian tree cover are present where geologic conditions force water to the surface (Figs. 7.7, 7.8). These channels are subject to irregular flooding and, thus, ideal habitats for pioneering riparian trees that can tolerate these conditions. Examples include cottonwoods, willows, and ash.

One example is seen in Fremont cottonwood (*Populus fremontii*), a large tree that can reach up to 60 feet in height (Fig. 7.9). It is easily recognized by its triangular leaves with a toothed margin (Fig. 7.10). This is the familiar cottonwood of the warm desert regions of California, Nevada, Utah, and Arizona. Cottonwoods get their name from the profusion of cotton-like seeds that they shed every spring. The local dominance of Fremont cottonwood in favorable habitats within our desert parks gives rise to the names Cottonwood Springs in Joshua Tree National Park and Cottonwood Canyon in Death Valley.

Riparian willows that form riparian thickets include red willow (*Salix laevigata*), sandbar willow (*Salix exigua*), and Goodding's black willow (*Salix gooddingii*). Both red and black willow are trees with a prominent main trunk. Red willow, which is characterized by leaves that are grayish or gray-white on their lower surface

Fig. 7.6. Colorado River, Chemehuevi. Photo by Allan A. Schoenherr.

Fig. 7.7. Amargosa River Canyon. Photo by Naomi Fraga.

Fig. 7.8. Mojave River, Afton Canyon. Public domain photo by Mark Wilson.

reaches heights of 20–30 feet or even taller under optimal growing conditions (Fig. 7.11). Goodding's black willow, in contrast, has leaves with a similar green color on both surfaces. It can be a large tree and reach heights up to 100 feet (Fig. 7.12) Sandbar willow is easily distinguished by long, thin, grayish leaves with silky hairs (Fig. 7.13). It has a shrubby growth form, with multiple main stems, and a height usually well below 15–20 feet. Other names for this species include narrow-leaved willow and coyote willow. The latter name derives from the fact that the shade cast by the shrubby growth provides a favored site for coyote dens. While these are the three common willows at lower desert elevations, several other willow species occur within the boundaries of the Mojave Desert, particularly along streams at montane or subalpine elevations on some of the higher mountains.

Another widespread tree in desert riparian woodlands is velvet ash (*Fraxinus velutina*), a species that can reach 50 feet or more in height. This riparian tree species that gives the name to Ash Meadows along the Amargosa River in Nevada, as described below. Velvet ash trees are easily recognized by their oppositely arrayed compound leaves with 5–9 lance-shaped leaflets (Fig. 7.14). The fruits, called samaras, are wind-dispersed gyrocopters with broad wings to give them aerodynamic lift. Velvet ash gets its common name from the young leaves which feel somewhat velvety.

Cottonwoods, willows, and ash are all riparian trees that lose their leaves during the winter months. While it may seem strange to have such moisture-loving species in the desert, the presence of a relatively permanent flow or groundwater pool of available freshwater provides conditions well suited for growth. So long as water is available, high summer temperatures present little or no threat. Similar desert riparian woodlands occur widely across the arid and semi-arid regions of the western United States where the conditions of geological and hydrological processes outweigh differences in climatic regime.

In addition to the riparian woodlands, open mesquite woodlands are often present in areas along river channels and floodplains with shallow groundwater. These stands include honey mesquite (*Prosopis glandulosa* var. *torreyana*) as described in Chapter 6. Also present in open or continuous stands is screwbean mesquite (*Prosopis pubescens*), known as tornillo in Spanish, which is also geographically widespread but much less common in California. It is easily recognized when fruits are present because of the shape of the pods with a tightly coiled pattern of growth. Screwbean mesquite is generally restricted in California to areas with permanent or semi-permanent groundwater, but generally is not able to root to depths more than about 10-15 feet.

A variety of human impacts including groundwater extraction, clearance for agriculture, recreational development, and the introduction of invasive species have dramatically reduced the extent of desert riparian and floodplain woodlands today. The most dramatic impact from the establishment and expansion of alien species has come from the introduction of saltcedar (*Tamarisk ramossisima* and *T. parviflora*). The ecology of saltcedar and its impact on desert riparian ecosystems is discussed in Chapter 12. Another invasive tree, Russian olive (*Elaeagnus angustifolius*), has also become established by escaping from cultivation. This small, usually

Fig. 7.9. Fremont cottonwood riparian trees in Lyon County, Nevada. Photo by Tim Messick.

Fig. 7.10. *Populus fremontii*, Salicaceae, Fremont cottonwood. Photo by Jim Morefield.

Fig. 7.11. *Salix laevigata*, Salicaceae, red willow. Photo by Len Mazur.

Fig. 7.12. *Salix gooddingii*, Salicaceae, Goodding's black willow. Photo by Robert Gustafson.

Fig. 7.13. *Salix exigua*, Salicaceae, sandbar willow. Photo by Matt Berger.

thorny shrub or tree can reach to 30 feet in height. It is easily recognized by its lance-shaped alternate leaves that exhibit a dense covering of silvery scales and creamy yellow flowers that appear in June and July. The fruits, produced abundantly in late summer, resemble olives and hence the origin of its name. It is a member of the mostly tropical family Elaeagnaceae.

Freshwater and Semi-Alkaline Seasonal Marshes

Small freshwater marshes occur in scattered locations across both the Mojave and Sonoran deserts. Sometimes these are local areas or oases where artesian springs bring water to the surface. In other cases, they occur along floodplains where backwaters, or ponded areas, form as desert stream and cut new channels. Some of the most prominent areas of freshwater wetlands are seen along the Amargosa River where it has surface flow in the area of Ash Meadows and Saratoga Springs (Fig. 7.15) in the eastern Mojave Desert and in the complex of springs in Cahuilla Basin of the Sonoran Desert (San Sebastien Marsh, San Felipe Creek, Carrizo Wash, and Harper's Well). Many of these springs are important conservation sites for desert pupfish, a significant and endangered group of freshwater fish that once occurred widely across the Pleistocene lakes of the Great Basin, Mojave, and Sonoran deserts.

Fig. 7.14. *Fraxinus velutina,* Oleaceae, velvet ash. Photo by Matt Berger.

Fig. 7.15. Saratoga Springs, Death Valley Nationa Park. Photo by Stan Shebs.

Fig. 7.16. Freshwater to brackish marshes with *Scirpus americanus* and *Anemopsis californica* near Zzyzx at Soda Lake. Photo by Todd Keeler-Wolf.

Fig. 7.17. *Phragmites australis*, Poaceae, common reed. Photo by Matt Berger.

Small wetland pools, with permanent water supplied by a complex hydrologic system of regional aquifers, promote a characteristic plant assemblages dominated by freshwater marsh species more typically encountered in non-arid areas of California and the western United States. The most prominent of these are bulrushes (*Schoenoplectus acutus* and *S. americanus*, formerly in the genus *Scirpus*), which reach 5–10 feet or more in height (Fig. 7.16). These members of the sedge family are recognized by the triangular shape of the stem cross-section, a character easily remembered by the mnemonic phrase, "sedges have edges."

Common reed (*Phragmites australis*) is a robust perennial grass with a remarkable range that extends to wetland habitats throughout the world, here common in desert marshes (Fig. 7.17). A third group of tall marsh species are the cattails (Typhaceae). The most common of these in our desert areas is the narrow-leaved cattail (*Typha domingensis*), which is distinguished by a bare area on the flowering stalks separating the male flowers above the female flowers below. The closely related broad-leaved cattail (*Typha latifolia*) lacks this separation (Fig. 7.18). All three of these groups reproduce vegetatively from underground rhizomes. They are able to survive the anaerobic conditions of waterlogged soils by using hollow stems to transport air to their roots.

Fig. 7.18. *Typha latifolia*, Typhaceae, cattail. Photo by Robert Gustafson.

Another common species of water-logged soils along streamsides and in marshes is yerba mansa (*Anemopsis californica*; Saururaceae). It forms continuous stands of low, herbaceous growth with basal leaves reaching up to 2 feet in height. The erect, conical heads of the flowering stalks are set off by showy white bracts (petal-like specialized leaves) at their base (Fig. 7.20). As with many other wetland species, yerba mansa has hollow stems and underground rhizomes that promote vegetative reproduction. Saltgrass (*Distichlis spicata*), described in Chapter 8, is common in alkaline marsh habitats.

Herbaceous areas of seasonal alkaline wetlands are often dominated by alkali dropseed (*Sporobolus airoides*), a tall bunchgrass up to 3 feet in height (Fig. 7.20), that is distributed across alkaline flats over broad areas of the southwestern United States. It is a summer-active grass, meaning that it exhibits C_4 metabolism and favors growth under high summer temperatures (see Chapter 3). It is recognized by its graceful, open seedheads with small reddish spikelets.

The Amargosa River flows underground in a southerly direction from its headwaters north of Beatty, Nevada. Its direction changes just south of Tecopa, California (Fig. 7.21), near the Dumont Dunes, where the river makes a u-turn and heads north into Death Valley National Park—terminating in Badwater Basin. Although the flow of the Amargosa River is primarily underground, there are sites where bedrock close to the surface has allowed the development of artesian springs with continuous flow. The Ash Meadow National Wildlife Refuge 90 miles northwest of Las Vegas protects 23,000 acres of wetland and desert habitat. Strata pushes fossil water, tens of thousands of years in age, to the surface. This nurtures a rich wetland complex including springs, seeps, river channels, and alkali meadows (Fig. 7.22).

There are many rare plant species associated with these perennially wet habitats. An example of a large perennial is copperwort (*Euphrosyne acerosa*). It is robust, reaching up to 3 feet in height in moist alkaline meadows where it forms large clumps of unbranched stems (Fig. 7.23). Numerous elongated clusters of minute flowers top each of the many stems. Copperwort is rare and restricted to the Ash Meadows area of Nevada and adjacent California along the Amargosa River with

Fig. 7.19. *Anemopsis californica*, Saururaceae, yerba mansa. Photo by Robert Gustafson.

Fig. 7.20. *Sporobolus airoides*, Poaceae, alkali dropseed. Photo by Naomi Fraga.

Fig. 7.21. Amargosa River at Tecopa. Photo by Stan Shebs.

Fig. 7.22. Ash Meadows Crystal Spring. Photo by Naomi Fraga.

a CNPS Rare Plant Rank of 1B: rare, threatened, or endangered in California and elsewhere. Similarly, Cooper's rush (*Juncus cooperi,* CNPS 4.3) is an herbaceous perennial that resembles a dense bunchgrass and reaches 3 feet in height—scattered in wet alkaline soils of the eastern Mojave Desert (Fig. 7.24).

The significance of these wetland habitats is seen in the numerous rare and, in some cases, locally endemic species of herbaceous perennials. Ash Meadows gumplant (*Grindelia fraxinipratensis*) is a robust herbaceous perennial in the Asteraceae reaching up to 3 feet (Fig. 7.25). It is rare and occurs only in the Ash Meadows area of Nevada and adjacent California along the Amargosa River with a CNPS Rare Plant Rank of 1B: rare, threatened,

Fig. 7.23. *Euphosyne acerosa*, Asteraceae, copperwort. Photo by Naomi Fraga.

Fig. 7.24. *Juncus cooperi*, Juncaceae, Cooper's rush. Photo by Naomia Fraga.

Fig. 7.25. *Grindelia fraxinopratensis*, Ash Meadows gumplant. Photo by Matt Berger.

or endangered in California and elsewhere. Tecopa salty birds-beak (*Chloropyron tecopense*) is a rare annual hemiparasite in the broom-rape family (Orobanchaceae) with a localized distribution in alkaline wetlands of the Tecopa marsh (Fig. 7.26). It has a CNPS Rare Plant Rank of 1B: rare, threatened, or endangered in California and elsewhere. Mojave nitrophila (*Nitrophila mojavensis*), described in Chapter 8, has a similar limited range. An interesting ecological note is that many of these specialized species flower in the summer, at the peak of extreme temperatures.

Alkali mariposa lily (*Calochortus striatus*) shows a similar restriction to springs and alkali seeps in the western Mojave Desert. It is easily recognized by its petals with lateral purple striations (Fig. 7.27). It also has a CNPS Rare Plant Rank of 1B: rare, threatened, or endangered in California and elsewhere.

Fig. 7.26. *Chloropyron tecopense*, Orobanchaceae, Tecopa salty birds-beak. Photo by Matt Berger.

Fig. 7.27. *Calochortus striatus*, Liliaceae, alkali mariposa lily. Photo by Robert Gustafson.

Chapter 8
Saline Habitats:
Playas, Saltbush Scrub, and Alkali Sinks

Remnants from the Saline Valley salt mine from which a tram was used to carry salt up and over the Inyo Mountains to the Owens Valley. Photo by Allison Poklemba.

Introduction

While most desert soils are mildly alkaline, localized saline habitats are widely present throughout the Great Basin, the Mojave Desert, and in parts of California's lower Sonoran Desert—although generally scattered in the latter. These saline areas are typically associated with dry playa lakes, topographic sinks, and the flood plains of the Mojave, Amargosa, and Colorado rivers. Poor drainage and subsequent evaporation, rather than elevation, are the key elements in the presence of saline habitats. Saline soils are found anywhere from below sea level in Death Valley to nearly 6,000 feet elevation in interior valleys of the Great Basin.

Playas

Playas occur in intermountain basins throughout the arid southwestern United States. These are flat areas that mark the lowest portion of interior desert basins and lack external drainage. Playas are characteristically underlain by stratified layers, clays, and other fine particles which allow the occasional ponding of runoff water on their dry surface. The fine-textured clays that form the playa's surface are deposited by water flow into these topographic basins. Such flow occurs from mountain runoff in wet years, from springs, or where ephemeral streams discharge onto the playa surface. Following the occasional wetting, the surface of the playa dries and becomes desiccated, forming polygonal cracks and fissures as clay-rich sediments shrink. These playas were the basins of large pluvial lakes during the Pleistocene (Fig. 8.1).

8.1. The Racetrack in Death Valley National Park is now a playa but originated as a pluvial lake formed in the Pleistocene. Photo by Robert Childs.

Salts commonly accumulate on playa surfaces through both evaporation of runoff waters and capillary rise of salty groundwater. Where groundwater is near to the playa surface, alkali salts such as sodium nitrate, sodium carbonate, and sodium bicarbonate precipitate out, forming a frothy-white coating on the playa surface (Fig. 8.2). While this surface appears dry and solid, attempting to walk across a moist playa surface produces a muddy experience—often associated with the loss of one's shoes. Playas with hard surfaces are typically those where the groundwater table is at least 15 feet deep. For both wet and dry playas, the surface layers of dry salts are easily eroded by wind and contribute much to the dust and haze in the Mojave region when late summer and fall winds are common. These fine particulates are associated with numerous health problems for desert residents.

8.2. Salt precipitate in Badwater, Death Valley National Park. Photo by Mark Bailey.

The high salt and clay content of playa mud, and the dry and hot conditions that prevail most of the year, prevent plants from establishing over most of the playa surface. However, the surface of a playa may not be completely homogeneous. Often sand accumulates in channels, fills desiccation fissures, or accumulates around spring mounds. Such sandy fissures allow local plant populations to become established. Nevertheless, plant growth is largely restricted to rings of salt tolerant vegetation around the playa (Fig. 8.3). This chapter describes the characteristic plant species for two of these ring zones—saltbush scrub and alkali sinks. Alkaline seasonal wetlands are described in Chapter 7.

8.3. Saline scrub meets creosote scrub. Photo by Phil Rundel.

Saltbush Scrub

Large desert playas tend to be defined by vegetation rings that form around their margins, with salinity as the key selecting factor. As you move along the lower bajada slopes or sandy flats approaching a playa, creosote bush typically drops out quite abruptly. This boundary for creosote closely approximates the geologic lakebed and lies well beyond the existing playa. While residual salinity may be one factor in limiting the occurrence of creosote bush, more important is the fine texture of the lakebed soils which provides poor mixing of soil gases. Below this boundary, creosote bush is replaced by a community called saltbush scrub with a dominance of various species of saltbush (Fig. 8.4). These saltbush habitats typically exhibit loamy soils with low levels of residual salinity originating from evaporation out of the geologic lakebed.

The saltbushes form the genus *Atriplex* in the goosefoot family or Chenopodiaceae. Some recent evolutionary studies place this family within a broader concept of the Amaranthaceae. Saltbushes as a group have a global pattern of distribution in saline coastal and interior arid habitats. While widely present in warm deserts, saltbush species attain increased importance in cold temperate desert ecosystems. Most shrubby saltbush species are dioecious, meaning that there are separate male and female plants. Both male and female flowers are relatively nondescript and appear during the warm late spring and summer months.

The leaves of most woody *Atriplex* species exhibit morphological and physiological characteristics which are adaptive in a hot, dry environment. Steeply angled leaves reduce midday solar interception yet result in relatively high interception when solar angles are low and atmospheric humidity is relatively high. Another morphological characteristic critical to their ecological success in saline soils is the presence of specialized multicellular hairs on the leaf surfaces which limit the effects

8.4. Saltbush scrub, Rosamond Dry Lake, Edwards Air Force Base. Photo by Phil Rundel.

of the potentially toxic accumulation of salts in their tissues. Each of these hairs has a stalk and an inflated tip called the bladder cell. These shrubs control tissue salt levels by sequestering sodium, potassium, and chloride ions in membrane-bound vacuoles within these bladder cells. The eventual rupture of bladder cells releases these salts back into the environment. Light reflectance from the surface of bladder cells covering the leaf surface gives saltbush species their characteristic silvery color (Fig. 8.5). Like a vertical leaf orientation, these silvery bladder cells reduce incident solar radiation during the summer months, increasing the efficiency of water use, and additionally limiting the absorption of potentially damaging ultraviolet light.

Most species of saltbush utilize C_4 metabolism, one of the specialized mechanisms of carbon fixation (described in Chapter 3). In these shrubs the C_4 metabolism is not utilized to produce unusually high rates of photosynthesis but instead to allow the plants to use water efficiently. This metabolism allows saltbushes to extend their growth well into the summer months when other competing shrub species have lost their leaves and become dormant.

Depending on conditions of soil salinity and moisture availability, there are at least seven *Atriplex* shrub species that attain localized dominance in saltbush scrub communities. Identifying these is challenging as they are all non-descript gray shrubs and lack showy flowers. These species are briefly described below, including several with broad ecological tolerances and ranges of distribution beyond alkaline soils. Shadscale (*Atriplex confertifolia*) is commonly the most abundant species in saltbush scrub (Fig. 8.6). It is a low woody shrub, seldom exceeding 2 feet in height, with branch tips that become notably spinescent as they age. It favors eroded sandy areas with shallow alkaline soils adja-

Fig. 8.5. Reflective bladder cells on Atriplex leaves. Photo by Tim Messick.

Fig. 8.6. *Atriplex confertifolia*, Chenopodiaceae, shadscale. Photo by Matt Berger.

Fig. 8.7. *Atriplex spinifera*, Chenopodiaceae, spinescale. Photo by Matt Berger.

Fig. 8.8. *Atriplex polycarpa*, Chenopodiaceae, allscale. Photo by Matt Berger.

cent to playas but may also be found on adjacent low dunes. Although shadscale is widely present in saltbush scrub across the Mojave Desert, its tolerance of low temperatures allows it to range into areas too cold for other Mojave Desert saltbush species. This species is best known as the dominant of shadscale scrub communities that cover broad saline basins of the Great Basin exposed to cold air drainage and subfreezing night temperatures (see Chapter 11).

Spinescale (*Atriplex spinifera*) is a moderate-sized shrub reaching 4–6 feet in height and characterized by sharp branch tips, hence its common name (Fig. 8.7). Leaves are often ovate with two basal teeth on older leaves. It typically occurs in relatively pure stands on mildly alkaline soils with a thin sand layer over impermeable clay layers below. These conditions are often present around the edges of playas or eroded flat plains. As sandy layers of soil deepen, spinescale begins to occur with other species, forming transitions to stands dominated by either shadscale or allscale.

Allscale (*Atriplex polycarpa*) is widespread throughout the California desert regions in mildly alkaline flats and playa depressions, often forming the outer-ring of saltbush scrub stands around playas. Unlike the more cold-tolerant shadscale, it does not occur at elevations above 5,000 feet. Allscale is a good-sized shrub, often reaching 4–6 feet in height, with small and narrowly oblong leaves with a short petiole (Fig. 8.8). Because of its palatability to cattle, it is sometimes called cattle spinach. Although often present in mixed Atriplex stands, allscale may also be found in relatively pure stands (Fig. 8.9). An interesting characteristic of allscale is it has been shown to change from male to female or back in a given flowering year depending on resource availability.

Parry's saltbush (*Atriplex parryi*) is a low spinescent shrub, 1–2 feet in height, often rounded in shape, that occurs widely on saline soils across the western United States (Fig. 8.10). It is distinguished from associated saltbush species by its heart-shaped leaves that are sessile and clasp the stems. Quailbush (*Atriplex lentiformis*), mentioned in Chapter 6, is commonly associated with mildly alkaline desert washes and wetlands around palm oases, and is often abundant in disturbed sites. It is a large sprawling shrub that is widespread on alkaline soils of the San Joaquin Valley and coastal southern California. Quailbush lacks spines and the large leaves are ovate to triangular, 0.5–2 inches in width, and with their surface covered by dense gray scales (Fig. 8.11).

The least ecologically specialized saltbush species is four-wing saltbush (*Atriplex canescens*) that inhabits a range of widespread, ecological communities over elevations from sea level to more than 8,000 feet. It is an upright shrub, 4–6 feet in height, with a scurfy, gray-green appearance common in many species of saltbush (Fig. 8.12). This color comes from evergreen leaves and young branches that are covered by specialized bladder cells which excrete salts from the plant tissues. Although mildly salt-tolerant, as are many other saltbush species, four-wing saltbush grows widely on sandy, well-drained desert soils as well. The name four-wing saltbush comes from its densely packed fruits on long stems that have four prominent wings displayed at 90° angles—arrayed around a central seed to promote wind dispersal. These fruits, which are persistent on the plant, resemble a mass of corn flakes. Again, like other species of saltbush, four-wing saltbush has separate male and female plants. Like allscale, individual plants can change sex. When drought or a heavy year of seed production stresses female plants, they change to male—with a lower need for resource allocation to fruits. As carbohydrate reserves are replenished in a future year, these male plants can change back to female. The fruits, leaves, and young stems of four-wing saltbush are all palatable, making this an important range plant for both wild and domestic animals.

Desert holly (*Atriplex hymenelytra*) is a large evergreen shrub, reaching 4–6 feet in height, that is widely distributed across the Mojave and Sonoran deserts in a variety of habitats—but less common in alkaline soils. Some of the most prominent stands of nearly pure desert holly are found at the base of alluvial fans in the northern half of Death Valley. The distinctive silver-white leaves are broadly oval but deeply toothed. Combined with the presence of red fruits, it is easily recognized (Fig. 8.13). The branch tips of desert holly are not spinescent.

There are two other shrubby members of the goosefoot family often present in saltbush scrub as well as in upland communities. Winterfat (*Krascheninnikova lanata*) and hopsage (*Grayia spinosa*) occur widely in creosote bush scrub, Joshua tree woodlands, and even pinyon-juniper woodlands (Chapter 4 and 11).

Budsage (*Artemisia spinescens*) is a small compact shrub, typically no more than a foot in height, which occurs widely across the Mojave Desert and Great Basin in stands of saltbush scrub. The inch-long spines along the stems of budsage, the source of the species name, represent the flowering stems from the previous year. The tiny palmately-divided leaves have a cobwebby appearance due to a dense covering of soft hairs and exhibit a strong fragrance (Fig. 8.14). Unlike the various species of saltbush, which are semi-evergreen, budsage is deciduous—losing its leaves each winter.

Alkali goldenbush (*Isocoma acradenia*) is a low and densely branched shrub occurring widely on alkaline soils in both the Mojave and Sonoran deserts (Fig. 8.15). The small, oblong leaves are typically toothed along the margin and distinctly dotted with small glands. Traditional uses include a tea to treat colds as well as an

Fig. 8.9. *Atriplex polycarpa*, Superior Valley, near Barstow, California. Photo by Gina Radieve.

Fig. 8.10. *Atriplex parryi*, Chenopodiaceae, Parry's saltbush. Photo by Matt Berger.

Fig. 8.11. *Atriplex lentiformis*, Chenopodiaceae, quail bush. Photo by Matt Berger.

Fig. 8.12. *Atriplex canescens*, Chenopodiaceae, four-wing saltbush. Photo by Jim Morefield.

Fig. 8.13. *Atriplex hymenelytra*, Chenopodiaceae, desert holly. Photo by Matt Berger.

Fig. 8.14. *Artemisia spinescens*, Astaraceae, budsage. Photo by Jim Morefield.

Fig. 8.15. *Isocoma acradenia*, Asteraceae, alkali goldenbush. Photo by Robert Gustafson.

insect repellent for horses. Unlike most desert species, alkali goldenbush flowers in late summer at the height of drought conditions with yellow flower heads.

The soils associated with many species of saltbush exhibit conditions that promote the development of what are called a *cryptobiotic crusts*, thin black mats formed of mixed cyanobacteria (blue-green algae) and lichens. These crusts are extremely important ecologically as many of the associated microorganisms are able to absorb and fix nitrogen from the atmosphere, and thus with time enrich the associated soils.

Alkali Sinks

Alkali sinks or saline scrub communities are present inside the ring of saltbush scrub, where salinity levels are higher and groundwater occurs near the surface. Saltbush gives way in this community through open stands of low, often succulent-leaved shrubs. Similar communities are present in topographically low areas where rainwater collects but does not penetrate the soil because of subsurface clay or caliche layers (Fig. 8.16). Here, as at the playa edge, dissolved salts wash into the area but remain behind as water evaporates. The resulting soils have a highly alkaline pH and high concentrations of sodium and chloride.

Perhaps the most widespread species of the alkali scrub plants is saltgrass (*Distichlis spicata*), a species also common in coastal salt marshes. Saltgrass forms broad mats using underground rhizomes (Fig. 8.17). To tolerate soils with high salinity, saltgrass possesses specialized structures called salt glands—located in rows parallel with the veins on both the upper and lower leaf surfaces. These glands possess a basal cell where salts collect. This cap cell forms part of the outer leaf surface and is the site of salt excretion. With a hand lens it is easy to see crystals of salt on the leaf surfaces above each salt gland. Lacking a hand lens, you can taste the salt with your tongue. Saltgrass has a broad global distribution and, like many grasses of subtropical origin, utilizes C_4 metabolism. It is not clear what ecological advantage that this provides in a saline desert environment.

Fig. 8.16. Alkali sink adjacent to Soda Lake, Mojave National Preserve. Photo by Stan Shebs.

Fig. 8.17. *Distichlis spicata*, Poaceae, saltgrass. Photo by Robert Gustafson.

Alkali heath (*Frankenia salina*, Frankeniaceae) is a widespread subshrub in saline soils of our desert regions and in coastal and interior salt marshes. Like saltgrass, it utilizes specialized salt glands to remove excess salt (Fig. 8.18). The low-growing plants form twiggy thickets. The laves are small and succulent-like while flowers are white, pink, or fuchsia. Alkali heath spreads by rhizome sand can cover large areas.

There are a number of alkali scrub species that utilize a second successful mechanism for tolerating high soil salinity levels—store excess salts in a way in which it does not affect cell metabolism. This is done by concentrating salts in membrane-bound cell structures called vacuoles, isolated from the cell's cytoplasm. Large storage vacuoles

Fig. 8.18. *Frankenia salina*, Frankeniaceae, saltbush. Photo by Robert Gustafson.

require large cells, which in turn lead to the formation of succulent tissues. Once the storage capacity of succulent leaves or stems is reached, these plants shed their salt-laden tissues and replace them. Most of the species with this trait are members of the goosefoot family (Chenopodiaceae), the same family as the saltbushes. As with saltgrass, many species of the succulent alkali scrub are the same or closely related to species present in saline wetlands of the San Joaquin Valley and coastal salt marshes.

Perhaps the most characteristic species of alkali sink ecosystems is iodine bush (*Allenrolfea occidentalis*), a widespread shrub across the southwestern United States and Mexico, that may form the dominant cover on saline soils of dry lake beds and desert washes. It is characterized by dense branches arising up to 6 feet from a woody base. The knobby stems are fleshy and jointed at the internodes between short, nearly round segments (Fig 8.19). This morphology has led some to describe the stems as a chain of small pickles. The leaves appear as flaky scales scattered across the surface of the stems. The blackish stems of iodine bush make it relatively easy to identify from a great distance by the dark hue which differs from that of surrounding species (Fig. 8.20). With close examination it is easily distinguished from the similar succulent-stemmed pickleweeds by its alternate branching and knobby joints. Cahuilla, Yuma, and Pima use the seeds of iodine bush as a grain to make bread, porridge, and beverages. The Seri of Mexico use it ceremonially.

Fig. 8.19. *Allenrolfea occidentalis*, Chenopodiaceae, iodine bush. Photo by Stan Shebs.

The pickleweeds are typically coastal salt marsh plants and are only rarely encountered in our saline desert habitats. Parish's pickleweed (*Arthrocnemum subterminale*) occurs all along the California coast as well as in alkaline wetlands of the San Joaquin Valley. This subshrub, with a woody base and jointed fleshy green stems, grows as low clumps up to 3 feet in width is known from scattered areas of the western Mojave Desert. The second species is the similar Pacific glasswort (*Salicornia pacifica*) which has a widespread distribution from coastal salt marshes to inland arid areas including a few desert sites in Death Valley.

Bush seepweed (*Suaeda nigra*) is a diffuse shrub or subshrub growing from a woody base and reaching 4 feet in height (Fig. 8.21). It occurs broadly across western North America in saline or alkaline soils. Although characteristically an inland species, it is occasionally found in coastal areas, like estuaries. Bush seepweed is genetically diverse and quite variable in appearance. Its foliage varies from hairy to hairless but is usually waxy. It may be green to red to dark purple in color, and sometimes almost black. The fleshy leaves are also variable in shape—ranging from linear to lance-shaped and flat to cylindrical. Nondescript

Fig. 8.20. *Allenrolfea occidentalis*, Badwater, Death Valley. Photo by Stan Shebs.

Fig. 8.21. *Suaeda nigra*, Chenopodiaceae, bush seepweed. Photo by Stan Shebs.

clusters of flowers occur in clusters along the upper stems with fleshy, rounded sepals. The succulent leaves of bush seepweed, like many other saline succulents, accumulate salts and in older leaves the salt content is high. Traditional uses include extracting a black dye from the stems and using it for basketry. This use gives rise to a second common name, ink-blite.

Greasewood (*Sarcobatus vermiculatus*) is a loosely branched spiny shrub 3–6 feet or more in height with solitary succulent leaves on elongate shoots of the current season growth (Fig. 8.22). It is one of the most common of western North American shrubs in alkaline habitats, growing both in relatively pure as well as mixed stands with saltbush or other shrub species over broad areas with alkaline soils across the Great Basin. It is frequently co-dominant with *Allenrolfea* in areas that support little else. While most characteristic in saline soils of the Great Basin outside of California, it is widely present in Death Valley and other parts of the northern Mojave Desert with a relict population in the Lucerne Valley of the western Mojave. Greasewood is reputed to be a phreatophyte—with a tap root extending deeply below ground. Although widely grazed by native animals, the foliage contains high concentrations of sodium and potassium oxalates which may be toxic to sheep.

Western nitrophila (*Nitrophila occidentalis*) is a low-trailing perennial up to 12 inches in height with paired branches and tiny, fleshy, opposite leaves (Fig. 8.23). It occurs widely across the Mojave Desert and Great Basin in relatively moist alkaline flats and meadows. Closely related is the rare Amargosa nitrophila (*Nitrophila mojavensis*), restricted to a few wetlands associated with the Amargosa River. It is locally abundant on barren alkali mud flats with a layer of encrusted salt over the topsoil (Fig. 8.24). It has a CNPS Rare Plant Rank 1B: rare, threatened, or endangered in California and elsewhere.

Although the dominant species of alkali sinks are relatively long-lived perennials, several herbaceous perennials and annuals are widespread and common. Alkali weed (*Cressa truxillensis*) is an herbaceous perennial in the morning-glory family (Convolvulaceae) that occurs widely across the western United States on saline and alkaline soils. It has a deep taproot and often grows trailing across the soil surface of moist alkaline flats (Fig. 8.25). Yellow pepper-grass (*Lepidium flavum*) is an annual member of the mustard family that trails along the ground where it forms large patches with dense clusters of small yellow flowers and rounded seedpods (Fig. 8.26). It is found at low- to moderate-elevations in alkaline flats, washes, and playa margins across our deserts—with a notable abundance in the western Mojave Desert and Death Valley. Mojave stinkweed (*Cleomella obtusifolia*) is a widespread annual species of alkaline flats. As its common name suggests, and as is typical for Cleomaceae, this species has an unpleasant, pungent smell. It is easily recognized by its hairy trifoliate leaves and four-parted yellow flowers (Fig. 8.27).

Fig. 8.22. *Sarcobatus vermiculatus*, Sarcobataceae, western nitrophia. Photo by Naomi Fraga.

Fig. 8.23. *Nitrophila occidentalis*, Chenopodiaceae, western nitrophila. Photo by Stan Shebs.

Fig. 8.24. *Nitrophila mohavensis*, Chenopodiaceae, Amargosa nitrophila. Photo by Stan Shebs.

Fig. 8.25. *Cressa truxillensis*, Convolvulaceae, alkali weed. Photo by James Andre.

Fig. 8.26. *Lepidium flavum*, Brassicaceae, yellow peppergrass Stan Shebs.

Fig. 8.27. *Cleomella obtusifolia*, Cleomaceae, Mojave stinkweed. Photo by Matt Berger.

Chapter 9
Sand Dunes

Kelso Dunes, Mojave National Preserve.
Photo by Michael Kauffmann.

Introduction

Desert dunes present a specialized and dynamic landform where windblown sands accumulate (Fig. 9.1). The key component of sand dunes, of course, is sand. While fine dust particles are easily lifted into the air, sand is not as easy to move as one might think. Winds of at least 15 miles per hour are generally necessary to move sand grains and even strong winds cannot lift sand higher than a few feet above the ground. Strong winds lift small sand grains a short distance and then drop them. When these grains hit the ground, they bump into other sand grains and cause them to jump and be caught themselves by the wind. This leapfrog motion of bumping and jumping is called saltation (Fig. 9.2). You can see this kind of movement on the windward side of the dune if you look closely at the dune surface. The hopping motion of individual sand grains is the most important mechanism for moving sand. Moreover, saltation allows larger grains of sand to move than would be possible from the wind alone.

Once sand begins to collect in a fixed location, small dunes form. As sand grains slowly work their way up the windward face of a dune they reach the crest, or top, of the dune. When these grains fall over the crest and start to pile up with protection from the wind, the leeward face of the dune becomes steeper and steeper. These piles of loose sand hold a slope and, depending on the sand's grain size and shape, have an angle of repose between 30–35°. When such an angle is reached, gravity steps in and causes the sand to slide and small avalanches occur. Sand along the dune crest may run down the leeward face like a small cascade, or the whole side may slip at once as a slump.

The repeating cycle of sand inching up the windward side to the dune crest, then slipping down the dune's slip face on the leeward side allows dunes to inch forward, migrating in the direction in which the wind blows. Thus, sand dunes are typically dynamic formations that are eroding on one side at the same time new

Fig. 5.1. Eureka Dunes, Death Valley National Park. Photo by Michael Kauffmann.

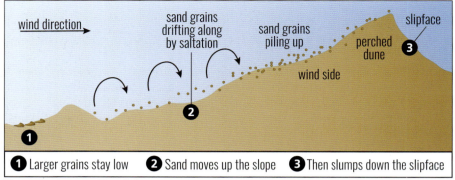

Fig. 9.2. Sand movement by saltation.

sand is being added on the windward side. When the input of sand is greater than the rate of loss, sand dunes move across the landscape. How fast a sand dune moves depends on wind speed, dune size, and plant cover. Deeply rooted plants growing on dunes stabilize sand and slow the movement of dunes.

Dunes come in many shapes and sizes. The simplest form, called a transverse dune, is a ridge formed perpendicular to the direction of a steady wind. Generally, the windward slope of a transverse ridge rises gently at an angle of about 15°, before falling off sharply on the leeward face. A barchan is a small crescent-shaped dune with arms bent to point downwind. Under conditions of changing wind direct, elongate linear dunes can form parallel with the wind direction (Fig. 9.3).

Walking along the upper windward face of a dune is relatively easy as the hopping motion of small sand grains removes small particles and compacts the dune surface. At the dune crest, this compacted surface layer may be quite thin, allowing your feet to break through to softer sand below. Finally, the steady avalanching of sand from the leeward dune face leaves the surface here very soft. Ripple marks that characteristically form across dune surfaces are essentially small transverse microdunes that develop perpendicular to surface winds (Fig. 9.4). The spacing of ripples, typically

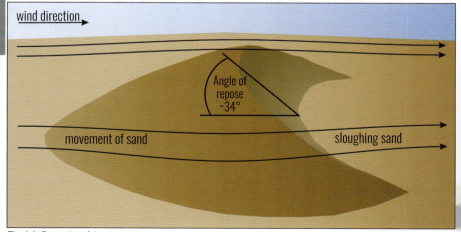

Fig. 9.3. Dynamics of dune movement.

3–8 inches between crests, is related to the average distance grains jump, which in turn is a function of wind velocity and size of the sand grains. Wind ripples are often spectacular and photogenic, especially with low sun angles at dawn or dusk, when the thousands of tiny sand ridges cast shadows. These ripple marks form and move remarkably rapidly, as one can see by how fast shallow footprints disappear from the sand surface. This movement is easily demonstrated experimentally by clearing a dune surface and marking the ripples with toothpicks or small twigs as they form.

Typically, desert dunes have a complex structure composed of stacked layers of sand deposits, each layer corresponding to a climate cycle within the last 10,000–25,000 years. During dry climate episodes, a decrease in stabilizing vegetation exposed surface sand to wind erosion, which ultimately brought the sand to the dunes. Wet glacial periods stabilize dune deposits and slow sand movement.

Fig. 9.4. Ripple marks in the sand, Algodones Dunes. Photo by Moe Donnelly.

Some desert dunes have an unusual characteristic of emitting low frequency sound when masses of sand are displaced. Most people are familiar with the squeaking sounds produced when one walks across wet beach sand. However, sounds produced by desert sand dunes are more a roaring or booming that has been described as kettledrums or a foghorn. Not all dunes have the capacity to produce such sounds. The relative rarity of booming desert sands throughout the world indicates that they form, or exist, under special and limited conditions. In California, only the Eureka, Panamint, Olancha, and Kelso dunes are known to make these sounds. The foremost requirement for the production of sound by desert sands appears to be the reworking of sand grains by wind to produce well-rounded, extremely smooth, and frosted quartz grains. The noise itself is thought to result from sand shear, or layers of sand grains, moving over one another. High dunes with steep, semi-stable slip faces that are easily put in motion produce the best sounds—but low humidity is critical. Generations of student field excursions to the Kelso Dunes have produced the belief that naked bodies sliding down the steep dune face at midnight produce ideal conditions for generating the booming sounds!

Adaptations to Dune Habitats

Life is difficult in the dune field, even for plants adapted to desert conditions, as the dune environment is unusually harsh. Plants must endure burial by moving sand, intense solar radiation, nutrient-poor soil, and extreme fluctuations of temperature. It is not surprising then that most plants growing in the dune areas are found not on the drifting dunes themselves, but in the protected hollows between dune ridges or around the edges of the dune field where the dunes are moving slowly. In the heart of the dune field it is a different story. Here the sand dunes are so large and dynamic that few plants survive.

Fig. 9.5. Mesquite coppice dunes, Mesquite Dry Lake. Photo by Julie Evens.

Unstable dune surfaces represent the greatest threat to dune plants. Only species that survive cycles of burial and erosion are successful in such dynamic habitats. One strategy for growing on moving dunes is to have a deep and extensive root system that can stabilize mounds of sand, thereby limiting erosion. So long as growth rates are fast these species can grow upward, expanding their mounds, as sands accumulate. Several woody desert species utilize this form of growth with mesquite (*Prosopis glandulosa*) and screwbean (*Prosopis pubescens*) serving as good examples (Fig. 9.5). These species are described in Chapters 6 and 7, respectively. A similar tolerance of irregular burial by moving sand is seen in dune eriogonum (*Eriogonum deserticola*), a long-lived woody shrub primarily restricted in California to Algodones Dunes. Large plants are tolerant of being cyclically buried and uncovered by moving sand, and large lateral roots that may extend for 10 feet or more (Fig. 9.6).

Fig. 9.6. *Eriogonum deserticola*, Polygonaceae, dune buckwheat. Photo by Joey Santore.

Another dune strategy is to have roots with abundant meristems and large carbohydrate reserves such that new shoots grow to replace those covered by drifting sands. Two sand-binding rhizomatous grasses are widely present in dune areas. These are big galleta (*Hilaria rigida,* Fig. 9.7) and desert panic grass (*Panicum urvilleanum,* Fig. 9.8). Both species

Fig. 9.7. *Hilaria rigida*, Poaceae, big galleta. Photo by Robert Gustafson.

Fig. 9.8. *Panicum urvilleanum*, Poaceae, desert panic grass. Photo by Julie Evens.

Fig. 9.9. *Stipa hymenoides*, Poaceae, Indian rice grass. Photo by Matt Berger.

Fig. 9.10. *Croton californicus*, Euphorbiaceae, sand croton. Photo by Robert Gustafson.

take advantage of rapid rates of growth and extensive development of underground rhizomes to survive in, and stabilize, dune sands. Both use C_4 metabolism, a metabolic system described in Chapter 3, that allows for higher rates of productivity and adaptation to solar irradiance. Big galleta is widely distributed throughout Mojave and Sonoran deserts in sandy soils of many plant communities, particularly creosote bush scrub and Joshua tree woodlands. Desert panic grass has an even broader range, occurring from the arid southwest of the United States to South America. Also commonly present, although more characteristic of other sandy desert scrub habitats, is Indian rice grass (*Stipa hymenoides*, Fig. 9.9), a species with typical C_3 metabolism. This bunchgrass is conspicuous during the early summer when the diffuse inflorescences from the previous year persists.

Sandy soils are highly porous and thus hold little water in their surface layers—providing serious problems of water stress for shallow-rooted plants. Because of the rapid rate in which water enters and percolates into sand, water typically collects at depth below dunes or at their lower margin. Phreatophytes, such as mesquite, root deeply to reach groundwater and tap this moisture. At the lower margin of the dune base, however, water is often present near the soil surface where it is available for many plant species.

The silvery coloration of the stems and leaves in many dune plants is an adaptation to the excessive solar radiation in desert regions. The leaves of some plants have a dense covering of fine hairs that give them their silvery appearance as well as a velvet-like softness. Other plants have tiny plate-like overlapping silvery scales that cover the leaves. Both these leaf surface forms aid plants in reflecting excess solar energy as well as helping control water loss. An example is seen in sand croton (*Croton californicus*), an undistinguished semi-woody gray shrub 2–3 feet in height (Fig. 9.10). It is a common sandy soil species that grows well in stabilized desert dunes as well as in sandy soils along the coast of southern California. Often individual shrubs collect sand around their base, forming low mounds. A close cousin, Wiggin's croton (*Croton wigginsii*) is a common species on the Algodones Dunes, but highly restricted in distribution. It has a CNPS Rare Plant Rank 2B: rare, threatened, or endangered in California; common elsewhere.

Adaptive traits for plant species surviving on sand dunes extend beyond their vegetative form and leaf morphology. Equally important are traits of seed germination. Species adapted to dune habitats generally have larger carbohydrate-rich seeds than their non-dune relatives—allowing for germination and successful growth of seeds buried well below the sand surface.

Dune Plants

The difficulty of establishment and survival on active dunes means that total plant cover is low. Active dune fields have virtually no plant cover, while older stabilized dunes may have larger areas of cover. These lower and relatively stable dune areas support a plant community that is transitional to that found in sandy soils of creosote bush scrub and desert washes. Creosote bush, with its drought adaptations, is a dominant species in these stabilized dune areas. Mesquite and screwbean are commonly found in stabilized dune areas, tapping groundwater pools below the dunes. The deep root systems of these species help stabilize sand by forming long-lived shrub mounds. Less common, but also present where soil moisture is near the surface, are arrow weed (*Pluchea sericea*) and desert willow (*Chilopsis linearis*). Both species are more characteristic of desert washes (Chapter 7).

One of the most spectacular wildflowers of sandy soils and sand dunes throughout the California deserts is dune evening primrose (*Oenothera deltoides*). It has showy, large, and fragrant white flowers that turn pinkish with age. This herbaceous perennial often grows in profusion on lower dune slopes—presenting a spectacular wildflower display (Fig. 9.11). The name evening primrose comes from the temporal pattern where flowers open in the evening for moth pollinators and close again in mid-morning. Other common names for dune primrose are desert lantern and birdcage primrose (because of the unusual form of the dried flowering stalk). The flower stalk has radiating branches extending in all directions along the ground. At the end of the spring flowering season, the greenish branches eventually dry and curl upward toward the central axis. Woody seed capsules that split into four prongs now occupy the positions where the large flowers used to be. This entire dried structure, up to a foot long, resembles a birdcage.

Frequently growing with dune evening primrose is desert sand verbena (*Abronia villosa*), an annual member of the Nyctaginaceae with

Fig. 9.11. *Oenothera deltoides*, Onagraceae, dune evening primrose. Photo by Morgan Stickrod.

Fig. 9.12. *Abronia villosa*, Nyctaginaceae, desert sand verbena. Photo by Robert Gustafson.

Fig. 9.13. Floral display at the Algones Dunes with *Dicoria canescens*, *Abronia villosa*, and *Oenothera deltoides*. Photo by Julie Evens. INSET: *Dicoria canescens* by Joey Santore.

Fig. 9.14. *Abronia pogonantha*, Mojave sand verbena, Nyctaginaceae. Photo by Robert Gustafson.

beautiful pink to magenta-colored flowers (Fig. 9.12). The many trailing stems of sand verbena grow outward for as much as 2 feet, with thick rounded leaves covered by sticky hairs along their length. This is an easy plant to recognize and perhaps the most photographed of all desert annuals. It is widely distributed in low sandy valleys and edges of dunes in lower elevations of both the Mojave and Sonoran deserts (Fig. 9.13). There are four other species of sand verbena in the desert areas of California. Mojave sand verbena (*Abronia pogonantha*) is a similar species with white to pale pink flowers (Fig. 9.14). It occurs in sandy areas across the Mojave Desert and into the foothills of the southern Sierra Nevada and adjacent San Joaquin Valley.

Desert lily (*Hesperocallis undulata*), one of the few desert bulb (geophyte) plants, is a slender, perennial herb (Fig. 9.15). It is a member of the Asparagacae, the family that includes agaves and yuccas. This widespread species occurs on dunes but is also common on sandy flats and mesas of creosote bush scrub and Joshua tree woodlands of the southern and western Mojave Desert, as well as the lower Sonoran Desert in California. It is described in more detail with other geophytes in Chapter 9.

Annual plants, which must reestablish their populations from seed each year, would seem to be poorly adapted to surviving in dune habitats. While this is generally true, there are a few annual species that are quite successful on sandy substrates such as dunes. An example of this mode of occurrence is seen in an unusual annual called desert twinbugs (*Dicoria canescens*) which forms thickets of many individuals in the desert sand. Unlike most annuals, it is aided in growth by a strong taproot and reaches heights up to 2–3 feet. This member of the Asteraceae has distinctive long and sharply toothed lower leaves and sharply toothed, contrasted with smaller and rounded upper leaves. Both leaf types are densely covered with white or gray hairs to reflect the sun (Fig. 9.13). Each plant can produce several whitish discoid flower heads which lack ray flowers. These heads often form closely associated pairs, a characteristic which is the origin of the name "twinbugs."

One of the most unusual dune plants of the lower desert is sand food (*Pholisma sonorae*), a bizarre root parasite that erupts with a head of scale-like leaves and flowers from the sand (Fig. 9.16). Most of the tissues of this strange plant lies in a succulent stem that extends as much as 3–6 feet below the sand surface where it attaches to roots of nearby host plants (Fig. 9.17). The common name comes from the fact that the fleshy tissue is eaten raw or roasted by Native American tribes including the Sand Papagos and Cocopas. The flavor of the stems is described as slightly sweet, with the texture of a crisp radish. Because of its limited range in the lower Sonoran Desert and specific habitat requirements it has a CNPS Rare Plant Rank 1B: rare, threatened, or endangered in California and elsewhere. A related species, desert pholisma (*Pholisma arenarium*), is widely distributed across southern California from coastal dunes to chaparral and eastward in sandy habitats across our desert region to Arizona.

Fig. 9.15. *Hesperocallis undulata*, Asparagaceae, desert lily. Photo by Robert Gustafson.

Fig. 9.16. *Pholisma sonorae*, Lennoaceae, sand food flowers. Photo by Robert Gustafson.

Fig. 9.17. *Pholisma sonorae*, underground stem. US Fish and Wildlife Service photo by Jim A. Bartel.

Death Valley Dunes

Death Valley National Park contains several areas of notable sand dunes. The most famous of these, but challenging to visit, are the Eureka Dunes in the northern portion of the park. Much more accessible and commonly visited are the Mesquite Dunes near Stovepipe Wells. Other dune fields include those in Saline Valley, the Panamint Dunes in Panamint Valley, and the Ibex Dunes near Saratoga Springs.

The Eureka Dunes lie in the remote Eureka Valley, an enclosed basin northwest of Death Valley at about 3,000 feet in elevation, bordered by the Inyo Mountains to the north and west and the Last Chance Mountains to the east (Fig. 9.1). The dunes cover an area only 3 miles long and one mile wide yet they are the tallest sand dunes in California and among the tallest in all of North America. They rise abruptly to more than 680 feet above the dry lakebed at their western base.

Several notable plant species are known only from here. The Eureka Valley dune grass (*Swallenia alexandrae*) is an unusual endemic genus with just this single species. The largest population is found on high, unstable areas of the Eureka Dunes, with other known stands located on smaller dunes on the west side of Eureka Valley and the adjacent Saline Mountains at elevations of 2,950–4,200 feet. This is a coarse perennial dune grass with a woody base and is often the only plant found on the less stable upper slopes of the dunes (Fig. 9.18). The dense root system of this species catches and holds drifting sand, forming stable hummocks up to 3 feet or more across. It is a federally listed endangered species with a CNPS Rare Plant Rank 1B: rare, threatened, or endangered in California and elsewhere.

Eureka Valley evening primrose (*Oenothera californica* subsp. *eurekensis*) is an

Fig. 9.18. *Swallenia alexandrae*, Poaceae, Eureka dune grass. Photo by Michael Kauffmann.

Fig. 9.19. *Oenothera californica* subsp. *eurekensis*, *Onagraceae*, evening primrose. Photo by Mike Splain.

Fig. 9.20. *Chaetadelpha wheeleri*, Asteraceae, Wheeler's skeletonweed. Photo by Joey Santore.

herbaceous perennial also endemic to the Eureka Dunes and federally listed as endangered. The leafy shoots sprout adventitious roots if they are covered by windblown sand, forming new shoots with rosettes of leaves at the tip (Fig. 9.19). It has a CNPS Rare Plant Rank 1B: rare, threatened, or endangered in California and elsewhere.

Dune broom (*Chaetadelpha wheeleri*), sometimes called Wheeler's skeletonweed, is a multi-branched perennial reaching to 3 feet or more in height from a stout rootstock that aids its survival in dune habitats (Fig. 9.20). This monotypic genus in the Asteraceae has simple white or pale purple flowers with five ray florets. It is common in the Eureka Dunes and surrounding alkali flats in the northern Mojave Desert.

Fig. 9.21. *Astragalus lentiginosus* var. *micans*, Fabaceae, shining milkvetch. Photo by Matt Berger.

Desert dunes are often home to rare and locally restricted taxa of *Astragalus*, commonly called milkvetch or locoweed. An example of this, representing a small conservation success story, is shining milkvetch (*Astragalus lentiginosus* var. *micans*). This is an erect perennial restricted to the stabilized lower slopes of the Eureka Dunes. Silky silvery hairs cover the stems and leaves, reducing solar radiation inputs to these tissues (Fig. 9.21). Once recommended for listing as a federally endangered species, shining milkvetch has rapidly expanded in formerly disturbed areas over the last two decades as off-road vehicle trespass has become less of an issue under management of the dunes by Death Valley National Park. It has a CNPS Rare Plant Rank 1B: rare, threatened, or endangered in California and elsewhere.

The Mesquite Dunes, located about 2 miles west of Stovepipe Wells, have their origin in winds blowing down Death Valley from the north, scouring and depositing sand from Mesquite Flat just to the northwest of the dunes. Standing less

Fig. 9.22. Mesquite Dunes, Death Valley, with bordering stands of mesquite. Photo by Morgan Stickrod.

than 200 feet high within the Death Valley basin, these dunes barely reach to sea level in elevation. The Mesquite Dunes are largely short transverse dunes, but their highest point is a star dune formed by four curving transverse dunes converging at a single point. With a mixed predominance of northwest and southeastern winds, the dunes are relatively stable in position. Bedrock below the dunes positioned high on the south side of the dunes directs ground water to drain into Mesquite Flat and collect near the soil surface. This has allowed the relatively profuse growth of creosote bush, screwbean mesquite (*Prosopis pubescens*), arrow weed (*Pluchea sericea*), and other desert plants (Fig. 9.22).

Kelso Dunes

The Kelso Dunes form the largest area of sand dunes in the Mojave Desert. The dune field covers 45 square miles or 29,000 acres, with the tallest dunes rising about 550 feet above the surrounding terrain (Fig. 9.23). The Kelso Dunes represent part of a much larger sand transport system that extends from the terminal area of the Mojave River near Afton canyon, eastward across the Devil's Playground region to the Kelso Dunes themselves where the Granite and Providence mountains form a barrier to prevailing winds. At present, only the area east of the Mojave River sink and the westernmost parts of Devil's Playground are continuing to receive new sand through this system.

Sand is no longer accumulating at the Kelso Dunes themselves. These dunes, and the sand flats of the Devil's Playground, represent relics of past geological conditions very different from those present today. One indication of this difference is that the four primary sand ridges running roughly parallel with each other show little relationship to current wind patterns.

Because of their size and relative protection within the Mojave National Preserve, these are an excellent place to see a diversity of dune life. However, unlike the Eureka Dunes and the Algodones Dunes described below, there are no plant species restricted to the Kelso Dunes.

Fig. 9.23. Kelso Dunes looking to the Devil's Playground, Mojave National Preserve. Photo by Michael Kauffmann.

Coachella Valley Dunes

The Coachella Valley was once dominated by large sand dunes lying to the east of Palm Springs. These formed from eastward transport of erosional sands brought into the upper valley from the Whitewater River. Today there is less than 5% of that habitat remaining in a protected condition. This remaining dune area, and the upwind area of sand generation that sustains these, are now protected as the Coachella Valley Preserve—covering 20,000 acres. The largest units of this preserve are centered on Thousand Palms Canyon which cuts through the Indio Hills on the northern edge of the Coachella Valley—midway between Palm Springs and Indio. This Preserve ranges from near sea level at its southern extreme to over 1,000 feet in the Indio Hills. An endangered plant in these dunes is the Coachella Valley milkvetch (*Astragalus lentiginosus* var. *coachellae*), a close relative of the Eureka Dunes milkvetch (Fig. 9.24). This species is largely restricted to the Coachella Valley in Riverside County, between Cabazon and Indio, with a few outliers to the east. It has a CNPS Rare Plant Rank 1B: rare, threatened, or endangered in California and elsewhere.

Fig. 9.24. *Astragalus lentiginosus* var. *coachellae*, Fabaceae, Coachella Valley milkvetch. Photo by USFWS.

Algodones Dunes

The Algodones Dunes lie approximately 25 miles west of the Colorado River and extend for 45 miles in a northwest to southeast direction along the margin of the Cahuilla Basin—a structural depression in southeastern California that extends northwestward to include the Salton Sea. These dunes, also referred to as the Imperial Dunes, range from 3–6 miles in width with individual dunes reaching 250 feet. Although much of the Salton Sea basin lies below sea level in a depression formed along the line of the San Andreas Fault, the base level of the Algodones Dunes

Fig. 9.25. Algodones Dunes. Photo by Morgan Stickrod.

Fig. 9.26. Algodones Dunes aerial view from Google Earth.

is well above sea level. The southeastern end of the Algondones Dunes extends 5 miles across the U.S./Mexico border to the edge of the Colorado River flood plain. The extensive Sierra del Rosario Dunes, part of the sand sea of the Gran Desierto, lie just across the border to the southeast—in northwestern Sonora, Mexico. Here they form a vast field of active dunes and stable sand sheets covering about 1,800 mi^2 or 1.15 million acres.

The major area of the Algodones Dunes consists of sand ridges extending from the southwest to northeast, perpendicular to the line of the dune system (Fig. 9.25). The steep southeast-facing slip faces of the dunes often overlook large sand-free depressions—which are thought to be exposed parts of the desert floor. Smaller crescent-shaped dunes are also present and show active movement.

Unlike some major dune systems that are located at the foot of a mountain range as a result of topographic effects on wind channels, the Algodones Dunes have formed primarily as a result of opposing seasonal winds. Winter winds come from the northwest, but often reverse to the southeast in summer (Fig. 9.26). The stronger winter winds bring sands from the basin of the Salton Sea and appear to be slowly pushing the dune system southeastward. Geologic evidence indicates that the dunes are now less active than in the past, and that the amount of sand in the dunes is not increasing significantly. There are two theories for the origins of the sands themselves. Many geologists believe that the sands largely originated from the eroded beaches of ancient Lake Cahuilla—a large Pleistocene forerunner of the Salton Sea. Recent studies suggest that the sand has more similarities to that transported by the Colorado River.

The Algodones Dunes receive only 2–3 inches of rainfall each year and are thus one of the driest areas of the Sonoran Desert in California. This extreme dryness, sharp seasonal temperature swings, and constantly shifting sands makes the Algodones Dunes a unique and difficult habitat for plants. During rains, the eastern side of the dunes acts as a natural dam—blocking waters flowing toward the Salton Sea from the Chocolate Mountains. This results in many small desert pools with moisture that supports a diverse wash-woodland community including desert ironwood and palo verde—providing diverse habitat structure and cover.

The Algodones Dunes are home to many rare, threatened, and endemic species of plants, lizards, and insects. The presence of these endemics has made land use management of the dunes a particularly contentious issue between off-road vehicle enthusiasts and environmental groups.

One of the rare endemic plants is Peirson's milkvetch (*Astragalus magdalenae* var. *peirsonii*), a silvery, perennial member of the pea family. It grows as tall as 2.5 feet and is notable among the many milkvetch species for its small leaves (9.27). The large seeds of Peirson's milkvetch (larger than any other milkvetch) are thought to be an adaptation to life as a dune plant. Large seeds have the carbohydrate resource to germinate and emerge from under several inches of sand. It has a CNPS Rare Plant Rank 1B: rare, threatened, or endangered in California and elsewhere.

Fig. 9.27. *Astragalus magdalenae* var. *peirsonii*, Fabaceae. Photo by Jim A. Bartel.

Algodones Dunes sunflower (*Helianthus niveus* subsp. *tephrodes*) is an attractive dune plant known in California only from these dunes. This silver-leafed member of the sunflower family inhabits the interior portions of the dunes at the bases along the sides of large dunes (Fig 9.28). It grows to more than 2 feet in height which is taller than its cousin *Helianthus niveus* subsp. *canescens*—widespread on dunes and low sandy places across the Sonoran Desert. Extremely tolerant of mov-

Fig. 9.28. *Helianthus niveus* subsp. *tephrodes*, Asteraceae, Algodones dunes sunflower. Photos by Matt Berger.

ing sand, Algodones dunes sunflower grows rapidly to avoid being buried. Interestingly, this sunflower has two distinct seasons of flowering—one from March to May and another from October to January—when it produces bright yellow daisy-like flower heads. It has a CNPS Rare Plant Rank 1B: rare, threatened, or endangered in California and elsewhere.

Giant Spanish needle (*Palafoxia arida* var. *gigantea*) is striking pink-flowered member of the sunflower family (Fig. 9.29). The typical form of this species is a widespread plant in sandy places throughout the California deserts, but this large and often perennial variety reaches as much as 6 feet high—three times the height of the typical form of the species. As is the case with many dune taxa, the seeds of the giant Spanish needle will germinate and emerge from depths much greater than the non-dune variety of Spanish needle.

Fig. 9.30. *Palafoxia arida* var. *gigantea*, Asteraceae, giant Spanish needle. Photo by Robert Gustafson.

Chapter 10
The Flowering Desert

A superbloom of desert dandelion (*Malacothrix glabrata*) in Red Rock Canyon State Park, California. Photo by Dylan Neubauer.

Introduction

Desert annuals and herbaceous perennials constitute the most diverse component of the flora of the California deserts. Yet, in a dry year, this remarkable diversity is hidden from view. These ephemeral plants are hidden as seeds in the soil for much of the year—dormant sometimes for years—awaiting the proper conditions to germinate, grow, and bloom. The presence of desert annuals becomes dramatic, however, in years with abundant rains when the desert comes alive with color flooding the landscape (Introductory image, Fig. 10.1).

While rain is a harbinger for flowering, there is no simple formula for predicting wildflower diversity and abundance. Flowering cycles and abundance are the result of the complex interactions of timing, amount, and frequency of rains through the fall and winter, as well as the occurrence of cold winter temperatures that could kill seedlings. The best flowering years typically occur when rains begin early and occur with regularity every few weeks through the fall and winter. These conditions promote early germination and survival throughout the fall and winter into spring. When similar rainfall totals occur in only a few heavy rains separated by long dry periods, many seeds that germinate die before reaching maturity. While

Fig. 10.1. View north from slopes of Shoreline Butte, Death Valley National Park, February 26, 2016, with desert sunflower (*Geraea canescens*). Photo by Dylan Neubauer.

most seed germination occurs following moderate rains in fall and early winter, modest germination may still occur with heavy spring rains that follow a dry fall and winter. Such conditions, nevertheless, do not promote mass flowering.

Years with the highest totals of rainfall from September to March clearly promote the highest densities and biomass of annuals but not necessarily the highest diversity of species. Experience suggests that under such conditions a few well-adapted species become abundant and crowd out other species. Maximum species diversity is typically associated with wet, but not the wettest, years.

While some desert annuals reach large size and flower in massive numbers in wet years, there are others that never become large. These are low-growing species aptly called "belly flowers," because you need to lie on your stomach to properly see them. Not surprisingly, the highest species richness of desert annuals is often found not in the showiest areas but, instead, where belly flowers are abundant. Such areas are commonly encountered in parts of the eastern Mojave Desert where three square feet can have more than 20 different species of desert annuals!

One important aspect of the timing of peak flowering in desert annuals and short-lived herbaceous perennials is elevation, which impacts when warm spring temperatures begin. The low-elevation Anza-Borrego Desert State Park is often in full flower by late February or early March (Fig. 10.2), while the higher elevations of the eastern Mojave Desert do not peak until April. There are multiple websites that track flowering conditions and provide weekly updates on the amount and diversity of flowering in various desert sites. Many state and national parks have their own listings of wildflower reports for their park.

Fig. 10.2 Spring bloom in Anza-Borrego Desert State Park. Photo by Moe Donnelly.

Of course, not all desert wildflowers bloom at the same time, even at a single locality. Some groups, such as the mustard family (Brassicaceae), are early bloomers. Consider the abundance of brassica, such as broccoli or cabbage, in the grocery store in winter—the same is true for wild species. Others, such as the sunflower family (Asteraceae), include species with deeper roots that flower in late spring or early summer. In addition to the typical winter-spring annuals, there is a small group of desert annuals that germinate not in the fall or winter but only following occasional monsoonal summer thunderstorms that reach California from the south or the east. These late-summer or fall bloomers are called summer annuals.

The length of the flowering season is also highly variable as it depends on soil moisture availability, the onset of high temperatures, and decreased rain in late spring or early summer. Thus, years with well-spaced winter rains may show strong flowering across two months or more, while this period may be compressed into only a few weeks if dry conditions follow early winter rains. To adapt to this variability from year to year, desert annuals may complete their life cycle in as few as 6–8 weeks under water stress and with optimal rainfall may survive for 4–6 months. Thus, some species might flower at 6 inches in height in a moderately dry year and 3 feet in height during an unusually wet spring. This means that height, commonly mentioned in the descriptions of individual species of desert annuals, is not always a reliable character.

Seedbanks and Germination

We know that mass blooming in the desert comes from the germination of seeds in the soil (Fig. 10.3). Research has focused on densities of soil seedbanks to answer the question: Can desert seedbanks be depleted if too many seeds germinate? Results have uncovered some astounding estimates of the abundance of desert seeds raging from relatively low densities of 1.5 million viable seeds per acre in open areas between desert shrub canopies to 10 million seeds per acre under the canopies of shrubs. If all these seeds germinated at the same time, more than 200 individuals per square foot would appear! It is even more fascinating to consider that these soil seedbanks exist despite the presence of rodents, birds, and harvester ants that make their living collecting and eating these seeds. When hundreds of thousands of desert annuals are flowering per acre in a favorable year, the yearly production of new seeds reaches tens of millions—which replenishes soil seedbanks.

As described above, desert annuals typically germinate after moderate fall or winter rains during relatively cool or even cold growing conditions. These plants persist through the winter as small vegetative rosettes or low clusters of leaves that are positioned close to the ground. Their microhabitat is heated by the sun and thus warmer than air temperatures just above. In this position, plants are potentially subject to freezing during frosts or desiccation with persistent drought. Dependent on elevation, the stems of these annuals begin to elongate and quickly grow to full size with increased solar radiation in the spring. The peak of flowering for desert annuals quickly follows as the stems reach their full height and flowerbuds form.

Seed germination in desert annuals is not simply a process where rain falls and seeds sprout, as we would see with beans or corn in our gardens. Certainly, some species do follow this pattern, particularly some species of native and alien grasses.

Figure 10.3. A diversity of wildflowers carpet the ground on the northern slope of Joshua Tree National Park near the Fortynine Palms Oasis, March, 2019. Photo by Jesse Miller.

More commonly, however, seeds of individual species have a physical or physiological dormancy that prevents them from germinating unless certain conditions are met. Physical dormancy typically involves a hard seed coat that keeps moisture from penetrating into the embryo and initiating germination. A good example of this system is in most legumes or other species whose microhabitats are the open areas between shrubs. Dormancy is broken by abrasion of the seed coat as it rubs against coarse soil particles when heavy rains flood surface soils. With such seed coats, there is often a built-in system of "bet-hedging" with some seeds weathering and germinating the first year while others requiring two or more years before the seed coat weathers sufficiently to allow germination. If conditions for growth and flowering are poor in the spring following germination, there are still seeds available to germinate in subsequent years when better conditions prevail.

A quite different germination strategy, called physiological dormancy, is found in many desert annuals whose favored microhabitat is the soil beneath the canopies of woody shrubs. This dormancy can be artificially broken by treating the seeds with plant hormones called gibberellins but not by simple watering or perforation of the seed coat. In nature, rains that wet the nitrogen-rich soils beneath shrub canopies set in motion bacterial processes that give off gaseous nitrogen compounds. The presence of these compounds breaks the dormancy and allows seeds to germinate when rains occur. This trait is widespread in members of the Hydrophyllaceae, Boraginaceae, and Plantaginaceae. It is noteworthy that many of these species are closely related the post-fire annuals in California's chaparral. Nitrogenous compounds present in ash produced post-fire in these fire-prone habitats initiate germination in chaparral annuals. A similar leachate used to wet soils under desert shrubs also breaks physiological dormancy, even though these desert habitats rarely experience fire. Based on these similar physiological results, it appears numerous chaparral annuals are progenitors to their desert cousins.

Superblooms

The amazing wildflower displays during a superbloom are not to be missed (Fig. 10.4). These events display mass flowering, coloring the landscape a myriad of vibrant colors. In these exceptional years, the superbloom extends beyond larger desert annuals to the smaller belly flowers as well. The critical mix of rainfall amounts, metered frequencies, warm spring temperatures, and abundant soil seedbanks act together to nurture germination to reproductive maturity. Intervening years with a modest- to poor-showing are more common. When rainfall is moderate and irregularly distributed, flowering is often uneven, producing wonderful displays in some areas and little in others. What follows are descriptions of the amazing array of desert annuals, grouped by family, that are found during superblooms and the years in between.

Figure 10.4. Antelope Valley Poppy Preserve, March 28th, 2018. Photo by Morgan Stickrod.

Sunflower Family (Asteraceae)

The sunflower family produces the most species as well as some of the most abundant desert annuals and herbaceous perennials of any family. Some of these species occur by the millions in a wet year, coloring the landscape for miles in every direction. The diversity of desert annuals in this family makes identification of individual species a challenge. One way to make this task easier is to separate species first by flower color and then by the form of the flower heads with respect to ray and disk flowers. This is by no means the perfect algorithm as the same genus may have species with yellow or white flowers and possess more than a single structure of flower head. Nevertheless, this approach is the most practical way to begin. The structure of flowers and flower heads in the Asteraceae is described in Chapter 4.

Yellow-Flowered Asteraceae

Desert sunflower (*Geraea canescens*) is a close relative of *Encelia* that can provide massive displays of yellow across the central and eastern Mojave Desert. Typically this species covers sandy flats under creosote bush scrub at elevations below about 4,000 feet (Fig. 10.5). Its leaves and stems are covered with soft hairs and it displays broad radiate flower heads about ¾ inches in diameter.

There are two additional daisies closely related to desert sunflower that, although uncommon, are perennials of special note. Panamint daisy (*Enceliopsis covillei*) is a spectacular perennial with flowering stems that are woody at the base and can reach heights of up to 40 inches (Fig. 10.6). Silvery, 3-veined, diamond-shaped leaves at the stem bases, with huge yellow flower heads that commonly reach 3–5 inches in diameter, make it distinct. It is relatively uncommon and known only from rocky slopes and canyons on the western face of the Panamint Mountains. It has a CNPS Rare Plant Rank 1B: plants rare, threatened, or endangered in California and elsewhere. The beauty and special qualities of Panamint daisy has led to its selection as the official logo for the California Native Plant Society. Closely related is nakedstem sunray (*Enceliopsis nudicaulis*), with a mounded growth form of basal leaves and leafless flower stalks up to about 16 inches in height (Fig. 10.7). Its leaves are a dull gray-green and ovate. The radiate yellow flower heads are 1½–3½ inches in diameter. Nakedstem sunray occurs infrequently in rocky canyons and bajada slopes in the mountains of the eastern and northern Mojave Desert, becoming more common to the east.

In a good blooming year the desert flora produces a number of small yellow flowered annuals that are challenging to separate. Goldfields (*Lasthenia californica*) is a familiar small annual that is widespread and showy in California grasslands and oak savannas—providing splashes of yellow on hillsides in a mosaic with blue lupines and golden California poppies (Fig. 10.8). However, this species extends into the western and southern Mojave Desert, with notable abundance in the Antelope Valley of Los Angeles County.

Woolly sunflowers (*Eriophyllum* sp.) are familiar in coastal California as semi-woody shrubs and subshrubs, but this genus includes several tiny annuals in our desert region. These annuals are all characterized by their small size, spoon-shaped leaves, and woolly hairs that cover their foliage. Two common species that easily qualify as belly flowers are Wallace's woolly daisy (*Eriophyllum wallacei*) and Pringle's woolly daisy (*Eriophyllum pringlei*), both of which colonize open sandy sites across our desert region. The former has flower heads with both disk and ray flowers produce singly on flower stalks (Fig. 10.9), while the latter has clusters of flower heads that lack ray flowers (Fig. 10.10). Similar in appearance is yellow syntrichopappus (*Syntrichopappus fremontii*), a small branched annual with yellow flower heads and spoon-shaped or wedge-shaped leaves (Fig. 10.11). It is widespread in occurrence across the Mojave Desert and resembles *Eriophyllum wallacei* but has only about half the number of ray flowers and favors rocky upland sites.

The genus *Leptosyne* (formerly *Coreopsis*) produces small yellow annuals with several species having a range that crosses the transition from the coastal foothills into the western Mojave Desert. Leafy-stemmed coreopsis (*Leptosyne calliopsidea*) produces individual stems up to 15 inches in height, each nearing an erect flower head. The head typically has eight large, bright yellow ray flowers and a center of up to 50 tiny yellow disc florets (Fig. 10.12). The basal leaves are slightly fleshy and

Fig. 10.5. *Geraea canescens*, Asteraceae, desert sunflower. Photo by Robert Gustafson.

Fig. 10.6. *Enceliopsis covellei*, Asteraceae, Panamint daisy. Photo by Robert Gustafson.

Fig. 10.7. *Enceliopsis nudicaulis*, Asteraceae, nakedstem sunray. Photo by Jim Morefield.

Fig. 10.8. *Lasthenia californica*, Asteraceae, goldfields. Photo by Robert Gustafson.

divided into several narrow lobes. There are several other annual species in our desert areas characterized by a small number of large, bright yellow ray flowers and a dense cluster of many yellow-orange disc flowers. Bigelow's coreopsis (*Leptosyne bigelovii*) has a range that includes the Coast Ranges of southern California and Mojave Desert (Fig. 10.13). California coreopsis (*Leptosyne californica*) is common in the western Mojave Desert and coastal areas of Southern California from Orange County south into Baja California

Desert marigold (*Baileya multiradiata*) is a short-lived perennial that reaches 10-20 inches in height, with white-woolly stems and gray-green pinnately-lobed leaves arrayed near the base of the plant (Fig. 10.14). It extends leafless flowering stalks with large and spectacular flower heads. Desert marigold is common in sandy and rocky flats on bajada slopes of creosote bush scrub and Joshua tree woodland in the eastern Mojave Desert. Closely related is lax flower (*Baileya pauciradiata*), an annual with smaller flower heads with fewer disk flowers and foliage covered by soft woolly hairs. The basal leaves of lax flower wither before the flowers reach maturity. Lax flower is limited to elevations below about 3,500 feet in the eastern Mojave and Sonoran deserts where it favors sandy soils and dunes.

There are many annual and herbaceous perennial species with yellow discoid flowers in addition to Pringle's woolly daisy mentioned above. Yellow-heads (*Trichoptilium incisum*) is a low annual reaching to 10 inches in height. Its deeply lobed basal leaves have a dense covering of curly hairs, while the globular flower heads occur singly on 1–4 inch long glandular-hairy stalks (Fig. 10.15). Except for their yellow color, these flowers might be mistaken for pincushion (*Chaenactis* sp.). Yellow-heads characteristically occur in areas of desert pavement and rocky bajada slopes of the southern Mojave and Sonoran Deserts.

Two other examples of discoid yellow-flowered species that are small but easily recognized are turtleback (*Psathyrotes ramosissima*) and mealy rosette or annual turtleback (*Psathyrotes annua*). Both form low, compact mats with the former having gray velvety leaf blades that resemble the scales of a turtle shell and the latter with sharply toothed gray-green leaves with less pubescence (Fig. 10.16). Turtle-

Fig. 10.9. *Eriophyllum wallacei*, Asteraceae, Wallace's woolly daisy. Photo by Robert Gustafson.

Fig. 10.10. *Eriophyllum pringlei*, Asteraceae, Pringle's woolly daisy. Photo by Robert Gustafson.

Fig. 10.11. *Syntrichopappus fremontii*, Asteraceae, yellow syntrichopappus. Photo by Stan Shebs.

Fig. 10.12. *Leptosyne calliopsidea*, Asteraceae, leafy-stemmed coreopsis. Photo by Robert Gustafson.

Fig. 10.13. *Leptosyne bigelovii,* Asteraceae. Bigelow's coreopsis. Photo by Robert Gustafson.

Fig. 10.14. *Baileya multiradiata*, Asteraceae, desert marigold. Photo by Robert Gustafson.

Fig. 10.15. *Trichoptilium incisum,* Asteraceae, yellow-heads. Photo by Robert Gustafson.

Fig. 10.16. *Psathyrotes ramosissima*, Asteraceae, turtleback. Photo by Stan Shebs.

back smells like turpentine, while mealy rosette has the odor of sweet vinegar. Both species have traditional uses including medicinal tea, a dressing for snake bites, and an eye wash. Turtleback has a wide distribution in sandy washes and flats below about 3,000 feet elevation from Death Valley south into Mexico. Mealy rosette has a more restricted geographic range in the Mojave Desert but has a broader ecological occurrence in habitats that include creosote bush scrub and alkaline soils of saltbush scrub (Fig. 10.17).

Many of our yellow Asteraceae species are characterized by their ligulate flower heads. This means they have a single bisexual flower type with a fusion of all five petals. One annual, capable of coloring large areas sandy flats and washes, as well as disturbed roadsides, is desert dandelion (*Malacothrix glabrata*). This is the most common among a group of six desert dandelion species that share the traits of milky sap and ligulate flower heads (Fig. 10.18). Desert dandelion has a rosette of basal leaves that forms early and then often becomes withered by the time that flowering occurs. Flowering stalks vary in height from a few inches to 16 inches in a year with good rains.

Yellow tack-stem dandelion (*Calycoseris parryi*), a small branched annual with milky sap that is easily confused with desert dandelion. Its common name comes from the presence of stalked glands, or tacks, along the stems. Yellow tack-stem occurs widely through warm desert communities on bajada slopes and washes. A related species, white-flowered tack-stem (*Calycoseris wrightii*), is named for its flower color and is more typical of the lower Sonoran Desert.

One more ligulate species with milky sap is scale-bud (*Anisocoma acaulis*), a low annual with a basal rosette of pinnately lobed or divided leaves. The yellow flower heads, about 1 inch in diameter, are borne singly on flowering stalks (Fig. 10.19). Scale-bud occurs widely on sandy soils of creosote bush scrub, Joshua tree woodland, and pinyon juniper woodland throughout our desert regions.

White-Flowered Asteraceae

White is the other common color for members of the Asteraceae. This white color is typically present in ray and ligulate flowers, but in many cases the disk flowers may also be yellow, presenting a yellow center to an otherwise white flower. Among the common groups of white-flowered radiate annuals are tidytips (*Layia* sp.). This group of 14 species has a distribution centered in California with wide geographic ranges that include our desert regions. The most common of these is white tidytips (*Layia glandulosa*), an erect annual that can reach up to 20 inches in height. It has purplish glandular stems with scattered long linear leaves, and broad flower heads up to 1 inch across with white ray flowers and a center of yellow disk flowers (Fig. 10.20). White tidytips occurs widely on sandy soils throughout our desert regions.

Emory rock daisy (*Perityle emoryi*) is erect with a brittle, glandular, and hairy stem with broad palmately-lobed leaves. The flowers are typical discoid daisy flowers with a small number of white ray flowers and numerous small yellow disk flowers (Fig, 10.21). Emory rock daisy is a common species across both the Mojave and Sonoran deserts at elevations below about 3,000 feet where it favors rocky canyon walls and boulder washes where water collects.

Two related annuals, with radiate heads of white flowers, are quintessential belly flowers. Desert star (*Monoptilon bellioides*) and small desert star (*Monoptilon bellidiforme*) are prostrate and only a few inches in height. The foliage of both species is covered by short bristly hairs with small, linear leaves tufted below the flower heads. The distinguishing feature separating the two species is the nature of the bristles on the pappus (sepal-like structure in Asteraceae flowers). Desert star has up to 12 simple pappus bristles (Fig. 10.22) while small desert star has only a single bristle tipped with a feather-like plume. Desert star may be abundant in sandy washes and gravelly flats below about 3,000 feet through both the Mojave and Sonoran deserts, while small desert star is more restricted—favoring sandy soils from 2000–4,000 feet in the Mojave Desert and the northern Sonoran Desert.

A common species with white discoid flowers is desert pincushion (*Chaenactis fremontii*). It is one of eight related species of pincushion in the California deserts. Most of these are annuals, although there are two species of perennial pincush-

Fig. 10.17. *Psathyrotes annua*, Asteraceae, mealy rosette. Photo by Stan Shebs.

Fig. 10.18. *Malacothrix glabrata*, Asteraceae, desert dandelion. Photo by Matt Berger.

Fig. 10.19. *Anisocoma acaulis*, Asteraceae, scalebud. Photo by Stan Shebs.

Fig. 10.20. *Layia glandulosa*, Asteraceae, white tidytips. Photo by Matt Berger.

Fig. 10.21. *Perityle emoryi*, Asteraceae, Emory rock daisy. Photo by Matt Berger.

Fig. 10.22. *Monoptilon bellioides*, Asteraceae, desert star. Photo by Matt Berger.

ion in the mountains of the eastern and northern Mojave Desert. Desert pincushion is an erect, branched annual that begins life with a basal rosette of leaves, which senesces as the stems mature and flowering begins (Fig. 10.23). The smooth stems lack hairs and produce single or multiple flower heads composed entirely of disk flowers. In favorable years, desert pincushion is found blooming in massive numbers across open sandy flats of creosote bush scrub and Joshua tree woodlands.

As with the yellow-flowered species of Asteraceae, there are several dandelion relatives with white ligulate flowers. One of the most prominent is gravel ghost (*Atrichoseris platyphylla*), a tall annual with a basal rosette of leaves and flowering stems that can reach 5 feet in height. The common name arises from the large white ligulate flower heads that appear to float in the air above the relatively invisible leafless stems (Fig. 10.24). The flowers have a sweet odor of vanilla. Gravel ghost occurs in massive numbers in sandy washes and dark volcanic soils of the eastern and northern Mojave Desert, most notably in open areas of Death Valley.

Desert chicory (*Rafinesquia neomexicana*) is a slender, erect annual up to 2 feet in height with a basal rosette of leaves that wither

10.23. *Chaenactis fremontii*, Asteraceae, desert pincushion. Photo by Robert Gustafson

Fig. 10.24. *Atrichoseris platyphylla*, Asteraceae, gravel ghost. Photos by Matt Berger.

Fig. 10.25. *Rafinesquia neomexicana*, Asteraceae. desert chicory. Photo by Matt Berger.

Fig. 10.26. *Eschscholzia glypyosperma*, Papaveraceae, desert gold poppy. Photo by Robert Gustafson.

Fig. 10.27. *Eschscholzia minutiflora*, little gold poppy. Photo by Matt Berger.

before flowers mature (Fig. 10.25). The weak stems, which like other members of the dandelion group have milky sap, commonly display a zig-zag form as they reach up through the canopy of sheltering shrubs. During the spring, desert chicory displays multiple heads of large and fragrant ligulate flowers. It is found widely in sandy and gravelly soils of creosote bush scrub and Joshua tree woodland throughout our desert regions. A closely related species, California chicory (*Rafinesquia californica*), extends its range into the desert but is more typical of coastal California shrublands. It is a sturdier species with a thick stem and small, relatively inconspicuous flowers that favors disturbed sites.

Desert Poppies (Papaveraceae)

The poppy family (Papaveraceae), like the evening primroses (Onagraceae), has four petals with radial symmetry. A prominent difference, however, is that the Papaveraceae generally have many stamens as opposed to four or occasionally eight in the Onagraceae. Another characteristic of most members of the Papaveraceae is the presence of only two sepals, which are shed as the petals develop and open.

The most prominent of our desert poppies, and our state flower, is the familiar California poppy (*Eschscholzia californica*). California poppies occur widely over grasslands and oak woodlands throughout California but are also notably abundant in the western Mojave Desert. Their orange to yellow flowers often color huge expanses of the landscape in favorable years, growing both as an annual or perennial. The Antelope Valley Poppy Preserve, near Lancaster, is famous for its spring displays of poppies. Interestingly, California poppies thrive with disturbance and regular grazing promotes the dominance of this species. The odd generic name commemorates a Russian naturalist and surgeon, Dr. Johann Friedrich Gustav von Eschscholtz who first collected this California poppy near San Francisco in 1815. Somehow the "t" in his name was lost in translation.

There are five other annual species of *Eschscholzia* in our desert regions. Desert gold poppy (*Eschscholzia glyptosperma*) is easily recognized by its cluster of basal rosette leaves and leafless stems, each supporting a single yellow-gold flower (Fig. 10.26). It is widely distributed in sandy washes and open flats of creosote bush scrub and Joshua tree woodland across the Mojave Desert and less commonly in the Sonoran Desert. Little gold poppy (*Eschscholzia minutiflora*) differs in having leafy flowering stems and smaller yellow flowers (Fig. 10.27). It favors sandy and gravelly flats from creosote bush scrub to pinyon-juniper woodlands across both of our desert regions. Parish's gold poppy (*Eschscholzia parishii*) is similar in appearance to little gold poppy, but with bright green or yellow-green leaves compared to the blue-green or grayish leaves of the latter species. It is found on sloping hillsides of creosote bush scrub in the southern Mojave and Sonoran deserts.

Fig. 10.28. *Argemone corymbosa*, Papaveraceae, Mojave prickly poppy. Photo by Matt Berger.

The poppy family also includes two species of prickly poppy, which are typically tall herbaceous perennials, up to 3 feet in height, with sharp spines along their stems and leaf margins. Mojave prickly poppy (*Argemone corymbosa*) is the smallest and characterized by orange sap (Fig. 10.28). It is widely seen along roadsides and valley bottoms of creosote bush scrub across the Mojave Desert. The second, and somewhat taller species, is chicalote (*Argemone munita*) which is characterized by spinier leaves and yellow sap. It has a much broader elevational range that extends to forest habitats over the Great Basin and beyond. Both species have large "fried-egg" flowers with white petals and clustered yellow stamens at their center.

Herbaceous Legumes (Fabaceae)

Unlike many of the woody desert legumes, all of the herbaceous legumes in our California deserts are members of the pea subfamily Papilionoideae. This group is characterized by a flower structure with bilateral symmetry and with the five petals arranged one as a banner, two as wings, and two joined together to form a keel. An important trait of the pea subfamily is a symbiotic relationship with rhizobium bacteria, which form colonies within the legume roots and fix atmospheric nitrogen. The host legume supplies the residence tissue with carbon and phosphorus, while the bacteria fix nitrogen and fertilize the soil around the plants. This is the same trait present in agricultural legume crops such as peas, beans, and alfalfa. Although water is the primary limiting factor for the growth of desert plants, nitrogen availability is also limiting during those months when water is available, especially in coarse or sandy soils with little organic matter. As a result, herbaceous legumes are classic colonizers of nutrient-poor sandy soils, roadsides, and other disturbed sites.

Lupines are iconic California wildflowers, and the deserts are home to many species. No less than 24 annual and perennial lupines occur within our desert boundaries, although many are more typical of southern California shrublands or mountains. There are more than 200 species of lupines in the world, with 71 species in California, making it one of our most species-rich genera. Interestingly, one of the other centers of lupine diversity is in the high elevations of the Andes of South America—a very different ecosystem.

While lupines as a group are easy to recognize with their palmate arrangement of leaflets, identifying individual species is quite challenging. Taxonomic keys to identifying lupines rely first on whether the plant is an annual or perennial, and then focus on morphological characteristics of the flowers and leaflets. The greatest lupine displays are seen with massive blooms of desert annuals. While perennial lupines are quite showy individually, they tend to occur in smaller numbers and thus seldom cover plains or hillsides like the annuals.

Arizona lupine (*Lupinus arizonicus*) is one the most common and conspicuous desert lupines when it blooms in sandy washes and open creosote bush scrub below 3,000 feet in the Mojave and Sonoran deserts (Fig. 10.29). It is particularly abundant in spring along roadsides. Although an annual, Arizona lupine is a robust plant that is typically 1–2 feet in height. Its stems and the underside of its green leaflets have long, spreading hairs. The purple flowers have a yellowish spot on each of the banners, which are the two petals that spread horizontally.

Desert lupine (*Lupinus shockleyi*) is a low growing annual, usually no more than 4–8 inches in height, which appears almost stemless (Fig. 10.30). It is a common species that occurs in open sandy soils and lower dune slopes below about 3,000 feet elevation over broad areas of both the Mojave and Sonoran deserts. The small

Fig. 10.29. *Lupinus arizonicus*, Fabaceae, Arizona lupine. Photo by Matt Berger.

Fig. 10.30. *Lupinus shockleyi*, Fabaceae, desert lupine. Photo by Matt Berger.

leaflets have silky flattened hairs on their lower surface but are hairless on their upper surface except at the margins. The spirally arrayed flowers are dark blue-purple or indigo.

Bajada lupine (*Lupinus concinnus*) is a small annual with densely hairy blue-green leaflets that occurs widely on bajada slopes in creosote bush scrub and Joshua tree woodland habitats across our desert and coastal region and eastward as far as New Mexico. It is particularly common in disturbed sites such as along roadsides and after fire. Bajada lupine has pinkish purple flowers, with banner petals displaying large cream-colored or yellowish centers, arrayed with a distinctive spiral, rather than whorls, on short flowering stalks (Fig. 10.31).

Fig. 10.31. *Lupinus concinnus*, Fabaceae. bajada lupine. Photo by Matt Berger.

Mojave lupine (*Lupinus odoratus*) is a showy species that occurs widely across sandy flats and open areas of the Mojave Desert at elevations up to 5,000 feet. This annual grows to 12 inches in height, with a cluster of basal leaves with bright green leaflets that lack hairs when mature. Its clusters of beautiful royal purple flowers with prominent white spots on the banner petals gives it the alternate name royal desert lupine (Fig. 10.32). The flowers have a distinctive odor of violets.

Fig. 10.32. *Lupinus odoratus*, Fabaceae, Mojave lupine. Photo by Jim Morefield.

We have three small herbaceous legumes, called dalea, in our desert flora. The most common is silky dalea (*Dalea mollissima*) which occurs widely across our Sonoran Desert region on coarse or gravelly flats and washes of creosote bush scrub at elevations below 3,000 feet. This mat-forming species sprawls over diameters of up to 12 inches, with blue-gray pinnately compound leaves dotted with black glands and covered with fine, soft hairs (Fig. 10.34). The small pea flowers are pink to white in color and produced on short dense spikes. The hairy prairie clover (*Dalea mollis*) is also common. It is similar to silky dalea but with leaflet margins that are entire and flat, as opposed to silky dalea which has leaflet margins that

Fig. 10.33. *Dalea mollisima*, Fabaceae, silky dalea Photo by Matt Berger.

are shallowly lobed or wavy. Hairy prairie clover favors sandier and lower elevation habitats that silky dalea. Although both species are relatively uncommon in dry years, they germinate and densely cover desert flats in years with abundant rainfall and are important for the nitrogen they fix. The closely related Parry dalea (*Marina parryi*) is a slender perennial herb with long hairy stems, reaching to 30 inches in height, with small, sparse, resin-dotted leaves. It is found across our low elevation deserts at elevations below 2,500 feet on rocky slopes or open washes. The small purple blue flowers are clustered in dense spikes.

The common names locoweed, rattleweed, and milkvetch all apply to members of the diverse genus *Astragalus*, with more than 2,000 species worldwide. With 94 species in California and 34 in our desert region, it is one of the most species-rich genera in California. Although a few species of *Astragalus* are distinctive, most are difficult to identify without examining both flowers and fruits. Our flora includes both annual and herbaceous perennial species, with most sharing a mat-like growth form and small pinnate leaflets. There are exceptions, however, with tall, relatively upright species. A characteristic feature of many species, and the source of the name rattleweed, comes from the inflated seed pods. When mature, pods rattle when blown by the wind. The name locoweed comes from the toxic accumulation of selenium in many species that poison cattle and cause them to behave strangely when eaten. Several species of perennial *Astragalus* are described in Chapter 9.

Layne milkvetch (*Astragalus layneae*) is a perennial commonly found in sandy washes and along roadsides across the Mojave Desert. It has an upright growth form, reaching 6 inches in height, with compact foliage covered with coarse gray hairs and spreading spikes of white flowers with purple tips on their petals. A notable characteristic of this species is the fruit structure, consisting of elongate pods up to 2 inches in length, which are curved into a crescent shape (Fig. 10.34). Two-seeded milkvetch (*Astragalus didymocarpus*), sometimes called slender white milkvetch, is a slender annual that grows erectly to a height of up to 12 inches under favorable conditions (Fig. 10.35). This is a wide-ranging species of open grassy, gravelly, or sandy flats across our deserts as well as into coastal areas of Southern

Fig. 10.34. *Astragalus layneae*, Fabaceae, Layne milkvetch. Photo by Matt Berger.

Fig. 10.35. *Astragalus didymocarpus*, Fabaceae, two-seeded milkvetch. Photo by Matt Berger.

California. It has green stems and leaflets covered lightly with small, stiff hairs. It produces dense heads of small purplish flowers that produce tiny spherical pods less than ¼ inch in diameter. These pods have just two seeds, giving rise to the common name.

Freckled milkvetch (*Astragalus lentiginosus*) is a widespread and highly variable species that has 19 described varieties in California, with 11 in our deserts. The common name comes from the strongly inflated pods with purple spots that look like freckles (Fig. 10.36). The common *A. lentiginosus* var. *variabilis* is found widely across the Mojave Desert in sandy washes and creosote bush scrub. *A. lentiginosus* var. *fremontii* grows commonly in open sandy and gravelly creosote bush scrub and Joshua tree woodland of the eastern Mojave Desert. *Astragalus lentiginosus* var. *albifolius,* with dense silvery foliage, is restricted to alkaline flats and clay pans of the Antelope Valley in the western Mojave Desert. Other varieties are highly localized and thus vulnerable to extinction.

Perhaps our most distinctive *Astragalus*, at least when flowering, is scarlet locoweed (*Astragalus coccineus*). This small, mounded perennial—lacking upright stems—produces brilliant red flowers, about 1½ inch in length, occurring in clusters of 3–10. The foliage is covered with dense, long hairs giving the leaflets a silvery appearance. The plump curved pods are 1–1 ½ inches in length and covered with long silky hairs (Fig. 10.37). This is a species of pinyon-juniper woodlands of the eastern and northern Mojave Desert. Newberry locoweed (*Astragalus newberryi*) is another pinyon-juniper species, with silvery foliage like that of scarlet locoweed. It differs in having persistent bases of the old leaves, giving the plant a shaggy appearance. Its flowers are smaller and pale purple or pink to white in color, and its pods are smaller.

Another large but less showy group of legumes in California were formerly placed in the genus *Lotus*. Recent molecular studies

Fig. 10.36. *Astragalus lentiginosus* var. *variabilis*, Fabaceae, freckled milkvetch. Photo by Matt Berger.

Fig. 10.37. *Astragalus coccineus*, Fabaceae, scarlet locoweed. Photo by Robert Gustafson.

Fig. 10.38. *Acmispon strigosus*, Fabaceae, stiff-haired lotus. Photo by Jim Morefield.

now indicate that the true *Lotus* are from the Mediterranean Basin. Our California species have been separated into two former subgenera, *Acmispon* and *Hosackia*. Most of our desert lotus are *Acmispon* and are easily distinguished from other herbaceous desert legumes by the yellow flowers present in almost all species. As with the lupines, *Acmispon* species include annuals, herbaceous perennials, and subshrubs. One of these desert subshrubs, desert rock pea (*Acmispon rigidus*), is described in Chapter 4. Our most common annual is stiff-haired lotus (*Acmispon strigosus*), a prostrate species with slender, often fleshy, stems with flowers born in stalked clusters (Fig. 10.38). As its common name indicates, its foliage has stiff, flattened hairs. A similar species is bird's foot lotus or foothill vetch (*Acmispon brachycarpus*), an annual with a prostrate growth form and dense, but not flattened, hairs. Its flowers occur singly in leaf axils rather than in clusters on stalks. Both species are widespread across our desert areas as well as other habitats in coastal foothills and valleys of California. In the desert they are commonly found on sandy flats, bajada slopes, and disturbed roadsides.

Desert Phacelias (Hydrophyllaceae)

The phacelia family includes diverse species that are a major component of the blue and purple desert annual blooms. The Hydrophyllaceae and the closely related Boraginaceae are characterized by radially symmetrical flowers arrayed in coiled spikes. The Hydrophyllaceae typically have five stamens that extend beyond the tubular flowering petals, and a stigma that is divided into two lobes. In the Boraginaceae the stamens are typically shorter than the petals and the stigma is undivided. In addition, the Hydrophyllaceae characteristically have deeply lobed or pinnately compound leaves, while the leaves of Boraginaceae are usually entire. Hydrophyllaceae have spherical fruit capsules, while the Boraginaceae have four small nutlets. An unscientific but useful rule of thumb is that blue to pink or purple flowers are usually members of the Hydrophyllaceae while white or yellow flowers are commonly Boraginaceae. Phylogenies based on molecular data are suggesting that the Hydrophyllaceae should be merged within a broader concept of the Boraginaceae but we retain the two as distinct families here.

Phacelias and several related genera form one of the most familiar groups of desert annuals. Desert *Phacelia* species produce some of the most spectacular and colorful displays in years with good rainfall, covering broad areas of flats and bajada slopes with masses of blue or purple flowers. Unlike some species of Asteraceae and Onagraceae, where a single species covers broad areas, flowering displays of phacelias typically include multiple species. *Phacelia* is one of the largest genera in California, with 93 species with 34 of these in our deserts. A characteristic of the genus is the presence of dense glandular hairs on the stems and foliage. A significant number of people are sensitive to the glandular secretions of phacelia and develop a rash similar to that of poison oak.

Most of our desert phacelias are erect annuals with distinctly divided basal leaflets and stem leaves that are deeply lobed. Perhaps our most common species is lace-leaf phacelia (*Phacelia distans*), whose common name describes the highly dissected, fern-like leaves (Fig. 10.39). It displays spikes of relatively small (¼–½ inch) pale blue to lavender flowers. Lace-leaf phacelia is a widespread and abundant on clayey and gravelly flats and slopes where it often blooms even in relatively dry years below the protective canopy of creosote bush. It has a broad distribution not only in our deserts but through our Mediterranean-type shrublands. Another wide-ranging species in both Mediterranean-type shrublands and a range of desert habitats is Fremont phacelia (*Phacelia fremontii*). This species has slightly succulent leaves, 2-5 inches in length, with deep lobes or divided leaflets with rounded segments. The purple flowers have unusual yellow bases on the upper surface of the petals. Desert Canterbury bells (*Phacelia campanularia*) is an erect annual with showy spikes of large deep blue flowers that are 1–1 ½ inches in diameter. It has large, elongate leaves with a saw-toothed margin with stems covered by glandular hairs (Fig. 10.40). This species occurs at relatively low elevations on sandy and gravelly flats and slopes in creosote bush scrub.

There are two common species of phacelia that are notable for their foul smell. Notch-leaved phacelia (*Phacelia crenulata*) is an erect but little branched annual with thick and densely glandular stems (Fig. 10.41). Its violet-purple flowers, with a touch of white at the petal base, highlight dark green leaves that are highly dissected into leaflets lobes with scalloped margins. The truly distinguishing feature of this plant is the unpleasant odor that has been described as "skunk in syrup." It is widespread across creosote bush scrub up into pinyon-juniper woodlands and beyond across the western United States. Similar in general form is specter phacelia (*Phacelia pedicillata*), another malodorous annual common in sandy washes and gravelly bajada slopes. It is distinguished by the ovate to rounded leaves on its stems, and basal leaves with rounded leaflets. The flowers are pinkish to pale blue. The glandular secretions can stain hands or clothing.

Fig. 10.39. *Phacelia distans*, Hydrophyllaceae, lace-leaf phacelia. Photo by Matt Berger.

Fig. 10.40. *Phacelia campanularia*, Hydrophyllaceae, desert Canterbury bells. Photo by Matt Berger.

Fig. 10.41. *Phacelia crenulata*, Hydrophyllaceae, notched-leaved phacelia. Photo by Stan Shebs.

Fig. 10.42. *Phacelia rotundifolia*, Hydrophyllaceae, round-leaf phacelia. Photo by Stan Shebs.

Fig. 10.43. *Emmenanthe penduliflora*, Hydrophyllaceae, whispering bells. Photo by Jim Morefield.

Fig. 10.44. *Nama demissa*, Hydrophyllaceae, purple mat. Photo by Stan Shebs.

Although purplish to blue flowers characterize most species of phacelia, there are several with white flowers. Round-leaf phacelia (*Phacelia rotundifolia*) is a small annual that favors rocky crevices and ledges of Joshua tree and pinyon-juniper woodlands of the Mojave Desert (Fig. 10.42). It has rounded, toothed leaves on petioles longer than the leaf blade, and small ¼ inch flowers that are white to pale pink. Ives phacelia (*Phacelia ivesiana*) is a low and branched annual with deeply divided lower leaves and white flowers with a pale-yellow throat. It favors dry sandy soils and dunes of the eastern Mojave Desert.

Another common species of waterleaf is confused with phacelia. Whispering bells (*Emmenanthe penduliflora*), the only species in its genus, is distinguished from *Phacelia* by yellow to cream-colored flowers that hang downward and persist in a dry form after flowering (Fig. 10.43). True phacelias have erect to spreading flowers and generally drop these flowers after maturity. Whispering bells is an interesting species because of its wide geographic and ecological range. In addition to its desert distribution, it is a common fire-following annual in California's chaparral, serpentine grasslands, and oak savannas.

Lastly, purple mat (*Nama demissa*) is an easily recognized prostrate spreading annual with a mat-like growth form (Fig. 10.44). In spring, masses of small rose-purple flowers decorate sandy and gravelly soils of creosote bush scrub below 4,000 feet.

Borage Family (Boraginaceae)

The traditional Boraginaceae have small white or yellow flowers arrayed in a coiled spike. The flowers are always radially symmetrical with five petals joined to form a tube over part of their length. The fruits form four small nutlets. Species of Boraginaceae are often difficult to identify without a hand lens, and the morphology of these nutlets is often important. The leaves of our desert borages are generally small and linear and covered with stiff hairs.

There are three commonly encountered groups of desert borages with small white flowers, collectively called forget-me-knots. The largest group is the genus *Cryptantha*, with 52 species across California and 29 in our deserts (Fig. 10.45). The second large group of species is formed by popcorn flowers (*Plagiobothrys* sp.), with about 39 species in California and 15 in the desert. The third group is *Pectocarya* with seven of its eight California species found in the desert. These genera are difficult to separate in the field. *Pectocarya* species are the most distinct with fringed margins on the nutlets (Fig. 10.46). *Cryptantha* and *Plagiobothrys* are even more difficult to distinguish, requiring a microscope to examine the attachment scars of the nutlets. Not surprisingly then, identification to species requires considerable experience.

There is, however, a highly distinctive borage, devil's lettuce or checker fiddlehead (*Amsinckia tessellata*), which is the only common desert borage with yellow flowers (Fig. 10.47). It is an erect annual with stems and linear leaves covered with stiff hairs. The foliage contains alkaloids and nitrates that make it poisonous to stock and an irritant to skin. Devil's lettuce is widely distributed in sandy and clay soils and notably thrives in sites disturbed by grazing.

Fig. 10.45. *Cryptantha barbigera*, Boraginaceae, bearded cryptantha. Photo by Jim Morefield.

Fig. 10.46. *Pectocarya recurvata*, Boraginaceae, arched-nut pectocarya. Photo by Matt Berger.

Fig. 10.47. *Amsinckia tessellata*, Boraginaceae, devil's lettuce. Photo by Matt Berger.

Phlox Family (Polemoniaceae)

The phlox family includes a variety of small but showy desert annuals. Many of these fit the description of belly flowers, with heights of no more than a few inches. The Polemoniaceae are separated from the closely related Boraginaceae (and the former Hydrophyllaceae now included in the borage family) by the flowering inflorescence in the form of what is called a cyme. A cyme is a branched inflorescence in which the central, or uppermost, flower opens before the outer flowers—in contrast to the coiled spike of flowers in the borage family. In addition, the Polemoniaceae has a stigma with three branches, Hydrophyllaceae has two stigma lobes, and Boraginaceae a single lobe. The flowers of Polemoniaceae typically have five stamens and five petals that are often joined to form a long floral tube. While most flowers have radial symmetry, some have bilateral symmetry.

Fourteen species combine to form the largest desert group in the phlox family. While once in a single genus, they are now split into *Linanthus* and *Leptisiphon*. All but two of these species are annuals. One of the traits that separates these from other genera of desert annual phloxes is the presence of opposite leaves that are often palmately lobed. Sand blossoms (*Linanthus parryae*) is a tiny tufted species, no more than 2-4 inches in height, with flowers that vary from deep blue to white within populations (Fig. 10.48). It is found in sandy soils in creosote bush scrub and Joshua tree woodland across the Mojave Desert, with notable populations in the western Mojave. Evening snow (*Linanthus dichotomus*) is a small erect annual, 4–8 inches in height, with wiry stems and large, white funnel-shaped flowers (Fig. 10.49). Its characteristic habitat is open spaces between shrubs in creosote bush scrub and Joshua tree woodland. It also grows beyond our desert regions in the coastal foothills where it is common in serpentine grasslands. After sundown thread-like plants transform to fields of fragrant bright white blossoms pollinated at night. These flowers begin to close soon after dawn and are fully closed by midmorning.

Fig. 10.48. *Linanthus parryae*, Polemoniaceae, sand blossoms. Photo by Robert Gustafson.

Fig. 10.49. *Linanthus dichotomus*, Polemoniaceae, evening snow. Photo by Jim Morefield.

Golden linanthus (*Leptosiphon aureus*) is a tufted species with bright yellow flowers (Fig. 10.50). It is locally common in sandy areas of creosote bush scrub and Joshua tree woodlands, as well as in coastal valleys. Mojave linanthus (*Leptosiphon breviculus*) is another erect annual with compact clusters of lavender to pink or whitish flowers. This is a higher elevation Mojave species found in dry, open areas including Joshua tree and pinyon-juniper woodlands.

The gilias, now split between *Gilia* and *Aliciella*, form another diverse group with 32 species in our desert region. One of the easiest species to recognize is broad-leaved gilia (*Aliciella latifolia*) because of its strong and unpleasant smell and broad basal leaves, 1–3 inches in length, with a strongly toothed margin (Fig. 10.51). The small, pink, tubular flowers are arrayed on erect flowering stems. Broad-leaved gilia is a common species in washes and rocky flats of creosote bush scrub across the Sonoran and Mojave deserts. Broad-flowered gilia (*Gilia latiflora*) has a basal rosette of large but deeply lobed or strongly toothed leaves covered with cobweb-like hairs. The tubular lavender flowers typically have a white throat and are loosely arrayed on erect stems. This gilia often blooms in massive numbers across sandy soils and washes of creosote bush scrub and Joshua tree woodland of the western and central Mojave Desert.

The related lilac sunbonnet (*Langloisia setosissima*) is a small, tufted annual that is the only member of its genus. It has large, white to pale blue flowers with petals up to 1 inch in length (Fig. 10.52). There are two distinct subspecies of lilac sunbonnet. The subspecies *punctata* is largely restricted in California to the Mojave Desert and has flowers with numerous tiny purple spots on their outer half and two yellow markings on the middle of each petal.

Fig. 10.50. *Leptosiphon aureus*, Polemoniaceae, golden linanthus. Photo by Stan Shebs.

Fig. 10.51. *Aliciella latifolia*, Polemoniaceae, broad-leaved gilia. Photo by Stan Shebs.

Fig. 10.52. *Langloisia setosissima*, Polemoniaceae, lilac sunbonnet. Photo by Stan Shebs.

Fig. 10.53. *Eriastrum eremicum*, Polemoniaceae, desert woollystar. Photo by Jim Morefield.

Fig. 10.54. *Loeseliastrum matthewsii*, Polemoniaceae, desert calico. Photo by Robert Gustafson.

Fig. 10.55. *Loeseliastrum schottii*, Polemoniaceae, little calico. Photo by Jim Morefield.

The subspecies *setosissima*, called bristly langloisia, lacks these distinctive spots and has a broader range—extending across both of our desert regions. Both subspecies favor sandy washes and gravelly slopes, but lilac sunbonnet is largely restricted to such habitats in creosote bush scrub while bristly langloisia extends to higher elevations.

The genus *Eriastrum* is a small but widespread group of Polemoniaceae characterize by spiny leaf-like bracts in the flower heads. Many of the six species in our desert regions these annuals are characteristically found on disturbed sites. One of the most common species is desert woollystar (*Eriastrum eremicum*), an erect to spreading annual, 2–12 inches in height, with linear-lobed leaves and stems that are generally covered with woolly hairs. The pale violet flowers have petals formed into two distinct lips, creating bilateral symmetry. Desert woollystar favors sandy soils at all elevations across creosote bush scrub to pinyon-juniper woodlands.(Fig. 10.53)

Although most members of the Polemoniaceae are characterized by flowers with radial symmetry, other exceptions are desert calico (*Loeseliastrum matthewsii*) and little calico (*Loeseliastrum schottii*). These are both small, tufted annuals no more than to 4–6 inches in height. Desert calico has rose-purple to white flowers with an upper lip of three joined petals with a maroon arch and large white spot and a lower lip of two separate petals with three lobes at their tips (Fig. 10.54). Little calico exhibits less pronounced bilateral symmetry with three lobes of white to pink upper petals and two lobes of lower petals (Fig. 10.55). Both species are locally abundant in sandy washes and bajada slopes of creosote bush scrub and Joshua tree woodland across the Mojave Desert. Both likewise occur in the Sonoran Desert, with the former largely restricted to the western portions.

Herbaceous Mints (Lamiaceae)

Opposite leaves and square stems are key characteristics of the mint family (see Chapter 4). Thistle sage (*Salvia carduacea*) is considered by many to be among the most beautiful species in the entire California desert flora (Fig. 10.56). It is locally abundant in sandy or gravelly soils of creosote bush scrub or Joshua tree woodlands in the western Mojave Desert as well as arid areas of the San Joaquin Valley and coastal ranges of southern California. The tall, white-woolly stems of thistle sage reach as high as 3 feet in favorable years. These stems arise from a basal rosette of pinnately lobed and toothed leaves. Along the stem, round clusters of lavender flowers have a platform of spiny, leaf-like bracts below the flowers.

Chia (*Salvia columbariae*) is a small annual ranging from 4–20 inches in height depending on growing conditions. This wide-ranging species occurs in abundance across the Mojave Desert in creosote bush scrub, as well as in many shrubland plant communities in southern California where it is a post-fire specialist. The plants have a basal rosette of twice-divided coarse-textured leaves, with flowering stalks bearing one or more cluster heads of blue two-lipped flowers (Fig. 10.57). Chia seeds are an important food source for Native Americans.

There are several other diminutive mint family species that occur in our deserts. Mojave pennyroyal (*Monardella exilis*) is an erect annual, up to 16 inches in height, with opposite lance-shaped leaves and clusters of small, white flowers with a whorl of purple streaked bracts below. Mojave pennyroyal is found in sandy washes of the western and central Mojave Desert, extending from creosote bush scrub up into Joshua tree and pinyon-juniper woodlands. Mock pennyroyal (*Hedeoma nanum*) is a low, densely-branched herbaceous perennial with oppositely-arrayed ovate leaves and purple flowers. In California, it is largely restricted to limestone outcrops in the eastern and northern Mojave Desert.

Fig. 10.56. *Salvia carduacea*, Lamiaceae, thistle sage. Photo by Matt Berger.

Fig. 10.57. *Salvia columbariae*, Lamiaceae, chia. Photo by Stan Shebs.

Penstemon Family (Plantaginaceae)

The penstemon family is large and diverse with many notable and showy desert annuals and herbaceous perennials. Like the mints, the family exhibits bilateral symmetry with two petals joined to form an upper lip and three joined below to form the lower lip. This type of symmetry has evolved to attract and facilitate pollination by insects and hummingbirds. Species in the penstemon family are readily distinguished from mints by the absence of aromatic foliage and the presence of stems that are round in cross-section, rather than square. The penstemon family has long been considered a rather eclectic group of taxa with mixed relationships. Taxonomists now place many genera once considered part of the Scrophulariaceae into the Plantaginaceae, including desert genera such as *Penstemon, Mohavea, Antirrhinum*, and *Holmgrenanthe*.

Perhaps the most familiar are in the genus *Penstemon*. This is a huge genus of large perennial herbs, subshrubs, and shrubs that includes 53 species in California and 19 in our desert regions. However, most of these desert species are found in the higher elevations of the Mojave and Great Basin deserts above creosote bush scrub and Joshua tree woodlands including Palmer's penstemon (*Penstemon palmeri*) (Fig. 10.58).

Ghost flower (*Mohavea confertiflora*) is an unusual erect annual with hairy foliage and alternate leaves. Its provocative common name comes from the presence of large pale-yellow flowers that are virtually translucent and "ghostly" in appearance. The flowers, up to 1.5 inches in diameter, flowers are borne singly in the axils of each upper leaf (Fig. 10.59). The flowers surprisingly contain no nectar. They appear to have evolved to resemble *Mentzelia involucrata*, a species in an entirely different family (see Fig. 10.83) with an overlapping range of occurrence. The nectar produced by *Mentzelia involucrata* attracts female bees of the genus *Xeralictus*Ghost

Fig. 10.58. *Penstemon palmeri*, Plantaginaceae, Palmer's penstemon. Photo by Robert Gustafson.

Fig. 10.59. *Mohavea confertiflora*, Plantaginaceae, ghost flower. Photo by Robert Gustafson.

flower favors washes and open flats in creosote bush scrub of the central and southern Mojave and Sonoran deserts.

Ghost flower is replaced in the eastern and northern Mojave Desert by a closely related species, lesser mojavea (*Mohavea breviflora*), with a smaller stature and bright yellow flowers. Both species appear, at first glance, to have radial symmetry but careful examination shows the two-lipped flower structure. A unique feature that separates the ghost flower species from other members of the genus is that only two of the stamens are fertile. The others two stamens are sterile structures called staminoids.

Fig. 10.60. *Antirrhinum filipes*, Plantaginaceae, twining snapdragon. Photo by Robert Gustafson.

An unusual close relative is twining snapdragon (*Antirrhinum filipes*), one of four snapdragon species that enter California's deserts. It is a slender annual that climbs up, into, and through the canopy of small shrubs (Fig. 10.60). An interesting feature is that not only do the thread-like stems twine around shrub branches but the flower stalks twine as well. The bright yellow flowers, about ½ inch in diameter, often have maroon spots on their lower lip.

Rocklady (*Holmgrenanthe petrophila*), is a rare, monotypic, herbaceous perennial restricted to limestone cliffs at 3,500–5,800 feet within Titus and Fall canyons in Death Valley National Park (see Chapter 2). This distinctive plant has broad yellow to whitish flowers and bristly toothed leaves with palmate veins. It has a CNPS Rare Plant Rank 1B: rare, threatened, or endangered in California and elsewhere.

Monkeyflower Family (Phrymaceae)

The monkeyflowers, which are common throughout the state, were formerly all placed in the genus *Mimulus* which included more than 60 species in California and 15 in the desert. Although once considered part of the Scrophulariaceae, there are unusual features of monkey flowers, including the presence of opposite leaves and four functional stamens with no sterile fifth stamen (staminode), that place them in the Phrymaceae.

The large, cosmopolitan genus *Mimulus* is now divided into several smaller genera. Yellow monkeyflower (*Erythranthe guttata*) is a familiar species in wet areas of coastal California as well as streamsides and other moist habitats in the desert (Fig. 10.61). Other desert monkeyflowers are in the genus *Diplacus*. Bigelow monkeyflower (*Diplacus bigelovii*), a small annual

Fig. 10.61. *Erythranthe guttata*, Phrymaceae, yellow monkeyflower. Photo by Robert Gustafson.

Fig. 10.62. *Diplacus bigelovii*, Phrymaceae, Bigelow monkeyflower. Photo by Matt Berger.

Fig. 10.63. *Diplacus rupicola*, Phrymaceae, Death Valley monkeyflower. Photo by Matt Berger.

Fig. 10.64. *Diplacus mohavensis*, Phrymaceae, Mojave monkeyflower. Photo by Naomi Fraga.

species with densely hairy foliage and large magenta flowers, occurs widely in washes on lower bajada slopes from creosote bush scrub to pinyon-juniper communities (Fig. 10.62). Two other notable species have restricted ranges. Death Valley monkeyflower (*Diplacus rupicola*) is a tiny perennial with unusual pink- to rose-colored flowers displaying a purple spot at the petal base with a yellow throat (Fig. 10.63). The ovate leaves are covered with tiny hairs. This species is restricted in distribution to limestone cliffs in and around Death Valley. It has a CNPS Rare Plant Rank 4.3: limited distribution. Mojave monkeyflower (*Diplacus mohavensis*) is a small tufted annual species distinguished by its maroon-colored tubular flowers with radial symmetry that differ from the typical two-lipped morphology of most species of monkeyflower (Fig. 10.64). It has a CNPS Rare Plant Rank 2B: plants rare, threatened, or endangered in California and elsewhere, and is restricted to the gravelly slopes of desert washes of the central Mojave Desert around Barstow.

Broom-Rape Family (Orobanchaceae)

There are several genera of parasitic plants that were traditionally placed in the Scrophulariaceae but are now in the broom-rape family or Orobanchaceae with other root parasites. Purple owl's clover (*Castilleja exserta*) is a California grassland species that extends its range into the western Mojave Desert. This is a showy annual species with bright magenta flowers with white or yellow markings on the petals (Fig. 10.65). It wet years it often occurs in dense populations that color the landscape. Like other root parasites it appears as any other plant, with foliage indicating the presence of chlorophyll and active photosynthesis. However, they supplement nutrient and carbohydrate supplies with parasitic roots that tap the below-ground tissues of other species.

Fig. 10.65. *Castilleja exserta*, Orobanchaceae, purple owl's clover. Photo by Matt Berger.

A related species of root parasite is desert paintbrush (*Castilleja angustifolia*), an upright perennial up to 18 inches in height. The bright red flowers of these species are often visible from a considerable distance (Fig. 10.66). Desert paintbrush is largely restricted to higher elevations of the Mojave Desert and Great Basin. In all, there are 11 species of *Castilleja* that occur in our desert regions.

Evening Primroses (Onagraceae)

This is an important group of desert flowers that are relatively easy to recognize. Distinctive characters include large and showy flowers with four petals and usually eight stamens with large anthers. The female stigma is also unusual in having either a

Fig. 10.66. *Castilleja angustifolia*, Orobanchaceae, desert paintbrush. Photo by Stan Shebs.

ball or hemispherical shape or being divided into four equal lobes. There are several other families of desert annuals that have four petals and may, at first, appear similar to the Onagraceae. One of these is the poppy family (Papaveraceae) with four showy petals that are often yellow or gold. Unlike the Onagraceae, all poppies have numerous stamens. Another common family with four petals is the mustard family (Brassicaceae). These seldom have the large showy petals of the evening primroses and have a unique arrangement of male flower parts—with four long and two short stamens.

The name evening primrose has traditionally been used for plants in two genera, *Camissonia* and *Oenothera*. The *Camissonia* group included species with a ball-shaped or hemispheric-shaped stigma while species of *Oenothera* have a four-lobed stigma. We now say *Camissonia* group, because this traditional genus has been split into nine different genera based on molecular studies. The evening primroses, and related species of Onagraceae, are one of the primary food plants of the sphinx

Fig. 10.67. *Chylismia brevipes*, Onagraceae, golden evening primrose. Photo by Stan Shebs.

Fig. 10.68. *Camissonia campestris*, Onagraceae, Mojave sun cup. Photo by Robert Gustafson.

Fig. 10.69. *Chylismia claviformis*, Onagraceae, brown-eyed primrose. Photo by Matt Berger.

moth. Years with abundant evening primrose blooms are correlated with millions of sphinx moth larvae feeding on these plants.

Camissonia, before its separation into multiple smaller genera, included 22 species with a range occurring, at least in part, in the desert—about ⅓ of the species in the genus. Our desert species are virtually all annuals and some occur in massive numbers coloring the landscape in years with good winter and spring rains. The showy flowers of the mustard-yellow species open widely during the day, brightly reflecting the sun and giving rise to the name sun cups.

One of the most spectacular species of this group is golden evening primrose or yellow cups (*Chylismia brevipes*), that color large areas of open washes and sandy or rocky bajada slopes of creosote bush scrub and Joshua tree woodlands with mass ivedisplays of flowers in a good flowering year. This is one of our taller species with plants reaching up to 2 feet in height under good growing conditions, and moderate sized yellow flowers about ¾ inch across with small red spots at the base of each petal (Fig. 10.67). Sand evening primrose (*Chylismia arenaria*) is a tall annual or bushy perennial up to more than 3 feet in height, with yellow flowers that open at dusk. This species is found in sandy washes and rocky slopes of creosote bush scrub in the Sonoran Desert. Mojave sun cup (*Camissonia campestris*) is an erect but delicate small annual that would be easy to miss until it bursts into spring bloom with large yellow flower up to 1½ inch in diameter, and like yellow cups having small red dots at the base of each petal (Fig. 10.68). This is an extremely widespread species occurring in sandy flats of creosote bush scrub and semi-arid grasslands across southern California.

While many species of the *Camissonia* group have yellow flowers which open at dawn, there is also a group of white-flowered species which typically open their flowers at night to attract moth pollinators. Brown-eyed primrose (*Chylismia claviformis*) is a variable species with flowers that range from bright yellow to white in color. This is a common species with a widespread range in sandy washes and slopes of creosote bush scrub and Joshua tree woodland, as well as widely in western North America (Fig. 10.69). Brown-eyed primrose is an erect species ranging in height from just a few inches to 24 inches depending on rainfall. Its common name comes from the presence of large brown or purple spots at the base of each petal, giving the flower a dark center.

Although most species of the *Camissonia* group have an erect growth form, there are several species with prostrate forms of growth lacking erect stems. One such rosette species is pale primrose (*Camissoniopsis pallida*), an annual found in sandy washes, flats and slopes from creosote bush scrub to pinyon-juniper woodland of our desert regions. The characteristic features of this plant are elongate entire margined leaves covered with dense flattened hairs (Fig. 10.70).

Bottlebrush primrose (*Eremothera boothii*) is another variable annual with white flowers that open at dusk. It ranges in height from as little as 4 inches to as much as 2 feet. Like many other species of evening primrose, it is found across our desert region in open areas of creosote bush scrub and Joshua tree woodland. The characteristic feature of this species is a curled spike of white to reddish flowers growing on stems with reddish lance-shaped leaves below (Fig. 10.72). A basal rosette of leaves is usually present in early

Fig. 10.70. *Camissoniopsis pallida*, Onagraceae, pale primrose. Photo by Matt Berger.

Fig. 10.71. *Eremothera boothii*, Onagraceae, bottlebrush primrose. Photo by Matt Berger.

Fig. 10.72. *Oenothera californica*, Onagraceae, California evening primrose. Photo by Matt Berger.

spring before the flowers mature.

The genus *Oenothera* forms a small group of species that includes annual, biennial, and perennial forms. California evening primrose (*Oenothera californica*) is a widespread and variable perennial with a range extending across much of the coastal foothills and desert areas of California in a range of habitats. It begins life as a rosette plant but gradually elongates a peeling leafy stem that trails for 30 inches or more along the ground (Fig. 10.72). The large white flowers open at night. The growth form of dune evening primrose (*Oenothera deltoides*) is different is being a loose rosette up to 3 feet in diameter and 1 foot tall in the center (Fig. 10.73). It is widely distributed across our desert regions on sandy slopes and dunes. When the plants die the stems curl upward and form a "birdcage" giving rise to a second common name of birdcage evening primrose.

Fig. 10.73. *Oenothera deltoides*, Onagraceae, dune evening primrose. Photo by Matt Berger.

Fig. 10.74. *Oenothera primiveris*, Onagraceae, yellow evening primrose. Photo by Stan Shebs.

Yellow evening primrose (*Oenothera primiveris*) is a prostrate species with bright yellow flowers that might be confused at first with *Camissonia*. The four-parted stigma is the distinguishing trait that separates these genera. Yellow evening primrose has a basal rosette of glandular leaves that are strongly toothed to pinnately divided into broad lobes (Fig. 10.74).

Desert Mustards (Brassicaceae)

Members of the mustard family form a third family that is characterized by flowers with four petals. In this family, the white or yellow flowers are generally small and clustered unlike the larger solitary flowers of the poppy family. The four petals are narrow at their base and spread more broadly toward their tips. Coupled with four long and two short stamens, these flowers have a distinctive character.

California spectacle-pod (*Dithyrea californica*) is a small annual whose common name comes from the appearance of its fruits with two flat rounded lobes that look like eyeglasses. Its trailing stems, that curve upward with clusters of small white flowers at their tips, are a unique growth form (Fig. 10.75). California spectacle-pod is found in sandy soils and washes of creosote bush scrub across both California deserts.

Slender bladderpod (*Physaria tenella*) is a tall, erect annual, up to 2 feet in height, with branched stems and long clusters of showy yellow flowers. The small spherical fruits that look like small beads at the ends of curved stalks are distinctive (Fig 10.76). Slender bladderpod is found in sandy soils and washes across creosote bush scrub in the eastern Mojave and northeastern Sonoran deserts. Yellow pepper-grass (*Lepidium flavum*) is a species that trails along the ground in sandy alkali soils forming patches up to 18 inches across (Chapter 8). The flowers are small but readily seen on the stem tips.

One of the most unusual and distinctive desert annuals is desert candle (*Caulanthus inflatus*). It is characterized by an inflated, hollow and leafless stems up to 2 feet in height (Fig. 10.77). Ovate to oblong dark-green leaves clasp the base of these stems. Desert candle is common on open, sandy plains in creosote bush scrub and Joshua tree woodland in the central and western Mojave Desert. There are nine species of *Caulanthus* in our desert region, including both annuals and herbaceous perennials, but none are as distinctive as desert candle. *Caulanthus* differs from other members of the mustard family because the sepals are yellowish or purple rather than green.

Buckwheat Family (Polygonaceae)

An important and diverse group of desert annuals and herbaceous perennials, but not as showy as others, is the buckwheat family. The shrubby California buckwheat (*Eriogonum fasciculatum*) is described in Chapter 4. This same genus, however, contains a diverse assemblage of smaller desert herbs. Flat-topped buckwheat (*Eriogonum deflexum*) is a tall annual, up to 2 feet in height. It has an erect flowering stalk arising from a basal rosette of small, kidney-shaped leaves. The tiny white- to pink-flowers are borne in a flat-topped crown, giving rise to the common name (Fig. 10.78). It occurs widely on sandy and gravelly flats of creosote bush scrub and Joshua tree woodlands. Much more unusual in appearance, and larger in size,

Fig. 10.75. *Dithyrea californica*, Brassicaceae, California spectacle-pod. Photo by Matt Berger.

Fig. 10.76. *Physaria tenella*, Brassicaceae, slender bladderpod. Photo by Matt Berger.

Fig. 10.77. *Caulanthus inflatus*, Brassicaceae, desert candle. Photo by Robert Gustafson.

Fig. 10.78. *Eriogonum deflexum*, Polygonaceae, flat-topped buckwheat. Photo by Matt Berger.

Fig. 10.79. *Eriogonum inflatum*, Polygonaceae, desert trumpet. Photo by Stan Shebs.

Fig. 10.80. *Chorizanthe brevicornu*, Polygonaceae, brittle spineflower. Photo by Stan Shebs.

is desert trumpet (*Eriogonum inflatum*), an herbaceous perennial that reach 3–5 feet in height. The unusual feature of this species is the presence of bluish-green flowering stems, arising from a basal rosette of leaves that are inflated at the stem nodes (Fig. 10.79). There is no clear understanding as to the adaptive advantage of these inflated hollow stems, but it seems possible that the entire stems serve as a raft to aid in seed dispersal when washes are flowing with water. Certainly, the stems also provide a photosynthetic surface. Beyond these, and the shrubby *Eriogonum deserticola* described in Chapter 9, there are more than 60 additional species of *Eriogonum* in California deserts.

Closely related is to *Eriogonum* is golden carpet (*Gilmania luteola*), a low branched annual that grows as a horizontal mat. It has stalked, ovate leaves and clusters of tiny yellow flowers. Although relatively abundant where it occurs, the range of this species, which represents an endemic genus, is restricted to five barren alkali slopes in Death Valley National Park (see Chapter 2).

If one thinks that *Eriogonum* species are not showy, there is a related group that is even more nondescript. The seven California desert spineflowers prefer some of the least hospitable barren slopes in the desert. Brittle spineflower (*Chorizanthe brevicornu*) is an erect annual, up to 20 inches in height, whose bare stems initially arise from a basal rosette of leaves (Fig. 10.80). This rosette withers and dies in early spring, leaving the plants leafless but with small leaf-like bracts at each branching node. Brittle spineflower has a broad geographical and elevational distribution on gravelly flats and rocky slopes across creosote bush scrub to pinyon-juniper woodlands. Devil's spineflower (*Chorizanthe rigida*) is a smaller erect annual with broadly elliptical leaves forming a basal rosette and along the stem. Secondary leaf nodes develop into hard spines as the plant develops, giving it a thorny appearance (Fig. 10.81). Devil's spineflower commonly occurs on desert pavement adjacent to creosote bush scrub in both the Mojave and Sonoran deserts.

Although most of the Polygonaceae are relatively nondescript, even when flowering, another member of the family is quite conspicuous. Desert rhubarb (*Rumex hymenosepalus*) is a tall herbaceous perennial, 2–4 feet in height, with stout reddish stems and large fleshy leaves up to 24 inches in length that arise from an underground cluster of tuberous roots (Fig. 10.82). These large leaves seem totally out of place in a hot desert environment but can maintain leaf temperatures below that of the air through rapid rates of transpiration. Desert rhubarb is found in sandy flats of creosote bush scrub and Joshua tree woodlands of the Mojave Desert.

Blazing Stars (Loasaceae)

The blazing star family is mentioned in Chapter 4 where several small shrub species were described. The family includes not only woody species but also a number of distinctive and showy annuals. The flower structure that characterizes the blazing star family is five petals, a single style, and numerous stamens. In desert species, flowers are either white or yellow and often have glossy petals. This flower form and bright appearance is the origin of the common name, blazing stars. Another family trait is the presence of well-developed and stiff hairs along the stem and leaf surfaces. These hairs allow stems to readily stick to clothing, giving rise to the name velcro plants. Hairs have evolved as stinging hairs in some species as with rock nettle (*Eucidne urens*) described in Chapter 4. However, stinging hairs are not present in any herbaceous desert species.

We have 20 species of blazing star, all members of the genus *Mentzelia*, that have a range in the California desert. Individual species are difficult to distinguish, with a microscope necessary to look at seed morphology. Native Americans utilize the seeds as a food source. Sand blazing star (*Mentzelia involucrata*) is branched annual with large, funnel-shaped white- to pale-yellow flowers that can reach more than 2 inches in width (Fig. 10.83). It has large, highly toothed basal leaves and small linear stem leaves. It occurs in a variety of habitats including creosote bush scrub and desert washes but is most common in the southern Mojave and Sonoran deserts (Fig. 10.84). Yellowcomet (*Mentzelia affinis*) is an erect annual with a basal rosette of leaves are up to about 6–8 inches in length and divided into lobes. The flower has five shiny yellow petals, each with an orange spot at the base. (Fig. 10.85). In a year with favorable rainfall it can reach to almost 3 feet in height, but only a few inches in a dry year. It has a broad distribution along the inner coast ranges of southern California and out into the desert areas.

While desert blazing stars are annuals, several are herbaceous perennials as well. Giant blazing star (*Mentzelia laevicaulis*) is an erect species, up to 3 ft or more in height, with a basal rosette of large, divided leaves and smaller, toothed stem leaves. It is one of most spectacular desert bloomers with huge, bright yellow flowers as much as 4–6 inches in diameter (Fig. 10.86). It is found in a variety of habitats at all elevation throughout our desert region and beyond.

Fig. 10.81. *Chorizanthe rigida*, Polygonaceae, devil's spineflower. Photo by Matt Berger.

Fig. 10.82. *Rumex hymenosepalus*, Polygonaceae, desert rhubarb. Photo by Matt Berger.

Fig. 10.83. *Mentzelia involucrata*, Loasaceae, sand blazing star. Photo by Robert Gustafson.

Fig. 10.84. *Mentzelia involucrata* in wash habitat. Photo by Stan Shebs.

Fig. 10.85. *Mentzelia affinis*, Loasaceae, yellocomet. Photo by Robert Gustafson.

Fig. 10.86. *Mentzelia laevicaulis*, Loasaceae, giant blazing star. Photo by Robert Gustafson.

Desert Milkweeds (Apocynaceae)

Almost everyone knows milkweeds, at least by name. The milky sap of the tissues of milkweed contains toxic compounds called cardiac glycosides. Monarch butterflies (*Danaus plexippus*) that feed on these tissues sequester these toxins in their bodies, making them unpalatable to birds. In addition to milky sap, a feature of milkweed is the large pods, usually several inches in length, that split open when mature and release large numbers of wind-dispersed seeds with hairy plumes. We have 12 species of milkweed in the California desert, although most of these are wide ranging species that are also found in the coastal and foothill areas of our state. Once separated as the family Asclepidaceae, the entire group is now in the Apocynaceae.

Desert milkweed (*Asclepias erosa*) is a true desert species. It is a tall perennial, up to 30 inches in height, with white woolly stems and large, broad leaves. Like most milkweeds, it produces dense heads of cream-colored flowers (Fig. 10.87). Desert milkweed favors dry slopes and washes from creosote bush scrub to pinyon-juniper woodlands. Rush milkweed (*Asclepias subulata*) is likewise a tall perennial, reaching up to 3 feet in height. Its common name comes from upright stems that are leafless for most of the year. It occurs in dry washes at low elevations in the eastern Mojave and Sonoran deserts.

There are several other milkweeds that are herbaceous climbers. Climbing milkweed (*Funastrum cynanchoides*) is one of two related species of vine-like milkweeds that often occur in dense colonies at the margins of washes where they clamber up and over woody species. The opposite-leaved foliage is ill-smelling, while the pink- to purplish-flowers are produced in small heads (Fig. 10.88). The range of this species in California is restricted to lower elevations of the eastern Mojave and Sonoran deserts below 2,000 feet. Climbing milkweed is an important food plant of the striated queen butterfly (*Danaus gilippus strigosus*), a relative of the monarch butterfly. Another climber is vine milkweed (*Funastrum utahense*) that occurs in dry, sandy or gravelly flats of the Mojave Desert across creosote bush scrub below 3,000 feet. It is readily separated from climbing milkweed by its yellow flowers that turn orange with age.

Fig. 10.87. *Asclepias erosa*, Apocynaceae, desert milkweed. Photo by Robert Gustafson.

Fig. 10.88. *Funastrum cynanchoides*, Apocynaceae, climbing milkweed. Photo by Robert Gustafson.

Geophytes

Geophytes are herbaceous perennials with underground storage organs like bulbs, corms, fleshy rhizomes or tubers that store carbohydrates, nutrients, and water. The above-ground portions of the geophytes dies back during adverse climatic conditions leaving only the storage organ in the soil until appropriate conditions for growth return. Geophytes are important components of the flora in temperate climates and are a notable component of the world's Mediterranean-type shrublands where summer drought is a seasonal stressor. However, the California deserts have relatively few geophytes. Many of the geophytes in California's deserts are also found in the Mediterranean-type shrublands or even in woodland. In fact, only a few geophyte species are found exclusively in our deserts.

In contrast, the winter-rainfall deserts of South Africa, the Mediterranean Basin, and Chile are rich in native geophyte species. In fact, 16% of the flora of the Succulent Karoo, the winter rainfall desert of South Africa, is comprised of geophytes. Most likely the unpredictable rainfall patterns of our deserts challenge geophyte's success. California deserts often have fall rains followed by lack of precipitation producing conditions where geophytes would be challenged to replace the stored carbohydrates pulled from the bulb for initial shoot growth.

Our most notable geophyte is the desert lily (*Hesperocallis undulata*), an unusual endemic found on sandy flats and dunes below 2,500 feet in the western and southern Mojave Desert and adjacent areas of the Sonoran Desert. A good place to see this species is at the Kelso Dunes in the eastern Mojave Desert, as described in Chapter 9. Desert lily arises from a large bulb, with a basal rosette of bluish-green leaves, 10–20 inches in length, with a distinctive wavy margin. These rosettes are distinct all other desert geophytes. The single flowering stalk reaches anywhere from 1–6 feet in height, depending on growing conditions, and bears clusters of large trumpet-shaped flowers that resemble small Easter lilies. The flowers have a strong, sweet fragrance that attracts hawk moths—the primary pollinators. Desert lily was once included in the lily family (Liliaceae) but is now placed in the Agave subfamily within the asparagus family (Asparagaceae).

Seven species of mariposa lily broadly enter our desert regions, but most of these range well outside of the desert. These are members of the genus *Calochortus*, a member of the Liliaceae, although sometimes placed in their own family (Calochortaceae). The common name comes from the Spanish word *mariposa* meaning butterfly. Desert mariposa lily (*Calochortus kennedyi*) is a showy species that grows on heavy soils with rocky or gravelly cover in creosote bush scrub, Joshua tree woodlands, and pinyon-juniper woodlands across the Mojave Desert at elevations of 2,000–6,500 feet (Fig. 10.89). It has a wide occurrence in arid areas of Mediterranean-type shrublands of southern California and across the southwestern United States. Each plant produces 1–2 large flowers with three orange petals and a black or purple spot at each petal base. It has narrow, grayish-green leaves with margins curled upward. A distinct variety of desert mariposa lily with yellow flowers occurs in the Providence and Clark Mountains of the eastern Mojave Desert.

Twining mariposa lily (*Calochortus flexuosus*) has pale lilac flowers and is found in creosote bush and sagebrush scrub above 2,000 feet in the eastern and northern Mojave Desert. It is a true desert species with an unusual vine-like growth form that winds its stem up to 20 inches through open shrub canopies or against cacti. Panamint mariposa lily (*Calochortus panamintensis*), also a lilac-colored species, is restricted to pinyon-juniper woodlands above 8,000 feet in the Panamint Mountains. Another desert species, alkali mariposa lily (*Calochortus striatus*), is described in Chapter 8. It is primarily restricted to springs and alkali seeps of the western Mojave Desert and is easily recognized by its petals with lateral purple striations.

Like mariposa lilies, there are eight species of wild onion (Amaryllidaceae) that occur within our California deserts but are not restricted to the deserts. Most of the desert onions are wide-ranging species that barely enter our desert regions and are more common in higher elevations elsewhere. These species are readily recognized by the onion or garlic odor of their foliage. Parish's onion (*Allium parishii*) prefers Joshua tree woodlands of the southern Mojave Desert and dark red onion (*Allium atrorubens*) occurs in pinyon-juniper woodlands and sagebrush scrub above about 4,000 feet in the eastern and northern Mojave Desert and adjacent Great Basin areas. Fringed desert onion (*Allium fimbriatum*) is a widespread species with a morphologically distinct variety that is restricted to creosote bush scrub and Joshua tree woodlands of the western Mojave Desert (Fig. 10.90).

Death camas (*Toxicoscordion brevibracteatum,* family Melianthaceae) is found in sandy areas of creosote bush scrub and Joshua tree woodlands of the western and southern Mojave Desert at elevations of 2,000–5,000 feet. It also extends into the arid woodlands of the Transverse Ranges. The large bulb of this species is up to 12 inches or more in diameter and produces a rosette of linear leaves, 6–12 inches in length, and a nearly leafless flowering stalk 12–20 inches in height. The small cream-colored flowers are produced in open clusters on the stems have similar petals and sepals forming six equal flower parts. The bulbs of death camas, and most if not all species of *Toxicoscordion*, contain poisonous alkaloids. Two other widespread species of *Toxicoscordion* enter the western margins of our desert areas but are not true desert species.

Fig. 10.89. *Calochortus kennedyi*, Liliaceae, desert mariposa lily. Photo by Robert Gustafson.

Fig. 10.90. *Allium fimbriatum*, Amaryllidaceae, fringed desert onion. Photo by Robert Gustafson.

Summer Annuals

Because the desert is a tough place to be in the hot summer, it is easy to overlook an interesting group of desert annuals with C_4 metabolism. These are plants that germinate and bloom after infrequent and irregular summer rains. Sometimes in July or August, convective summer thunderstorms move into the California deserts from Arizona or Mexico—especially in the eastern margins. Because summer rain is infrequent, C_4 annuals are relatively uncommon in the western Mojave Desert (see Chapter 3) but become more common moving eastward. Although we have few species of summer annuals compared to the diverse spring annual flora, C_4 annuals can carpet large expanses of creosote bush flats and upland slopes. This metabolic system allows these summer annuals to attain high rates of photosynthesis and productivity, while still maintaining a favorable water balance.

Some summer annuals are low in stature but the majority are relatively tall, reaching to heights as much as 12–30 inches. In contrast to winter annuals, basal rosettes of leaves are generally lacking, undoubtedly due to the high soil surface temperatures of midsummer. Many species have weedy characteristics, becoming most abundant on disturbed ground, as with certain C_4 grasses that are an important component of this flora.

The smallest and yet showiest of our summer annuals is chinchweed (*Pectis papposa*), one of the few members of the Asteraceae with C_4 metabolism. In some years, with widespread summer storms, chinchweed blooms in such numbers it paints yellow across creosote bush scrub and Joshua tree woodlands in the central and eastern Mojave and Sonoran deserts (Fig. 10.91). Chinchweed has a low spreading or mounding growth form and small, narrow leaves with pungent, spicy-smelling glands (Fig. 10.92).

Fig. 10.91. *Pectis papposa* in wash drainage. Photo by Naomi Fraga.

Fig. 10.92. *Pectis papposa*, Asteraceae, chichweed. Photo by Robert Gustafson.

Another family of C_4 annuals is the four-o'clock family (Nyctaginaceae). This is the familiar desert dune family that contains sand verbena (Chapter 10). Although most genera of Nyctaginaceae use typical C_3 photosynthetic systems, there are two desert genera with C_4 metabolism. The more common group is the spiderlings (*Boerhavia* sp.), with five desert species. All regional spiderling species have tiny, pale pink to white bell-shaped flowers no more than 1/8 inch in length, which may be present from September to December. Slender spiderling (*Boerhavia triquetra*) is the most common species (Fig. 10.93). It is an erect annual, up to 2 feet in height, with sticky areas along the slender stems between nodes. It is found widely and abundantly in creosote bush scrub and Joshua tree woodlands of the southern Mojave and Sonoran deserts. Windmills (*Alliona incarnata*) is an annual or short-lived perennial with slender, glandular stems that trail along the ground. What appears to be a single, radially symmetrical magenta-colored flower in are actually clusters of three bilaterally symmetrical flowers growing together. Windmills favor sandy soils in creosote bush scrub across the southern Mojave and Sonoran deserts.

C_4 metabolism has evolved at least five times in the pigweed family (Amaranthaceae). We have two lineages represented in our desert flora. Fringed amaranth (*Amaranthus fimbriatus*) is a tall, slender annual that reaches 3 feet in height from August –November (Fig. 10.94). Small, separate male and female flowers are produced in clusters along a terminal spike. Fringed amaranth is one of seven species in this genus that are found in our desert region, all with a similar range to other C_4 annuals. Although an annual, the tall stalks are persistent and often evident in the following spring. *Amaranthus* is the same genus that includes the grain amaranth, a plant domesticated thousands of years ago by the Aztecs and other New World cultures.

Honey-sweet (*Tidestromia subfruticosa* var. *oblongifolia*) is another C_4 plant in the Amaranthaceae. It is a distinctive herbaceous perennial with a rounded growth form that reaches as much as 2–3 feet in height. The large, ovate leaves are covered with whitish-gray hairs and display an unusual pattern of venation (Fig. 10.95). Honey-sweet is found widely in washes, dune areas, and on rocky bajada slopes of the eastern Mojave Desert as well as south in the Sonoran Desert.

Among our showiest desert annuals, but relatively uncommon, are species of devil's claw (Proboscidea sp.). These unusual members of the unicorn-plant family (Martyniaceae) also utilize C_4 metabolism and thus summer flowering. There are two species of devil's claw whose range extends across the Sonoran Desert. Pink devil's claw (*Proboscidea parviflora*) is an attractive, pink-flowered annual. Yellow devil's claw (*Proboscidea althaeifolia*) is a brilliant, yellow-flowered perennial. Both species have a sprawling growth form with large, moist, and sticky-lobed leaves. The large bilaterally symmetrical flowers, up

Fig. 10.93. *Boerhavia triquetra*, Nyctaginaceae, slender spiderling. National Park Service photo.

Fig. 10.94. *Amaranthus fimbriatus*, Amaranthaceae, fringed amaranth. Photo by Stan Shebs.

Fig. 10.95. *Tidestromia subfruticosa* var. *oblongifolia*, Amaranthaceae, honey-sweet. Photo by Robert Gustafson.

Fig. 10.96. *Proboscidia parviflora*, Martyniaceae, pink devil's claw. Photo by Robert Gustafson.

Fig. 10.97. *Euphorbia albomarginata*, Euphorbiaceae, rattlesnake weed. Photo by R. Gustafson.

Fig. 10.98. *Bouteloua barbata*, Poaceae, six-weeks grama. Photo by Robb Hannawacker.

to 1½ inch across, look like those of jacaranda and other flowers in the related bignon family (Bignoniaceae). The pink devil's claw (*Proboscidia parviflora*) is an annual that prefers disturbed sites along roads while the yellow devil's claw is a perennial with a stout tap root that prefers dunes (Fig. 10.96). The origin of the rather sinister name devil's claw is because of the long, woody capsules, up to 3–4 inches in length, which split open at one end to form a pair of curved claws. These claws readily cling to the hooves of grazing animals, or your shoes if you are not watching where you step. Since these claws don't fit the hooves of native grazing animals, scientists have speculated that this form evolved to facilitate dispersal by giant ground sloths and other Pleistocene megafauna that are now extinct.

Our C_4 herbaceous desert flora contains 16 native species of spurge (*Euphorbia*) once placed in the genus *Chamaesyce* (Euphorbiaceae). These are prostrate or low growing annuals and herbaceous perennials that flower almost any month of the year (Fig. 10.97). Most have broad ranges, extending well outside of our desert region with several non-native species also widely naturalized. One of the distinctive features of the spurges is the milky sap contained in their stems. What appears to be a single flower in spurges is instead a cup-like structure called a *cyathium* that holds a central female flower surrounded by several male flowers. The structures that look like petals are extensions of the cyanthium. Rattlesnake weed (*Euphorbia albomarginata*) is a widespread, prostrate perennial whose common name arises from its use to treat rattlesnake bites. Desert spurge (*Euphorbia micromera*) is another common prostrate annual.

A large portion of our desert grasses exhibit C_4 metabolism which is consistent with their active summer growth. Two annual species of C_4 grasses are also common in our desert region where they appear after summer rains These are needle grama (*Bouteloua aristidoides*) and six-weeks grama (*Bouteloua barbata*, Fig. 10.98). Both species which have broad geographic ranges that extend well beyond desert environments. The small seeds of these species are produced in massive numbers in years with summer rains and provide an important food source for desert harvester ants. Four other species of grama grasses in California are all perennials

Chapter 11
The Great Basin

A pinyon-juniper woodland in the Panamint Range. Photo by Mark Bailey.

Introduction

Plant communities characteristic of the Great Basin are present at higher elevations of the eastern Mojave Desert. These include shrublands dominated by a single species as with blackbrush scrub, shadscale scrub, and sagebrush steppe, Another characteristic assemblage are the pinyon-juniper woodlands with moderately diverse assemblages of associated shrub species. While many of the Great Basin species described in this chapter have a broad range across the Western U.S., the intent is to focus on areas of Great Basin occurring within the broader area of the Mojave Desert region. An extensive area of Great Basin communities in California (outside of the geographical context of this book) is present in the Inyo and White Mountains north of Death Valley, and northern and northeastern California from the Cascade Range of Siskiyou County eastward to the Modoc Plateau.

Blackbrush Scrub

Blackbrush scrub forms a transitional community in the eastern Mojave Desert between creosote bush scrub and Joshua tree woodlands communities below to colder temperature-adapted Great Basin shrublands and woodlands above (Fig. 11.1). It typically occurs on shallow, rocky soils of flats and plateaus—often in areas with calcareous soils—at elevations between 3,800–6,000 feet. Rainfall averages 9–10 inches, which is higher than that of typical Mojave Desert communities. A diversity of shrub and herbaceous species are typically present in blackbrush scrub. These are almost equally split between species with an affinity to creosote bush scrub communities at lower elevations and the pinyon-juniper woodland above.

Fig. 11.1. Blackbrush (*Coleogyne ramosissima*) scrub is often a transition to pinyon-juniper woodlands, here in the New York Mountains, Mojave National Preserve. Photo by Michael Kauffmann.

The dominant shrub species in this community is blackbrush (*Coleogyne ramosissima*), an unusual member of the rose family (Rosaceae) representing a relatively ancient lineage with no close modern relatives. Generally, blackbrush scrub is recognized by a strong and monotonous dominance of blackbrush itself, which may cover as much as 50 percent of the ground surface with 10–30 percent coverage being more typical. Blackbrush is easily recognized by its densely branched, dark gray twigs which age to black. This black color is even more evident after desert rains. The shrubs are typically low-growing and seldom exceeding 3–4 feet in height. The small, thick leaves are arranged in clusters on the stems with spinescent branch tips, and a rolled-over leaf margin. Masses of yellow flowers cover the branches in spring (Fig. 11.2). A distinctive trait of blackbrush flowers, that separates it from other shrubby members of Rosaceae, is the presence of four sepals (petals are absent) rather than the typical number of five. Because of ancient ancestral lineage of *Coleogyne*, there is controversy surrounding its evolutionary affinities.

Fig. 11.2. Coleogyne ramosissima, Rosaceae, blackbrush. Photo by Stan Shebs.

Because blackbrush scrub occurs in dense stands with short distances between shrub canopies, fire will readily burn through stands. Blackbrush does not resprout and its soil seed banks are destroyed by fire. Combined with seeds that are poorly dispersed, stand recovery after fire is a slow process requiring many decades. In some areas the transitions between existing blackbrush stands and areas burned as long as 50 years ago are quite distinct. Short-lived shrubs, subshrubs, and perennial grasses typically colonize these burned areas. Red brome grass (*Bromus rubens*) has aggressively invaded many parts of the eastern Mojave Desert in recent decades including blackbrush scrub (Chapter 12). This highly flammable invasive grass promotes fires and is responsible for the decline of many blackbrush stands. However, in the absence of fire, blackbrush is quite long-lived for a small shrub—reported to reach up to 400 years.

Shadscale Scrub

Shadscale scrub is a Great Basin community that forms a transition between creosote bush scrub and sagebrush steppe in many areas of the eastern and northeastern Mojave Desert. In its typical form, shadscale scrub is a community of low, small-leaved shrubs that are often spinescent. It occurs widely across much of the Great Basin including eastern California where it commonly dominates in broad desert valleys with alkaline soils. At its southern range in the eastern Mojave Desert, however, it occurs on steep mountain slopes with heavy rock soils. It forms a significant community cover over much of the upper Owens Valley north of Bishop. It is also found on rocky slopes of the Inyo and Panamint ranges and widely in the Black and Funeral mountains east of Death Valley. Smaller stands of shadscale scrub occur in the western Mojave Desert around the lake playas at Edwards Air Force Base.

The relationship of shadscale scrub to creosote bush scrub in the northern Mojave Desert often reflects patterns of average minimum temperature more than elevation alone. There is commonly a bimodal pattern of distribution of shadscale scrub, with open stands of shadscale in heavy soils around playa lakes where cold air drainage produces low winter temperatures. Shadscale again returns as much as 3,000 feet higher at elevations with denser stands on rocky slopes. Intermediate elevations, with less extreme winter temperatures, support creosote bush scrub or blackbrush scrub.

Shadscale (*Atriplex confertifolia*) is the dominant species and gives this community its name—as described in Chapter 8. It is a low, spiny shrub typically reaching no more than 3 feet in height (Fig. 11.3). The stems are stiff and widely divergent with sharp spine-like tips. Like other species of saltbush, shadscale foliage has a distinct silver-gray appearance, small gray-green linear leaves about half an inch long, and a hairy surface. The spiny nature of shadscale becomes particularly apparent in winter when shadscale loses the majority of its leaves. While it may superficially resemble its relative four-wing saltbush (*Atriplex canescens*), shadscale is readily separated by its spinescent branches, small oval leaves, and fruits with two wings rather than four.

Fig. 11.3. *Atriplex confertifolia*, Chenopodiaceae, shadscale. Photo by Matt Berger.

Although shadscale is generally dominant, associated shrub species include other members of the Chenopodiaceae such as winterfat, hopsage, and green molly (*Kochia americana*). These communities also support numerous species of herbaceous perennials but relatively few annuals. This low composition of annual species is consistent with the Great Basin shadscale scrub alliance.

Sagebrush Steppe

Sagebrush steppe has an extraordinarily wide geographic range over which it exhibits considerable ecological plasticity. It extends across much of the arid western United States, occurring at elevations from 1,000 to more than 10,000 feet. It is common on the arid desert-facing slopes of the Transverse Ranges and across higher elevations of the eastern Mojave Desert. In California, Great Basin sagebrush does not form its own community as it does across much of the Great Basin. It occurs as a scattered component of pinyon-juniper woodlands in the eastern Mojave Desert, but seldom attains dominance (Fig. 11.4). Relatively pure stands are limited to granitic soils of the Kingston Range at elevations of 4,500–7,000

Fig. 11.4. Transition from Great Basin sagebrush to Utah juniper in Death Valley National Park. Photo by Julie Evens.

feet. These stands of sagebrush steppe have relatively poor species diversity. An extension of Great Basin sagebrush steppe continues along the eastern slopes of the Sierra Nevada and higher elevations of the White and Inyo mountains. Additional stands of sagebrush steppe are found on the arid slopes of the Transverse Ranges, most notably in the western Tehachapi Mountains.

Great Basin sagebrush (*Artemisia tridentata*) is easily recognized by its fragrant wedge-shaped leaves tipped with three distinct lobes, hence *tridentata* (Fig. 11.5). Although leaf area is reduced in the cold winter months, the plant retains foliage throughout the year. The individual shrubs are commonly 3–4 feet in height but may be considerably taller where higher levels of moisture are available. As with pinyon pines and junipers, Great Basin sagebrush is intolerant of fire and relies on wind-blown seeds from outside the burned area for reestablishment. In contrast to this fire intolerance, some of its common shrub associates resprout successfully after fire.

Great Basin sagebrush provides critical habitat for many bird species including the endangered sage grouse. Although sheep graze moderately on young foliage, sagebrush is toxic to cattle. Deer avoid sagebrush in the summer months due to the high volatility of oils but during winter months, when oil concentrations decrease, the seed heads of sagebrush become an important food source for deer and other ungulates. We can only speculate about sagebrush's

Fig. 11.5. *Artemisia tridentata*, Asteraceae, Great Basin sagebrush. Photo by Stan Shebs.

palatability in the past to the extinct American camels, horses, and ground sloths that called this region home in the Pleistocene Epoch. The volatile oils of Great Basin sagebrush sometimes cause an allergic reaction in humans..

The most abundant shrub associate is bitterbrush (*Purshia tridentata*). This common species shares a leaf morphology with Great Basin sagebrush in having three lobes at the leaf-tip of its small, aromatic leaves. Unlike the gray leaves of Great Basin sagebrush, bitterbrush leaves have a dark green upper surface and dense, white, and woolly lower surface (Fig. 11.6). Leaves produced in early spring are shed with the onset of summer drought, but leaves produced later in the growing season overwinter and remain functional into the following year. Thus, the species is functionally evergreen

Despite a bitter taste that gives rise its common name, bitterbrush is palatable to grazing animals because of a special trait—high protein leaves. These proteins are produced as a result of ample nitrogen availability from a symbiotic relationship with nitrogen-fixing bacteria associated with root nodules. These bacteria fix nitrogen directly from the atmosphere which is why bitterbrush is an effective colonizer of road cuts and other disturbed areas. Although bitterbrush struggles to resprout after fire events it is more responsive than Great Basin sagebrush. Some plants resprout after fire, while seedlings establish from seed caches left by rodents.

Fig. 11.6. *Purshia tridentata*, Rosaceae, bitterbrush. Photo by Jim Morefield.

Another common associate is yellow rabbitbrush (*Ericameria nauseosa*) which occurs widely across the arid western United States over a broad range of elevations. This is a tall shrub with numerous parallel, erect branches reaching to 5–8 feet in height. The narrow, linear leaves—which are lost under summer drought conditions—are much less apparent than the sticky, gray stems covered with a fine felt layer of woolly hairs. This shrub flowers in summer, sporting dense heads of small, yellow composite flowers from September through October (Fig. 11.7). Rabbitbrush is most evident along roadsides and other areas disturbed by overgrazing, vehicle activity, or fire. The colonizing ability of rabbitbrush and its deep root system make this an important species for erosion control. The name rubber rabbitbrush is sometimes used and comes from the extractable latex in the stem. This latex was unsuccessfully experimented with during World War II as a possible source of rubber.

Fig. 11.7 *Ericameria nauseosa*, Asteraceae, yellow rabbitbrush. Photo by Jim Morefield.

Pinyon-Juniper Woodlands

Pinyon-juniper woodlands, often called dwarf conifer woodlands because of the low stature of the trees, are present across the higher mountainous elevations of the Great Basin and Colorado Plateau (Fig. 11.8). It is estimated that more than 50 million acres of pinyon-juniper occurs in the Intermountain West—from eastern Oregon through Nevada, Utah, Arizona, and New Mexico. There are extensive areas of pinyon-juniper woodlands in the higher ranges of the eastern Mojave Desert and northward in the Inyo and White mountains across to the Panamint Range. Additionally, relict populations of pinyon-juniper woodlands occur on the arid slopes of the Transverse and Peninsular ranges near the western margins of the Mojave Desert and extend westward into the Tehachapi Mountains.

The specific pinyon and juniper species associated in these woodlands differs across the Intermountain West and adjacent northwestern Mexico. These include combinations of four pinyon and four juniper species. However, the associations in the eastern Mojave Desert are much simpler. Almost all California stands of pinyon-juniper woodland have singleleaf pinyon (*Pinus monophylla*) as the co-dominant (Fig. 11.9). Over most of the range of pinyon-juniper woodlands in the western United States, however, the dominant pine is Colorado pinyon (*Pinus edulis*). This a pine with fascicles containing two needles (Fig. 11.10). It reaches its most westward distribution in the New York Mountains, barely entering California. A third pinyon species is present along the Peninsular Ranges of southern California and southward into Baja California, Mexico. This is the Parry pinyon (*Pinus quadrifolia*) a *mostly* four-needled pine (Fig. 11.11). Further south in the Sierra Juárez, five-needles become normal and this may be a new species once formally described but is now retained within the Parry pinyon complex.

Utah juniper (*Juniperus osteosperma*) is the codominant species over much of our higher elevation pinyon-juniper woodlands. It has a distribution largely

Fig. 11.8. Western juniper (*Juniperus occidentalis*) dominate the Great Basin woodlands of Modoc County, in far northeastern California. Photo by Michael Kauffmann.

Fig. 11.9. *Pinus monophylla*, Pinaceae, single-leaf pinyon. Photo by Jim Morefield.

Fig. 11.10. *Pinus edulis*, Pinaceae, Colorado pinyon. Photo by Matt Berger.

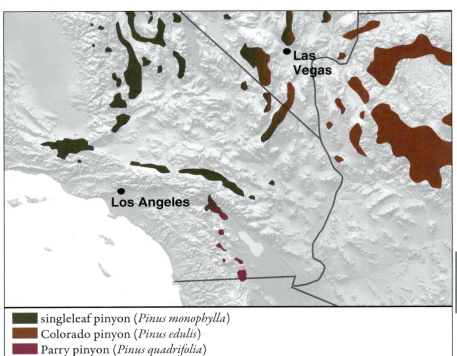

■ singleleaf pinyon (*Pinus monophylla*)
■ Colorado pinyon (*Pinus edulis*)
■ Parry pinyon (*Pinus quadrifolia*)

Fig. 11.11. Pinyon pine distribution adapted from *Conifers of the Pacific Slope* by Michael Kauffmann, 2013.

restricted to the Great Basin and does not reach the interior slopes of the Transverse Ranges in California (Fig. 11.12, 11.13). It is a single-stemmed tree with oppositely arrayed pairs of scale-like leaves lacking a prominent leaf gland with both male and female structures on the same plant (Fig. 11.14). California juniper (*Juniperus californica*) forms lower-elevation desert woodlands on the arid interior slopes of the Transverse Ranges at the western margin of the Mojave Desert. This species is shorter than Utah juniper with a range associated more typically with Mediterranean-type shrublands rather than the desert. It does occur in scattered areas in the eastern Mojave Desert. In addition to its shrubby growth form with multiple stems, California juniper is identified by scale leaves occurring in whorls of three with prominent resinous glands at their centers—and the presence of separate male and female plants (Fig. 11.15).

Our pinyon-juniper woodlands in the eastern Mojave Desert typically occur from 5,000 feet at the upper margin of creosote bush or blackbrush shrublands (see below) to the crest of the mountains. Pinyon-juniper woodlands are equally at home on a variety of parent materials including granite to limestone. Typically, they occur on steep, rocky slopes with poor soil development. The depth of the soil varies, but they are typically well drained and relatively low in fertility.

While the name pinyon-juniper woodland suggests that both a pinyon pine species and juniper species are both present, this not always the case. Both Utah juniper and California juniper are significantly more tolerant of soil drought than singleleaf pinyon and thus occur at lower elevations. This pattern is seen along

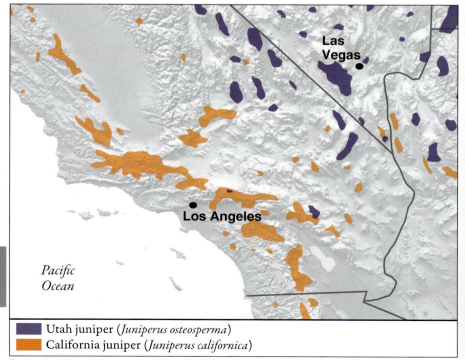

Fig. 11.12. Juniper distribution adapted from *Conifers of the Pacific Slope* by Michael Kauffmann, 2013.

Fig. 11.13. *Juniperus osteosperma*, Ivanpah Range, Mojave National Preserve. Photo by Todd Keeler-Wolf.

Fig. 11.14. *Juniperus osteosperma*, Cupressaceae, Utah juniper. Photo by Jim Morefield.

Fig. 11.15. *Juniperus californica*, Cupressaceae, California juniper. Photo by Michael Kauffmann.

Highway 14 in the Antelope Valley on the northern slopes of the San Gabriel Mountains where California juniper is abundant at elevations as low as 2,800 feet with pinyon pines absent. Singleleaf pinyon, however, becomes dominant at higher elevations where summer drought stress is less severe.

The lower elevational range of pinyon-juniper woodlands in the eastern Mojave Desert is found in the Granite Mountains, where good infiltration of rainfall into the rocky slopes allows the development of pinyon-juniper woodland as low as 4,200 feet. At the other extreme, single-leaf pinyon occurs as high as 10,000 feet in the White Mountains—well beyond the upper elevational range of Utah juniper.

Fires are relatively infrequent in pinyon-juniper woodlands, historically occurring at intervals of 150–300 years or more under natural conditions. Although lightning strikes are relatively common in the woodlands, the open stand structure does not readily allow the spread of fires. Individual pinyons are known to live for as long as 500 years or more. When conditions do allow a fire to burn through stands of pinyon and juniper, the impacts are severe, often with high tree mortality. Recovery of these stands typically requires the development of a lower shrub layer to act as nurse plants for conifer seedlings, and requires decades.

Seed dispersal of pinyon pines is closely tied to the activities of avian dispersers. Both Clark's nutcrackers and pinyon jays cache the fleshy pinyon nuts in the soil. Some of these seeds are unused and serve to establish new cohorts of seedlings. Although less important, rodents may also serve as pinyon nut dispersers. The dispersal modes of juniper seeds are less well studied but coyotes are known to eat juniper fruits.

Pinyon pines play a significant role in the life of Native Americans living around these woodlands. Pinyon nuts provide fine caloric content and continue to be gathered today in many areas. The wood is utilized for fuel, construction poles, roof beams, and materials for tools. The pitch from pinyon trees is used for medicinal purposes and for glue in jewelry making.

Extensive areas of pinyon-juniper woodland in the western Great Basin were harvested by Euro-American settlers in the late 19th and early 20th century to provide charcoal and fuel for the mining industry. The hierarchy of preference for firewood was first curl-leaf mountain mahogany (described below), then Utah juniper, and finally pinyon pine. This extensive clearing had profound effects on many areas of pinyon-juniper woodland that remain today. On top of this harvest, extensive bark beetle attacks have killed thousands of pinyon pines, increased fuel loads, and leading to increased fire frequency. The introduction of annual cheatgrass (*Bromus tectorum*) over the past century has also increased fire frequencies well beyond those occurring under conditions pre-contact (see Chapter 12).

Woody Shrubs of Pinyon-Juniper Woodlands

The understory of pinyon-juniper woodlands typically displays a diverse community of shrubs, cacti, and perennial herbaceous species—while annual plant diversity is low. The mixed flora of woody shrubs seen in pinyon-juniper stands of the eastern Mojave Desert represent a mix species of with three broad biogeographic patterns of distribution. The first group, comprising the great majority of pinyon-juniper shrub species, is composed of wide-ranging shrubs that occur broadly across the Great Basin and are well-adapted to severe winter temperatures. While some of these species extend down into Joshua tree woodlands, they are more characteristically Great Basin species. Two families, the Rosaceae and Asteraceae, are particularly well represented. A second group includes a small number of species with biogeographic affinities to chaparral ecosystems that occur in scattered locations across the Mojave Desert within, or adjacent to, pinyon-juniper woodlands. The third group is formed of shrub species typical of creosote bush scrub and Joshua tree woodlands in the Mojave Desert that reach their upper elevational limits in these woodlands (see Chapter 4).

Several common Great Basin shrubs in pinyon-juniper woodlands are members of the rose family (Rosaceae) and related to *Purshia tridentata*. Cliffrose (*Purshia stansburiana*) shares many ecological features including the ability to fix nitrogen. Its common name is derived from its abundant, fragrant flowers, 0.5–1 inch in diameter, with its frequent occurrence on steep slopes or cliffs. The small leaves of cliffrose typically have five terminal lobes that extend back to half or more of the leaf length. Small glandular hairs that cover the leaf surface make them sticky to the touch. An interesting feature of the seeds of cliffrose are the plume-like hairs attached to the seed (Fig. 11.16). These hairs act in two ways. First, they are tiny parachutes and aided by wind for dispersal. Secondly, once the seed lands in the soil the blowing wind twists the hair like a drill, rotating it to push the seed into the soil.

Fig. 11.16. *Purshia stansburiana*, Rosaceae, cliffrose. Photo by Stan Shebs.

Another rosaceous shrub with a broad range across the aridlands of the western United States is Apache plume (*Fallugia paradoxa*). This densely branched shrub reaches 4–6 feet in height, with distinctive, small, wedge-shaped leaves with 3–7 lobes and a margin rolled under toward the lower surface (Fig. 11.17). These leaves are densely hairy above but covered with rust-colored scales below. For much of the year, Apache plume is a relatively nondescript mound of branches with tiny leaves—and may lose all of its leaves under dry summer conditions. In May to June, however, it changes appearance as masses of large rose-like flowers, 1 inch in diameter, cover the stems. Even more dra-

Fig. 11.17. *Fallugia paradoxa*, Rosaceae, Apache plume. Photo by Stan Shebs.

matic are the clusters of small seeds, each tipped with a feathery pinkish plume 1–2 inches in length. Although drought tolerant, Apache plume favors semi-riparian sites along the margins of arroyos or washes where water collects following rains. Unlike Great Basin sagebrush, Apache plume is one of the few pinyon-juniper shrubs that resprouts after fire.

Fern bush (*Chamaebatiaria millefolium*) is a rosaceous shrub of higher mountain areas of the Great Basin—ranging from Wyoming and Texas west to California and reaching elevations as high as 11,000 feet. Fern bush is an erect shrub 3–6 feet in height, with twice-divided lobes of fern-like leaves that give rise to its common name (Fig. 11.18). Despite the delicate form of the leaves, they are relatively leathery and semi-evergreen. Perhaps the most definitive identification traits are the presence of a sticky resin that covers leaf and young stem surfaces as well as the reddish, shredding bark on the woody stems. A simple touch of foliage will generally necessitate washing your hands. Although rarely abundant, fern bush is widely present on a range of parent soil materials including volcanic to limestone. It is a good colonizer of disturbed sites including roadsides and lava flows.

Fig. 11.18 *Chamaebatiaria millefolium*, Rosaceae, fernbush. Photo by Jim Morefield.

Other members of the Rosaceae include mountain mahogany (*Cercocarpus* sp.) which are successful colonizers of rocky slopes, a trait related to the ability to fix atmospheric nitrogen using symbiotic bacteria in root nodules. This symbiotic relationship is the same as that described above for *Purshia* species. Curl-leaf mountain mahogany (*Cercocarpus ledifolius*), a widespread shrub or small tree distributed across the arid mountain ranges of the Great Basin where it occurs from pinyon-juniper habitats up into ponderosa or subalpine forests (Fig. 11.19). It often forms closed canopy stands of arboreal growth up to 30 feet in height and

Fig. 11.19, *Cercocarpus ledifolius*, Rosaceae, curl-leaf mountain mahogany. Photo by Jim Morefield.

Fig. 11.20. *Cercocarpus ledifolius* var. *intricatus*, Rosaceae little-leaved mountain mahogany. Photo by Stan Shebs.

attains great ages. In California it is widespread in the Inyo and White mountains and present, but relatively uncommon, in pinyon-juniper woodlands of the eastern Mojave Desert. It is also found on arid slopes of the Transverse and northern Peninsular ranges. On these sites it prefers slopes or rocky outcrops with little or no soil development.

Little-leaved mountain mahogany (*Cercocarpus ledifolius* var. *intricatus*) is a form restricted to limestone and dolomite soils in the eastern Mojave Desert but may occur on other substrates across the Great Basin of Nevada and Utah. The growth form is much more compact than that of curl-leaf mountain mahogany, reaching only 3–10 feet in height in mature shrubs (Fig. 11.20). As its name suggests, a character separating this variety from curl-leaf mountain mahogany is the small size of the leaves—less than a half inch in length compared to leaves up to 1.5 inches long in the latter species. In addition, the leaf margins of little-leaved mountain mahogany are curled back toward to the point of almost obscuring the lower leaf surface.

Returning to members of the Asteraceae, there are two species of semi-evergreen *Ericameria* that are typical of pinyon-juniper woodlands of the eastern Mojave Desert. Both are rounded shrubs up to about 3 feet in height, with colorful displays of yellow composite flowers in spring. The most distinctive of these species is wedgeleaf or cliff goldenbush (*Ericameria cuneata*) with relatively broad wedge-shaped leaves (Fig. 11.21). This species is widely distributed around pinyon-juniper woodlands, where it often colonizes rock crevices of cliffs and outcrops. A second common species in pinyon-juniper woodlands is turpentine bush (*Ericameria*

Fig. 11.21. *Ericameria cuneata*, Asteraceae, wedgeleaf goldenbush. Photo by Jim Morefield.

Fig. 11.22. *Ericameria laricifolia*, Asteraceae, turpentine bush. Photo by Stan Shebs.

laricifolia), a rounded shrub up to 3 feet in height with aromatic foliage smelling like turpentine. It likewise has narrowly linear leaves up to about ¾ inch in length (Fig. 11.22). It is also found in higher elevations of creosote bush scrub. Several species of *Ericameria* in creosote bush scrub and Joshua tree woodlands were described earlier in Chapter 4 including interior goldenbush (*Ericameria linearifolia*) which can extend into pinyon-juniper woodlands.

Although recent molecular studies have suggested that most species in the genus *Chrysothamnus* cannot be separated from the related goldenbushes (*Ericameria*), a few species remain within a more constrained concept of *Chrysothamnus*. Two of these species of rabbitbrush occur at higher elevations in the pinyon-juniper woodlands of the eastern Mojave and Great Basin. Green rabbitbrush (*Chrysothamnus viscidiflorus*) is small shrub up to 3 feet in height with a broad elevational range extending from pinyon-juniper woodlands up into alpine fellfields. The sticky leaves have a characteristic twisted appearance, like a loose corkscrew (Fig. 11.23). It is abundant in the Inyo and White mountains but occurs only in the New York and Kingston mountains of the eastern Mojave Desert and west across the Tehachapi Mountains.

Fig. 11.23. Chrysothamnus viscidiflorus, Asteraceae, green rabbitbrush. Photo by Jim Morefield.

The genus *Tetradymia*, known as horsebrush or cottonthorn, includes ten aridland species of Asteraceae from the western United States, of which seven are present in our deserts—most notably in higher elevation Great Basin communities. Horsebrush species are typically woody shrubs, 3–4 feet in height, with the notable traits of spiny stems (not all species) and small branches covered by dense

Fig. 11.24. *Tetradymia axillaris*, Asteraceae, long-spine horsebrush. Photo by Jim Morefield.

Fig. 11.25. *Tetradymia canescens*, Asteraceae, spineless horsebrush. Photo by Jim Morefield.

mats of cottony hairs. The branch spines of most species are formed by persistent leaf veins that harden after the blades are shed in summer. Thus, spines are absent from the current year branches. The mats of woolly hairs, that give rise to the name cotton-thorn, are the persistent bristles of the pappus from the base of the discoid flower heads. The most important traits are the presence or absence of spines and the amount and form of pubescence on leaves.

Four species of horsebrush are commonly encountered in pinyon-juniper woodlands and sagebrush steppe of the eastern Mojave Desert and associated Great Basin communities. Two of these, long-spine horsebrush (*Tetradymia axillaris*, Fig. 11.24) and striped horsebrush (*Tetradymia argyraea*), have characteristic spines. Cotton-thorn is widespread at higher elevations in the Mojave Desert, often associated with sagebrush steppe or saltbush scrub. Striped horsebrush is infrequent on gravelly and rocky slopes and ridges in pinyon-juniper woodlands and occasionally extends lower in elevation into Joshua tree woodlands in the eastern Mojave Desert. Its name comes from the pattern of alternating woolly and hairless stripes of stem surface. Two other species that lack spines are widespread in pinyon-juniper woodlands, sagebrush steppe, and shadscale scrub. Spineless horsebrush (*Tetradymia canescens*) is characterized by leaves densely covered with white woolly hairs (Fig. 11.25). Little horsebush (*Tetradymia glabrata*) is most typical of pinyon-juniper woodlands but can be found in higher elevation Joshua tree woodlands. As its species name suggests, the leaves of little horsebrush lack dense hairs.

Broom snakeweed (*Gutierrezia sarothrae*) is a low subshrub described in Chapter 4 with a range extending broadly from the shortgrass prairies of Kansas and Oklahoma west to arid areas of California—where it is common in many communities including pinyon-juniper woodlands. It forms a sprawling mound, 1–2 feet in height, with small linear leaves. Clusters of small yellow flowers cover the plants in summer. Unlike many of the Great Basin shrubs which are evergreen or semi-evergreen, broom snakeweed is drought-deciduous, losing its leaves in our area under dry summer conditions. The foliage is toxic to domestic grazing animals, containing compounds called saponins which are bitter and can rupture red blood cells. Because of this toxicity, broom snakeweed increases rapidly in heavily grazed woodlands.

Several members of the Chenopodiaceae are common associates of pinyon-juniper communities. Most notably four-wing saltbush described in Chapter 8. Also present is one of the least charismatic but most ecologically significant shrub species—winterfat (*Krascheninnikovia lanata*). The long generic name, of Russian origin, replaces two former names—*Eurotia lanata* and *Ceratoides lanata*. Winterfat has a broad range across aridlands from southern Canada and Texas westward to the Mojave Desert (see Chapter 4) where this highly branched, low shrub reaches no more than about 3 feet in height. Despite its relatively small size, individual plants are thought to live well over 100 years. The linear-shaped leaves of winterfat, up to an inch in length and with margins prominently curved back and under, are covered by a dense mat of star-shaped white hairs. This mat of hairs gives the plant a silvery appearance. Flowering begins in late spring when separate and nondescript male and female flowers remain on the plant and form on short spikes at the tips of the vegetative branches. Dense tufts of hair at the basis of these flowering spikes gives the upper half of the plant a woolly appearance. The seeds, also covered with white hairs, mature over the summer and largely remain on the plant through the winter. The ecological significance of winterfat lies with its importance as a food source for elk, mule deer, bighorn sheep, and jackrabbits.

There are several relatively uncommon but interesting shrub species found within the pinyon-juniper woodlands of the eastern Mojave Desert. Narrow-leaved yerba santa (*Eriodictyon angustifolium*) is a shrubby member of the borage family (Boraginaceae) reaching 4–6 feet in height, with stiff sticky stems with long, linear leaves coated with resin on the upper surface (Fig. 11.26). It is more abundant in Great Basin areas of Nevada, Utah, and Arizona and is known in California only from the Granite and New York mountains where it occurs in canyon bottoms with coarse boulders and slopes on both granite and limestone. It has a CNPS Rare

Fig. 11.26. *Eriodictyon angustifolium*, Boraginaceae, narrow-leaved yerba santa. Photo by Matt Berger.

Fig. 11.27. *Philadelphus microphyllus*, Hydrangeaceae, little-leaf mock orange. Photo by Stan Shebs.

Fig. 11.28. *Jamesia americana*, Hydrangeaceae, five-petal cliffbush. Photo by Stan Shebs.

Fig. 11.29. *Fendlerella utahensis*, Hydrangeaceae, yerba desierto. Photo by Matt Berger.

Fig. 11.30. *Buddleja utahensis*, Scrophulariaceae, Utah butterflybush. Photo by Todd Keeler-Wolf.

Plant Rank: 2B: rare, threatened, or endangered in California; common elsewhere. The leaves of this and other species of *yerba santa* are used to brew an herbal tea.

Three winter-deciduous shrubs in the mock orange family (Hydangeaceae) are widely distributed across the mountains of the arid western United States and are present in local, moist habitats within the pinyon-juniper woodlands of California. Little-leaf mock orange (*Philadelphus microphyllus*) is a rounded shrub reaching to 4 feet or more in height (Fig. 11.27). It is found in the San Jacinto and Santa Rosa Mountains in the west to the Providence, New York, and Clark mountains in the eastern Mojave Desert. It favors rock crevices on steep, north-facing slopes. The showy, creamy-white flowers are produced in clusters of three from buds in the previous year stem-tips. The sweet fragrance of these flowers gives the group the name mock orange.

The two other members of the mock orange family are smaller. Five-petal cliffbush (*Jamesia americana*) is a shrub up to 3 feet in height that favors moist cliff faces and cliff bases. It is found in pinyon-juniper and higher elevation pine forests of the Inyo, White, and Grapevine mountains—extending eastward as far as Colorado. The flowers are like little-leaf mock orange but waxy and less fragrant. Additionally, flowers of little-leaf mock orange typically have only four petals while those of five-petal cliffbush have five (Fig. 11.28). A smaller shrub in this family that is much more limited in distribution is yerba desierto (*Fendlerella utahensis*) which is largely restricted to limestone soils in the desert ranges of the northern Mojave around Death Valley and in the Providence, Clark, and Kingston ranges of the eastern Mojave Desert. This is a low shrub no more than about 12 inches in height (Fig. 11.29).

Utah butterflybush (*Buddleja utahensis*) is found in dry, well-drained gravelly areas on bajadas formed of limestone or volcanic rocks in the lower pinyon-juniper zone and upper Joshua tree woodland. This member of the

Scrophulariaceae is a densely branched shrub with elongate, blue-gray leaves with wavy margins, rolled edges, and a covering of thick woolly hairs (Fig. 11.30). Clusters of small, yellow flowers form along the tips of the outer stems, with male and female plants differentiated.

Two species of barberry, with widespread ranges across the Great Basin, are found in pinyon-juniper woodlands and adjacent chaparral areas of the eastern and southern Mojave Desert. These are members of the Berberidaceae, a family widely cultivated in California. Both are large shrubs, 5–10 feet or more in height, with leathery divided leaves with sharp spines along their margins. Desert barberry (*Berberis haematocarpa*) has 3–5 leaflets and an elongate overall leaf shape such that the length is more than three times the leaf width (Fig. 11.31). The species name refers to the blood-red to purple color of the berries. Fremont's barberry (*Berberis fremontii*) has 3–7 leaflets and a broader leaf shape with the length less than three times the width (Fig. 11.32). Its fruits are more yellowish-red.

Fig. 11.31. *Berberis haematocarpa*, Berberidaceae, desert barberry. Photo by Matt Berger.

Five species of ephedra are described in Chapter 4. One species of this odd group of gymnosperms is a common understory shrub in pinyon-juniper woodlands. This shrub is green ephedra (*Ephedra viridis*), with a broad range from eastern Oregon and Texas westward across the Great Basin. In addition to its higher elevation habitat, green ephedra is readily differentiated from the Mojave Desert species by its erect growth form, 2–5 feet in height, and up to 10 feet in diameter with bright green stems (Fig. 11.33). As with other *Ephedra* species, the leaves are reduced to tiny deciduous scales, and positioned in opposite pairs at each branch node. A thick, brown leaf base remains after the leaves are shed. Green ephedra is relatively tolerant of fire, resprouting readily from underground meristems.

Fig. 11.32. *Berberis fremontii*, Berberidaceae, Fremont's barberry. Photo by Matt Berger.

Chaparral Elements

Broad areas of transition between more arid desert communities and more mesic chaparral communities occur along the western margin of the Mojave Desert on the inner slopes of the Transverse Ranges or along the eastern slopes of the Peninsular Ranges on the margins of the Sonoran Desert. In

Fig. 11.33. *Ephedra viridis*, Ephedraceae, green ephedra. Photo by Matt Berger.

Fig. 11.34. *Arctostaphylos pungens*, Ericaceae, pointleaf manzanita. Photo by Matt Berger.

these areas one can find a mix of typical chaparral and desert species growing in close proximity. More surprising, however is the presence of many drought-resistant chaparral species growing within areas of pinyon-juniper woodlands of the eastern Mojave Desert. Scattered stands of these chaparral elements are found in the Granite, Mid Hills, and New York mountains. These areas are generally characterized by favorable water availability that has allowed the localized survival of these elements as relictual populations disjunct from a broader distributional range during wetter periods of the past. Soil substrate and local hydrological conditions of these sites clearly aid in increasing water availability, as present in the geologic structure of the Granite Mountains—with numerous springs due to the effective infiltration of rainwater into the soil. The limestone soils in the New York Mountains have a water-holding capacity greater than that of adjacent soils derived from granitic and volcanic parent materials.

Several chaparral species have broad geographic distributions that cross the arid deserts and extend as far to the east as Texas and northern Mexico where they form open chaparral-like stands in arid mountain regions with strong summer rainfall regimes unlike the Mediterranean-type climate of California. An example is pointleaf manzanita (*Arctostaphylos pungens*). This evergreen shrub extends from the Transverse and Peninsular ranges of southern California to the mountains of Arizona, New Mexico, and Texas into northern Mexico. This species is easily recognized by its vertical leaf orientation, sharp pointed leaf tip, and shiny red bark (Fig. 11.34).

Another species with a similar broad ecological and geographic range extending from southern California to northern Mexico is Mojave ceanothus (*Ceanothus pauciflorus*). This is a shrubby to semi-arboreal species that can reach up to 10 feet in height. It was formerly considered a variety of the chaparral species *Ceanothus greggii*. It occurs on rocky slopes and ridges along the desert transition areas of the Transverse Ranges, but is rare in the eastern Mojave, known only from the New York Mountains where it is locally abundant. Mojave ceanothus has small evergreen leaves arranged oppositely along the stems (Fig. 11.35).

Two other members of the Rhamnaceae, the same family as *Ceanothus*, are typical chaparral species that are common on rocky slopes and canyon bottoms of pinyon-juniper woodlands up to elevations of about 6,500 feet in the eastern Mojave Desert. Hollyleaf redberry (*Rhamnus ilicifolia*) is a tall shrub that is widespread in chaparral and oak woodlands of California and is frequently encountered in the higher mountain ranges of the eastern Mojave (Fig. 11.36). Hoary coffeeberry (*Frangula californica* subsp. *ursina*) is a variety of a typical chaparral shrub found widely in pinyon-juniper woodlands of the Providence, New York, and Clark mountains. As the common name suggests, the leaves of this species have a dense covering of white hairs on their lower surface (Fig. 11.37). This desert variety is separated from the southern California populations by having a finely-toothed leaf margin.

Two species of oaks (Fagaceae) are found in pinyon-juniper woodlands. Canyon live oak (*Quercus chrysolepis*) is a familiar evergreen oak in southern California where it grows widely in moist mountain canyon areas (Fig. 11.38). Its range extends from southern Oregon throughout the Mediterranean-type climate regions of California and then across the Mojave Desert into Arizona. It is found on boulder slopes, arroyos, and canyon bottoms in the higher ranges of the eastern Mojave Desert. The second oak species present in pinyon-juniper woodlands is desert scrub oak (*Quercus turbinella*), an evergreen shrubby to sometimes tree-like species that often forms dense thickets across its range from Colorado to Texas and south to Arizona (Fig. 11.39, 11.40). In California it is locally common in arroyos, canyon bottoms, and coarse rocky slopes of the New York Mountains. Desert scrub oak has a CNPS Rare Plant Rank of 4.3 because of its limited distribution in California.

Another widespread species from coastal foothill areas of California is

Fig. 11.35. *Ceanothus pauciflorus*, Rhamnaceae, Mojave ceanothus. Photo by Matt Berger.

Fig. 11.36. *Rhamnus ilicifolia*, Rhamnaceae, hollyleaf redberry. Photo by Robert Gustafson.

Fig. 11.37. *Frangula californica* subsp. *ursina*, Rhamnaceae, hoary coffeeberry. Photo by David Greenberger.

Fig. 11.38. *Quercus chrysolepis*, Fagaceae. canyon live oak, Photo by Morgan Stickrod.

Fig. 11.39. *Quercus turbinella*, Fagaceae, desert scrub oak. Photo by Michael Kauffmann.

Fig. 11.40. Desert scrub oak (*Quercus turbinella*) and canyon live oak *(Quercus chrysolepis)* are joined by a variety of coastal chaparral plants, including manzanita, yerba santa, ceanothus, and coffeeberry in Caruthers Canyon, New York Mountains, Mojave National Preserve. Photo by Michael Kauffmann

skunkbush (*Rhus aromatica*), whose common occurrence in and around pinyon-juniper woodlands is indicative of local water availability. This shrub forms small thickets around springs, washes, and boulder slopes where it may reach 4–6 feet or more in height. The leaves of skunkbush, shed in winter, are distinguished by three prominent leaflets (Fig. 11.41). Although resembling poison oak, and in the same family (Anacardiaceae), skunkbush does not cause skin dermatitis. Poison oak itself (*Toxicodendron diversilobum*) barely enters the desert in chaparral and woodland transitions at the southwestern margin of the Mojave Desert.

Ashy silktassel (*Garrya flavescens*) is perhaps not strictly a chaparral species—as its range extends from coastal California into higher areas of the Great Basin in Utah and Arizona. This shrub is recognized by its opposite, evergreen leaves and silky spikes of hanging flowers that droop for about 4 inches below the branches (Fig. 11.42). Male and female flowers occur on different plants. Ashy silktassel is found commonly in the higher ranges of the eastern Mojave Desert on both calcareous and granitic soils of canyon bottoms and rocky slopes.

White Fir-Pinyon Woodland

An unusual community, best described as white fir-pinyon woodland, is found in a few, small upper elevation areas in the three highest mountain ranges of the eastern Mojave Desert. This assemblage of shrub and tree species here represents a montane community typical of higher elevations in more mesic mountain ranges. It extends over no more than a combined 250 acres across the north-facing slopes of the Clark, Kingston, and New York mountains. Present in these stands are several shrub species that are widespread in montane areas of California but not normally associated with desert areas. Utah serviceberry (*Amelanchier utahensis*) is a winter-deciduous member of the rose family that forms a sprawling shrub that reaches 20 feet or more in height under optimal conditions. The plants are conspicuous in spring when covered by white flowers before the leaves appear (Fig. 11.43). The purple berries are edible

Fig. 11.41. *Rhus aromatica*, Anacardiaceae, skunkbush. Photo by Matt Berger.

Fig. 11.42. *Garrya flavescens*, Garryaceae, ashy silktassel. Photo by Stan Shebs.

Fig. 11.43. *Amelanchier utahensis*, Rosaceae, Utah serviceberry. Photo by Jim Morefield.

Fig. 11.44. *Holodiscus discolor*, Rosaceae, small-leaved creambush. Photo by Jim Morefield..

Fig. 11.45. *Acer glabrum*, Sapindaceae, mountain maple. Photo by Jim Morefield.

Fig. 11.46. *Fraxinus anomala*, Oleaceae, singleleaf ash. Photo by Jim Morefield.

to wildlife and humans alike and have even been used to make wine. It serves as an important browse plant for desert bighorn sheep, mule deer, and elk. Native Americans in the Great Basin dry the berries and mixed them with buffalo meat to make pemmican. Also in the rose family is small-leaved creambush (*Holodiscus discolor*), a low winter deciduous shrub (Fig. 11.44) whose range extends on north-facing slopes as low as 4,500 feet. Both Utah serviceberry and small-leaved creambush have broad ranges across moist conifer forests of the Sierra Nevada, through the Pacific Northwest, and much of the mountainous areas of the western United States.

A relatively rare occurrence here of an otherwise common species in mountains of the western United States is mountain maple (*Acer glabrum*). This winter-deciduous shrub or shrubby tree (Sapindaceae) has a broad range extending from southeastern Alaska to New Mexico but is an unexpected member in this dry white fir-pinyon woodland (Fig. 11.45). Another unusual member of the community is singleleaf ash (*Fraxinus anomala*), a tall shrub or small tree in the olive family (Oleaceae) up to 20 feet tall that occurs frequently on rocky canyon bottoms and steep slopes at higher elevations. It likewise is a winter-deciduous species that is rare in California but extends across the Great Basin in similar habitats. It is unique among ash species in having simple leaves without separate leaflets (Fig. 11.46).

Two related shrub species (Grossulariaceae) present in the white fir-pinyon woodlands are wax currant (*Ribes cereum*) and desert gooseberry (*Ribes velutinum*). Currants lack spines, while gooseberries have spines. Wax currant is a deciduous species with a wide range across mountain areas of the western United States. The foliage has an aromatic scent with both leaves and stems displaying visible resin glands.

The stems lack spines and prickles. The leaves are rounded with shallow lobes which are toothed along the edges and flowers are reddish in color (Fig. 11.47). In contrast, desert gooseberry is a multi-branched arching shrub that may reach up to 6 feet in height. Nodes along the stems display sharp spines ¾ inch in length. The thick leaves have a rounded shape with 3–5 lobes and flowers are pale white to yellow in color (Fig. 11.48). Desert gooseberry typically occurs at lower elevations of pinyon-juniper woodlands and even sagebrush steppe across much of the Great Basin.

Two-thirds of the area of white fir-pinyon woodland occurs in the Clark Mountains where there are more than 1,000 white fir (*Abies concolor*). About 500 white fir trees occur over 30 acres in the Kingston Mountains, while only about 30 white fir trees are present over several acres in the New York Mountains. These sites, at elevations from about 6,000–7,600 feet, collect spring snowfall despite only receiving about 9–13 inches of annual precipitation. This is a surprisingly small amount of moisture to support the growth of white fir. It is interesting to note that these white firs are members of the Rocky Mountain variety (var. *concolor*) rather than the Sierra Nevada variety (var. *lowiana*), and thus represent an intermountain west biogeographic element.

The largest white firs are up to 65 feet in height with diameters up to 36 inches, indicating relatively good growing conditions (Fig. 11.49). Associated with the firs in these stands are singleleaf pinyon pines and Utah juniper, both of which reach sizes here larger than in typical pinyon-juniper woodlands. Associated with the white fir, pinyons, and juniper are a variety of shrub species that favor relatively moist sites. Most of these are species found in the upper elevations of pinyon-juniper woodlands, but a few are largely restricted to these small stands. Although white fir is absent from the White and Inyo mountains and other ranges around Death Valley, moist canyons at the upper end of the pinyon-juniper woodlands in these mountains support a community much like the white fir-pinyon woodland of the eastern Mojave Desert—with many of the same shrub species present.

Fig. 11.47. *Ribes cereum*, Grossulariaceae, wax currant. Photo by Robert Gustafson.

Fig. 11.48. *Ribes velutinum*, Grossulariaceae, desert gooseberry. Photo by Robert Gustafson.

Fig. 11.49. In the Kingston Range, scientists undertake a seed collection mission of the rare white fir (*Abies concolor*) to preserve the genetics of this isolated population. Photo by Duncan Bell.

Bristlecone-Limber Pine Forests

One of the most unusual forest types on Earth grows on the highest summits of California's desert ranges. Steeped in myth and legend, Great Basin bristlecone pine (*Pinus longaeva*) are long-lived, multi-stemmed trees that attain ages approaching 5,000 years (fig. 11.50). Needles are old as well, being retained for as much as 40 years. Clark's nutcrackers and other birds disperse, cache, and are thus responsible for new seedling spread and establishment. At 10,000 feet and higher, they are found in the White, Grapevine, Inyo, Last Chance, and Panamint mountains in California and in similar habitats in Utah and Nevada. Rocky Mountain bristlecone pine (*Pinus aristata*) is found in similar habitats across Colorado, New Mexico, and on the San Francisco Peaks in Arizona. These pines are of an ancient lineage that emerged around 40 million years ago. Other relatives include the California endemic foxtail pine (*Pinus balfouriana*) and pinyon pines.

Fig. 11.50. *Pinus longaeva*, Pinaceae, Great Basin bristlecone pine. Photo by Matt Berger.

Fig. 11.51. *Pinus flexilis*, Pinaceae, limber pine. Photo by Michael Kauffmann.

Fig. 11.52. Great Basin bristlecone pines and limber pines decorate the ridgelines below Telescope Peak (11,043 feet) in Death Valley National Park. Photo by Matt Berger.

A similar species, limber pine (*Pinus flexilis*), is often found in the same stands as Great Basin bristlecone pine. These shade-intolerant, slow-growing, and long-lived trees attains 60 feet in height and may live to 1,000 years (Fig. 11.51). While preferring foothill communities further north, in California it is a true summit species found across the Transverse and Peninsular ranges; southeastern Sierra Nevada; and the Inyo, White, Sweetwater, Glass, and Panamint mountains of the desert above 9,000 feet. At the margins of these forests, in high-elevation meadows with deep, well-drained, carbonate-rich soils the California endemic Rothrock's sagebrush (*Artemisia rothrockii*) is found. This shrub lives to 40 years and grows to 2 feet in height (Fig. 11.52).

These ancient conifers have played a crucial role in our understanding of the past with the emergence of dendrochronology. Due to the resinous wood, cold and arid habitats, and slow wood decay, dendrochronologists have been able to go back in time from the present to 6828 BCE (8,850 years!) by aligning tree rings of living and long-dead bristlecone pines. They have also dated living trees to almost 5,000 years. The Schulman Grove in the White Mountains is readily accessible by car and includes both bristlecone and limber pines. For the more adventurous, the higher elevation Patriarch Grove, at about 11,000 feet, contains the oldest known trees on a stark dolomite substrate that is inhospitable to limber pines.

Fig. 11.52. *Artemisia rothrockii, Asteraceae*, timberline sagebrush. Photo by Jim Morefield.

Fig. 11.53. Ancient bristlecone pine like these live ones, along with the downed wood, are used for cross-dating research. Photo by Jim Morefield.

Chapter 12
Conserving the California Desert

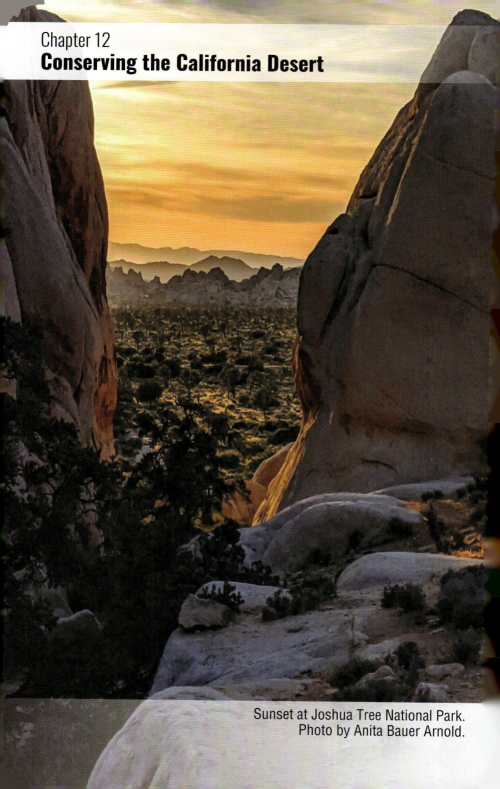

Sunset at Joshua Tree National Park.
Photo by Anita Bauer Arnold.

Introduction

This book is a celebration of California's deserts through the lens of the plants that call this beautiful and vast landscape home. In the last chapter, we look to the future of the desert by exploring the past, present, and future of land management with a proactive view to protect biodiversity.

First Peoples

The California desert region has a human history that extends back thousands of years. Numerous Native Americans Tribes constructed both seasonal and permanent village sites near water from which they could hunt and forage. Rather than living as isolated tribes, these groups established elaborate trading routes with footpaths across the deserts (Fig. 12.1). Among the tribal groups in the Mojave Desert pre-contact were the Vanyume (Desert Serrano), Kawaiisu, Kitanemuk, Koso, Southern Paiute bands, and Chemehuevi. Among those in the Sonoran Desert were the Cahuilla, Yavapaiv Apache, Western Shoshone, Xawitt kwñchawaay, and Quechan. They established similar socio-economic systems and seasonal, semi-permanent villages. Most tribes were hunter-gatherers with resource collection carried out by family groups foraging over wide areas. However, tribes along the Colorado River practiced agriculture—growing melon, corn, pumpkin, and beans. Trade routes extended widely and reached as far as the Pacific coast.

Fig. 12.1. The Chemehuevi artists who chiseled these petroglyphs lived in the region now designated as the Mojave National Preserve for thousands of years pre-contact. These petroglyphs are a testament to their relationship with the land and the diversity of life they shared it with. Photo by Michael Kauffmann.

Euro-American Era

Trails established by Native Americans were used by the Spanish in the middle 16th century to cross from settlements in Arizona and Mexico to coastal areas of California. Despite forays through these areas by explorers, soldiers, and Mormon settlers, there was little Euro-American interest in the desert itself. It was not until statehood for California that the railroad and hydrological surveys of the southwestern United States promoted a strong interest in desert resources. This began with a focus on precious metals such as gold and silver, but the mining industry soon expanded to include more exotic minerals such as borax. At the same time, ranching operations expanded over extensive areas of the desert and the less arid western desert margins.

Another critical change in the exploitation of desert resources and land use came with the construction of canals to bring water into the California desert. The construction of the Los Angeles Aqueduct began in 1905 and was completed in 1913—bringing water more than 220 miles from the Owens Valley to Los Angeles. The All-American Canal, built by the United States Bureau of Reclamation in the 1930s and completed in 1942, brought water from the Colorado River to Imperial County and allowed the development of large, irrigated agricultural lands. Railroads continued to control large areas of land between the two World Wars, but an increasing appreciation of desert biota and natural resources led to the establishment of three large parks in the 1930s. These are Anza-Borrego Desert State Park and what were initially Joshua Tree and Death Valley national monuments.

With the end of World War II and the developing era of the automobile, cheap gasoline, and cross-country highways, the California deserts experienced a renewed focus of development as highway towns and resorts were planned and constructed. This development was encouraged by the first widespread application of air conditioning in homes, making desert living much more attractive in places like Palm Springs. At the same time, pressure for more public ownership of desert lands led the U.S. federal government to pass the Small Tract Act of 1938, which opened hundreds of thousands of acres to 5-acre homesteading contingent on the building of a structure no smaller than 12 x 16 feet. No water or electrical utilities were required. This act was repealed in 1976 but has left a legacy of thousands of decaying desert shacks. The experience of World War II also led the government to withdraw large tracts of desert lands from public access to provide for military training grounds and for the development of weapon technologies.

In 1976, Congress established the 25-million-acre region of desert, stretching from the Mexican border north to Death Valley and the eastern Sierra Nevada Mountains, as the California Desert Conservation Area. The Bureau of Land Management (BLM) was assigned to manage this scenic and biologically important area. However, limited resources and conflicting priorities at the BLM limit the effectiveness of this designation.

The passage of the California Desert Protection Act in 1994, following eight years of difficult negotiations, was a landmark event in the conservation of desert ecosystems and their biodiversity. This legislation accomplished four major steps in improving the protection and management of desert resources. It greatly broadened the boundaries of what had been Death Valley and Joshua Tree national monuments and designated them national parks. It additionally established the 1.5 million-acre Mojave National Preserve, protecting a key area of the eastern Mojave Desert. Nearly 3.5 million acres of BLM land were protected as wilderness. BLM land was also transferred to the State of California to expand Red Rock Canyon.

Landownership and Resource Management

The vast majority of California desert lands are owned by the U.S. government and managed by various federal agencies (Fig. 12.2). These agencies include the BLM, the National Park Service, and the Department of Defense. Each of these federal agencies has a different mission, with often conflicting objectives, including resource management, resource extraction, recreational use, and military training

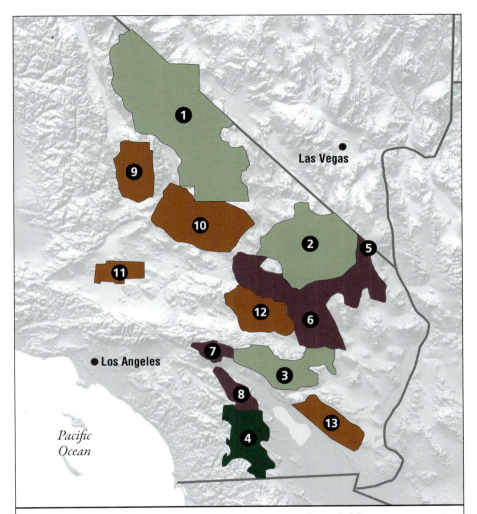

Fig. 12.2. California Desert Land Management.

and preparedness. An example of the complexity of resource management is seen with the BLM. Under Federal policy, the BLM is mandated to maintain environmental quality and to protect rare and endangered species, while at the same time accommodating multiple uses such as mining, grazing, water extraction, and recreation. Many of these uses are damaging to sensitive desert habitats and conflict with conservation goals. Moreover, limited budgets constrain the BLM further because proper land management and enforcement of regulations over huge areas is not feasible. Despite these limitations, BLM has classified large portions of the California desert region as wilderness areas, protecting them from disturbance because of their ecological, geological, scenic, and/or historical values.

The proportion of federal ownership is high in the Mojave Desert with its national parks and military lands comprising 80 percent of the total area. The BLM is the largest land manager for the Mojave, overseeing approximately 8 million acres, or 41 percent of the area. The National Park Service manages Death Valley National Park, Joshua Tree National Park, Mojave National Preserve, and several smaller areas of conservation lands that together account for 26 percent of the region. The Department of Defense manages five military bases, briefly described below, that cover about 13 percent of the region. California state agencies control another 2 percent of the land area. Only about 18 percent of the land belongs to private landowners or municipalities.

The area of land owned by the federal government is smaller in the Sonoran Desert of California where extensive irrigated agricultural lands are under private ownership. BLM is also the largest land manager with about 2.9 million acres, or 43 percent of the area. Department of Defense lands account for about 460,000 acres, or 5 percent of the region. Joshua Tree National Park spans the transition from the Mojave to the Sonoran Desert with slightly less than half the park, about 340,000 acres, in the Sonoran Desert. Anza Borrego Desert State Park encompasses over 600,000 acres, or nearly 9 percent of the region. A number of other public landholdings occur around the Salton Sea, with the California Department of Parks and Recreation, the California Department of Fish and Game, and the U.S. Fish and Wildlife Service managing the sea and adjacent lands.

A large area of California's desert has received international recognition for its conservation significance. In 1984, UNESCO designated a *Mojave and Colorado Deserts Biosphere Reserve* to promote biodiversity conservation. The biosphere reserve includes Death Valley National Park, Joshua Tree National Park, Anza Borrego Desert State Park, and the Santa Rosa and San Jacinto national monuments. This designation, however, has no legal status with respect to management policies.

Death Valley National Park

Death Valley National Park, the largest in the continental United States, covers 3.4 million acres. It encompasses almost all of Death Valley, Saline Valley, a large part of Panamint Valley, and portions of several surrounding mountain ranges. The area was first protected in 1933 as a national monument, and in 1994 the monument was expanded to include Saline and Eureka valleys and redesignated as a national park. The Badwater Basin is 282 feet below sea level, making it the second-lowest point in the Western Hemisphere and the lowest point in North

America. The remarkable biodiversity of Death Valley results, in part, from the diverse topography and geology, as well as its location between the Mojave, Sonoran, and Great Basin deserts. Habitats range from the saline flats around Badwater to vast creosote bush scrub and Joshua tree woodlands. Park boundaries extend to elevations of 5,475 feet at Dante's View on the eastern edge and to Telescope Peak at 11,049 feet on the western boundary. Approximately 95 percent of Death Valley National Park is designated as wilderness.

Mojave National Preserve

Mojave National Preserve, established in 1994, is a unit of the National Park Service encompassing 1.6 million acres (Fig. 12.3). It is roughly bounded to the north and south by Interstates 15 and 40, and to the east by the California–Nevada border. Although geographically centered on the eastern Mojave Desert, the preserve includes a broad range of elevations including lowlands at 880 feet near Baker to an elevation of 7,929 feet at the summit of Clark Mountain. Substrates are also highly varied and include dry playa lakebeds, granites, volcanics (domes, lava flows, and cinder cones), and sedimentary deposits. The Providence Mountains even have limestones as seen in the spectacular Mitchell Caverns. The Kelso Dunes, at the western margin of the preserve, are the largest aeolian dune system in the Mojave Desert, covering about 29,000 acres. The University of California's Sweeney Granite Mountains Desert Research Center and California State University's Soda Springs Desert Studies Center at Zzyx are also within the park boundaries. Approximately 700,000 acres of the preserve are designated as wilderness.

Joshua Tree National Park

Joshua Tree National Park was first designated a national monument in 1936, and later upgraded to national park status in 1994. It includes over 791,000 acres of federal land, with 430,000 acres designated as wilderness. The park is named

Fig. 12.3. Entrance to the Mojave National Preserve. Photo by Michael Kauffmann.

for the stands of Joshua tree (*Yucca brevifolia*) that extend across the northern half of the park. One of the significant aspects is its position straddling the boundary between the Mojave and Sonoran deserts. The higher elevation northern and western areas are the southern extension of the Mojave Desert, while the lower elevation eastern and southern areas are part of the Sonoran Desert. The Little San Bernardino Mountains, which run through the southwest edge of the park, reach elevations high enough to support pinyon-juniper woodlands. Among the outstanding scenic features are the eroded granite rock formations that were uplifted by tectonic forces 250 to 75 million years ago. The oldest exposed rock formations are gneiss that were formed 1.7 billion years ago. Five of the park's six mountain blocks—the Little San Bernardino, Hexie, Pinto, Cottonwood, and Eagle—are geological components of the east-west trending Transverse Ranges which also includes the San Bernardino, San Gabriel, and Tehachapi Mountains. The Coxcomb Mountains, at the eastern margin of the park, run north–south and are geologically part of the Basin and Range Province.

Big Morongo Canyon Preserve

The Big Morongo Canyon Preserve is a 31,000 acre preserve managed by the BLM to protect a unique area of riparian woodland in the Little San Bernardino Mountains, north of Palm Springs, in the transition from the Mojave to Sonoran desert. Big Morongo Canyon preserves a large area of cottonwood and willow riparian ecosystems with important wildlife habitats that offers some of the best neotropical bird watching around.

Red Rock Canyon State Park

Red Rock Canyon State Park covers approximately 27,000 acres of spectacular rock formations and badlands in the western Mojave Desert just north of the town of Mojave (Fig. 12.4). The original park area was almost tripled in size in 1994 when the California Desert Protection Act provided for the BLM to transfer

Fig. 12.4. Red Rock Canyon State Park. Photo by Naomi Fraga.

16,665 acres to State Parks. One of the prominent features of Red Rock Canyon are exposed cliffs with folded layers of red and white sediments capped with more resistant black basalt and pink volcanic tuff. These sedimentary and igneous layers were deposited in an ancient lake basin millions of years ago and have subsequently been lifted by the multiple fault systems in the area. Streams and rivers have carved the canyons to form what we see today.

Mojave Trails, Sand to Snow, and Castle Mountains National Monuments

A California Desert Protection Act of 2010 proposed the establishment of three new National Monuments but failed to win approval in the U.S. Senate. In 2016, before leaving office, President Barack Obama used the Antiquities Act to declare the establishment of these three protected areas, creating Mojave Trails (Fig. 12.5), Sand to Snow, and Castle Mountains national monuments. Together these cover more than 1.8 million acres and link existing national parks and conservation areas. The first two are managed by the BLM while the third is managed by the National Park Service.

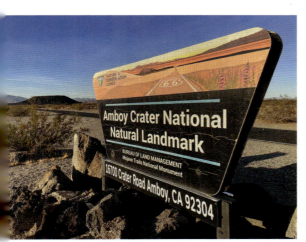

Fig. 12.5. Mojave Trails National Monument at Amboy Crater. Photo by Michael Kauffmann.

Santa Rosa and San Jacinto Mountains National Monuments

The Santa Rosa and San Jacinto Mountains national monuments were established by Congress in 2000 to preserve the significant biological, cultural, recreational, geological, educational, and scientific values of the Santa Rosa and San Jacinto mountains (Fig. 12.6). The boundary of the national monument encompasses about 272,000 acres, including 65,000 acres within the San Jacinto Ranger District of the San Bernardino National Forest, and 89,500 acres within the BLM California Desert Conservation Area. Although the area of this National Monument extends to

Fig. 12.6. Santa Rosa and San Jacinto national monuments as seen from Coyote Canyon. Photo by Karen Orso.

high elevations and includes extensive montane conifer forests, the lower elevations cover broad areas of alluvial fans and bajadas with creosote bush scrub, and several California fan palm oases. The National Monument includes two federal Wilderness Areas: the Santa Rosa Wilderness (61,600 acres of BLM and Forest Service lands) and the San Jacinto Wilderness (19,470 acres of Forest Service lands). The national monument boundaries also surrounds lands owned and administered by the Agua Caliente Band of Cahuilla Indians, California Department of Parks and Recreation, California Department of Fish and Game, other agencies of the State of California, and private landowners. Much of this area was originally designated as the Santa Rosa Wildlife Area to protect the largest herd of peninsular bighorn sheep (*Ovis canadensis nelsoni*) in the U.S.

Anza-Borrego Desert State Park

Covering approximately 600,000 acres of eastern San Diego County and adjacent areas of Riverside and Imperial County, Anza-Borrego Desert State Park is the largest in the California system and second in size of any state park in the United States, with only the Adirondack Mountains Park in New York larger. The name of the park commemorates Juan Bautista de Anza, a Spanish explorer who set out with an expedition in 1774 from the settlement of Tubac in southern Arizona and crossed the Colorado River into the Sonoran Desert of California. He traveled on to the Mission San Gabriel and eventually up the coast to Monterey before returning. Lying in the western portion of the Salton Sea basin, Anza-Borrego highlights the flora of the Sonoran Desert area of California with many subtropical species, such as palo verde and ocotillo, that do not occur in the colder Mojave Desert. *Borrego* is the Spanish word for the desert bighorn sheep, which are found in the park.

Military Land Management

Military training activities utilize large areas of the Mojave Desert and smaller areas in the Sonoran Desert. In total, military bases occupy more than 3 million acres, or about one-sixth of the total land area. Interestingly, these bases include some of the most pristine habitats because of their protection from public access. However, there is typically no formal protection for these quality habitats. There are five major military bases in our desert regions.

Naval Air Weapons Station at China Lake, located in the north-central Mojave Desert covering portions of San Bernardino, Inyo, and Kern counties, has an area of about 1.1 million acres. It is the largest single holding of the U.S. Navy, comprising 38 percent of the total Navy land holdings in the entire world.

Edwards Air Force Base, situated in the western Mojave Desert, just south of the town of Mojave and north of Lancaster in the Antelope Valley, covers about 308,000 acres. This includes Rogers Dry Lake (28,000 acres), the largest dry lake bed in North America, and Rosamond Dry Lake (13,400 acres). Because of Rogers Dry Lake's history in the space program, it was declared a National Historic Landmark.

Fort Irwin National Training Center, located approximately 37 miles northeast of Barstow in the central Mojave Desert, includes a total area of about 740,000 acres and is the center for desert training for the United States Army.

Marine Air Ground Task Force Training Command at Twentynine Palms covers an area of 915,000 acres within the Morongo Basin and the high desert region of the Mojave Desert. The military uses the airfield at Twentynine Palms for flight training, dating back to World War II. This core area and adjacent lands were designated as the Marine Corps Training Center at Twentynine Palms in 1952, and additional lands were added in subsequent years,

Chocolate Mountain Aerial Gunnery Range, located on the east side of the Salton Sea in Imperial County, California is a 456,000 acre restricted area under the jurisdiction of the U.S. Navy and Marines used for bombing and aerial gunnery practice.

Conserving Our Desert Flora

From a botanical perspective, there are two important aspects of conserving and protecting our California's desert ecosystems. The first of these is from the ecosystem-level perspective that seeks to protect community structure and dynamics, allowing these to operate sustainably. Because of their low levels of productivity, desert ecosystems typically have poor resilience to major disturbance. Intact populations of living plants have significant impacts on habitat-water relations and nutrient dynamics in desert ecosystems. Accumulation of dead plant material, organic matter, and associated nutrients around the bases of long-lived desert shrubs is critical to these ecosystems. A classic example is in the slow rate of reestablishment of plant cover in ghost towns abandoned a century or more ago.

The second aspect to desert conservation is from the floristic perspective which focuses on the preservation of biodiversity and protection of rare species. Nearly 100 taxa of desert plants are identified by either the Federal Government or the State of California as rare, threatened, or endangered. There are several forms of rarity. It can result from any one or combination of a limited geographic range, a highly specific habitat requirement, or a small population size. Many rare species are restricted to localized desert habitats such as wetlands, dunes, riparian corridors, and unusual soils that have ecological significance

The California Native Plant Society has developed a rating system classifying the form and significance of rarity in the native flora (rareplants.cnps.org).

- Rank 1A: Plants presumed extirpated in California and either rare or extinct elsewhere
- Rank 1B: Plants rare, threatened, or endangered in California and elsewhere
- Rank 2A: Plants presumed extirpated in California but common elsewhere rare
- Rank 2B: Plants rare, threatened, or endangered in California but common elsewhere
- Rank 3: Plants about which more information is needed, a review list
- Rank 4: Plants of limited distribution, a watch list

Major threats to the conservation of California desert ecosystems come from a variety of causes. These include impacts from invasive non-native plant species, fire, expanding urbanization and development, groundwater depletion and associated loss of riparian habitat, mining operations, inappropriate off-road vehicle use, excessive livestock grazing, and solar and wind power development.

Invasive Plants

It was once thought that the environmental stressors in desert ecosystems made them relatively immune to competition from invasive plant species. Our experience over the last three decades, however, has shown this is incorrect. Not only have many non-native invasive species becoming widely established in California deserts, but moreover some of these are having major impacts on ecosystem structure and dynamics. The dynamics of species invasion are complex and influenced by global change.

Two grass species from the Mediterranean Basin have invaded vast areas of the Mojave and Sonoran deserts over the past four decades and dramatically transformed the native vegetation structure through both abundance and wildfire impacts, as described below. Cheatgrass (*Bromus tectorum,* Fig. 12.7) and red brome (*Bromus rubens,* Fig. 12.8) and have been present in California since the arrival of the first Spanish missions in the late 18th century when they were inadvertently brought into the state with the establishment of the California missions. These grasses found a welcoming habitat in California's oak savannas and grasslands where they rapidly expanded across the state and eventually into the deserts.

Two other abundant non-native grasses in our lower desert areas are Arabian schismus (*Schismus arabicus*) and Mediterranean schismus (*Schismus barbatus*). These are closely related winter annual grasses that are geographically segregated in the Old World between the Near East and the western Mediterranean. Both are thought to have become widely established in California in the first half of the 20th century. During years of favorable winter rains, these grasses are abundant

Fig. 12.7. *Bromus tectorum*, Poaceae, cheatgrass. Photo by Matt Berger.

Fig. 12.8. *Bromus rubens* offers flammable fuels in the open spaces between desert shrubs. Photo by Stan Shebs.

and form dense carpets across flat, sandy terrains. The prostrate stems spread out close to the ground, effectively preventing many native annuals from becoming established. Although low in stature, the biomass accumulated in the grasses can be sufficient to carry a fire between individual woody shrubs.

Other non-native plant species are currently expanding their ranges and population densities. Of particular concern are two members of the mustard family, Sahara mustard (*Brassica tournefortii*) and shortpod mustard (*Brassica incana*). The former is the most serious problem. Sahara mustard is a robust winter annual reaching up to 18 inches in height (Fig. 12.9). It favors sandy, disturbed soils at low elevations, but its range is expanding in recent decades to colonize undisturbed soils and rocky hillsides. Sahara mustard is now abundant in the Coachella, Borrego, and Imperial valleys of California, especially in areas with wind-blown sediments where it may form monocultures. It is thought to have been inadvertently introduced in the early 20th century when date palms were brought to the Coachella Valley from the Middle East. Sahara mustard was considered a relatively infrequent species until the late 1970s. Once established, it crowds out native annuals and comprises as much as three-quarters of the spring biomass of annual plants. Like the invasive annual grasses, the dry summer biomass accumulation of Sahara mustard becomes a fire hazard.

Fig. 12.9. *Brassica tournefortii*, Brassicaceae, Sahara mustard. National Park Service photo.

Another invasive species, which has become one of our most abundant desert annuals, is redstem filaree (*Erodium cicutarium*). It is a relative of geranium that is also from the Mediterranean Basin. Despite its abundance, redstem filaree is currently more benign in its effect on native ecosystems. Although it may have some impact in competition with native annuals, it furnishes forage for desert tortoise and other wildlife. Redstem filaree was one of the early non-native plants to invade western North America and was introduced to California during the early 1700's by passing Spanish explorers.

Fig. 12.10. *Salsola tragus*, Chenopodiaceae, Russian thistle. National Park Service photo.

Russian thistle (*Salsola tragus*) is the familiar tumbleweed found collecting along fence lines in disturbed desert areas (Fig. 12.10). It is a large and deeply rooted annual that breaks free on maturity in late summer and tumbles across the landscape spreading seeds as it moves. Russian thistle utilizes C_4 metabolism and is thus best adapted to summer growth under high temperature conditions, as described for other native C_4 desert annuals in Chapter 10. This weed grows fast but is not yet considered to have severe ecological impacts on other species. Wild Western movies with Wyatt Earp or Jesse James often had windblown tumbleweeds included in their set design. Interesting however, Russian thistle was not introduced to the United States until 1874 and was not widespread until the 1890s, well after the era of the western gunfighters.

Fire

There is little evidence suggesting fire was anything but a rare event in the low- to mid-elevations of the Mojave and Sonoran deserts prior to a half century ago. However, this is shifting and now new factors are contributing to increased fire frequency in the desert. These include climate change, extensive drought, convective air currents, and anomalous late spring rainfall. The latter contributes to anomalous growth of both native and non-native plants—which are believed to be increasing the spread of fire.

Although lightning associated with convective thunderstorms in summer provided a potential for fire, fires did not historically spread as fast as today because there was less connectivity between flammable materials across the open spaces. This began to changed in the late 1970s with the invasion of annual grasses, *Bromus rubens* and *Schismus*. Wet years with plentiful rainfall supported these grasses, but nitrogen accessibility limited their success. This changed with decades of nitrogen deposition associated with air pollution moving eastward from the air shed of the greater Los Angeles Basin. A series of wet years in the late 1970s made it apparent that non-native annual grasses were becoming widely established. Today, these non-native grasses are abundant in wet years and can comprise as much as 95 percent of the annual plant biomass in creosote bush scrub and Joshua tree woodlands.

Many woody species lack the fire-adaptive traits of either a woody root crowns or fire-stimulated seed germination that we see in chaparral shrubs. Thus, these

Fig. 12.11. Joshua trees killed in the 2007 Covington fire in Joshua Tree National Park. National Park Service photo by Robb Hannawacker.

shrubs are poorly adapted to resprouting or establishing seedlings after fire. Seedling recruitment for native perennials may require decades to a century or more. Short time intervals between fires, and the rapid reestablishment of annual non-native grasses, leads to continued dominance of invasive grasses. Thus, these species enter a negative feedback loop with more frequent wildfires.

Records for lightning-ignited fires in Joshua Tree National Park suggest that before 1965 such events typically burned less than a quarter acre. After this, records show fires becoming more common. In 1979 the Quail Mountain fire burned 6,000 acres and in 1995 the Covington fire burned 5,000 acres (Fig. 12.11). In 1999 the Juniper Complex fire, the largest fire in the history of the park, burned almost 14,000 acres of Joshua tree and pinyon-juniper woodlands. However, the most dramatic fire event in the Mojave Desert occurred in August 2020 when lightning ignited invasive annual grasses near Cima Dome in the Mojave National Preserve (Fig. 12.12). Before the fire was finally contained it had burned more than 43,000 acres of Joshua tree woodland. It is estimated that as many as 1.3 million Joshua trees were killed in the fire.

Fig. 12.12. Dome fire, August 2020. National Park Service photo by Barbara Michel.

Prior to Euro-American settlement blackbrush shrublands, at transition areas between the Great Basin and Mojave deserts, are thought to have experienced infrequent low-intensity fires with fire-free intervals as long as centuries. Low, fine fuel loads between shrubs likely limited fire spread except during extreme fire weather conditions. With Euro-American settlement, burning increased to remove blackbrush to expand areas for livestock grazing. These activities contributed to invasion of nonnative annual grasses (*Bromus tectorum* and *B. rubens*). This invasion has set up a cycle of shorter fire-return intervals, degradation of shrublands, and an associated loss of woody species lacking fire-adapted traits. Similarly, sagebrush steppe is similarly sensitive to frequent fires, with Great Basin sagebrush only rarely able to resprout after fire. A single fire event can convert sagebrush steppe to non-native annual grassland.

Non-Native Invasive Trees

Invasive species problems in the California deserts are not restricted to grasses and herbs. Saltcedar, or tamarisk, (*Tamarix ramosissima*) and related species of tamarisk from the aridlands of Africa pose serious problems (Fig. 12.13). Saltcedar was brought to the southwestern United States to control erosion and shield roads and railroad lines from moving sand. Today, however, saltcedar has replaced cottonwoods and willows in much of the riparian habitats, most notably along watercourses such as the Mojave and Amargosa rivers. It has become virtually ubiquitous along the flood plain of the Colorado River.

The saltcedar invasion problems are many. Areas with saltcedar have experienced dramatic changes in geomorphology, groundwater availability, soil chemistry, fire frequency, plant community composition, and native wildlife diversity. Geomorphological impacts of saltcedar result from the trapping and stabilizing of alluvial stream sediments, which results in narrowing of stream channels and associated flooding intensity. The alteration

Fig. 12.13. *Tamarix ramosissima*, Tamaricaceae, saltcedar. National Park Service photo.

of natural flow regime favors invasive tamarisk over native vegetation, in part because some native species are adapted to a seasonal flooding regime for dispersal and germination.

Because of its high transpiration rates and extensive cover, saltcedar also lowers water tables. In areas where groundwater levels are declining, saltcedar out competes water-stressed native trees by extending its root systems more deeply than willows, cottonwoods, and many other riparian tree species. Another competitive advantage is its ability to tolerate moderately alkaline soils by sequestering salts in its leaf tissues. When these tissues are shed, salts become concentrated in surface soil horizons, thereby degrading soil conditions for native plants. In many places, tamarisk has completely replaced native cottonwood, willow, and mesquite and grows in dense monocultures. Even where native riparian trees remain, tamarisk usually grows among them. It is also found along other waterways and aquatic habitats, including irrigation canals and springs where it provides lower-quality habitat than native trees for nesting birds and other wildlife.

Russian olive (*Elaeagnus angustifolia,* Elaeagnaceae) grows as a tree or shrub and is found in disturbed, seasonally moist places in the Mojave Desert (Fig. 12.14). Once established near springs, this invasive tree quickly crowds out native species. It regenerates under a wide variety of floodplain conditions with little or no mortality after seedling development. Once established, it crowds out native cottonwoods and willows.

Fig. 12.14. *Elaeagnus angustifolia*, Elaeagnaceae, Russian olive. Photo by Oftersheimer Dünen, Public Domain.

Urbanization and Development

Varying levels of urbanization and development have occurred in our desert region for many years but has been concentrated in only a few areas. The western Mojave Desert, because of its proximity to the greater Los Angeles urban center, has experienced tremendous growth over the last few decades—which is expected to continue. In recent decades these incorporated cities grew at rates double that

Fig. 12.15. Joshua tree woodland disappearing in the Antelope Valley. Photo by Todd Keeler-Wolf.

statewide. The sprawling form of suburban development has removed and fragmented extensive areas of desert habitat, particularly in the Antelope Valley (Fig. 12.15). Associated with this development is the increased construction of roads, power lines, pipelines, and other infrastructure that has further intensified habitat fragmentation.

Significant population growth, however, has not been present to the same extent in the eastern Mojave of California where there is little human infrastructure. However, major population growth has occurred across the California-Nevada line in Las Vegas and Pahrump. This growth has significant environmental effects on air quality and groundwater supplies nearby.

Although the Sonoran Desert region is likewise sparsely populated over extensive areas, there are two regions where population growth and land-use conversion has been extensive. The first of these is the Coachella Valley. Home to a series of fast-growing communities that stretch from Palm Springs through Cathedral City, Rancho Mirage, Palm Desert, and Indian Wells eastward to Indio, new residential and resort complexes with golf courses have expanded steadily over recent decades. They now are moving further up the canyons onto the lower slopes of the Peninsular Range and replacing natural communities. Outlying agricultural communities such as Mecca, Coachella, and Thermal are not yet seeing this degree of development.

Major population growth has also occurred in southern Imperial County where agricultural development has expanded southeast of the Salton Sea from Brawley and El Centro to near the United States–Mexico border including the cities of Calexico and Mexicali. Imperial County has 600,000 acres of land under cultivation for vegetable crops and alfalfa.

Groundwater Depletion and Loss of Riparian Habitat

Development also increases pressure to drawdown groundwater supplies. Groundwater pumping for domestic, agricultural, and industrial uses across both the Mojave and Sonoran deserts has lowered groundwater levels significantly in many areas. As groundwater levels drop, there is a depletion of water supplies for riverbeds, springs, and seeps—all of which are integral for the survival of animal species. Diminished groundwater also impacts riparian corridors and can cause the decline of cottonwoods and willows and facilitates their replacement by invasive species such as the deep-rooted saltcedar. If the depletion is severe enough to significantly lower water tables, even the native deep-rooted phreatophytes like mesquite species are affected.

Groundwater depletion has caused major ecological impacts along the Mojave River and imperils the riparian habitat and wetlands of the Amargosa River. Continuing depletion of major Amargosa River aquifers to serve expanding urban development and agriculture in Nevada has the potential to have major impacts in Ash Meadows, the Amargosa Canyon, and Death Valley National Park along this corridor.

Mining Operations

Mineral commodities extracted from the Mojave Desert include lead, zinc, gold, silver, copper, sand, gravel, limestone, gypsum, sodium, lithium, and borates. The desert also provides minerals from evaporative deposits that are used in filtration systems, chemical refining, ceramics, and drilling muds. In 1990, nearly 40 percent of the gold extracted in California came from the Mojave Desert and gold mining continues to be economically important in the region today. Mining has had harsh, localized environmental impacts, most notably in the Mojave Desert. Mining roads, tailing mounds, pits, ore piles, and chemical runoff at mine sites produce long-lasting scars on the natural landscape (Fig. 12.16). Additionally, open pit mining and dry-lakebed mineral projects produce fine particulate dust that quickly spreads over large areas, presenting a health hazard for humans. Uncovered ponds of toxic leachates from mineral refining impact waterfowl and other species.

Some active mines within protected areas will be returned to public ownership when mining is no longer active. An example of this is the Castle Mountain Mine

Fig. 12.16. Large mine in the Mojave Desert near Amboy, California. Photo by Michael Kauffmann.

area, an open pit gold mine in the southern Castle Mountains, which has approval to excavate nearly 10 million tons of ore through 2025, The national monument proclamation states that after mining and reclamation are completed, or after 10 years if no mining occurs, the land is to be transferred to the National Park Service. This policy should be encouraged for other lands with active mining claims.

Illegal Off-Road Vehicle Use

Off-road vehicles negatively impact natural ecosystems in numerous ways and creates long-lasting scars (Fig. 12.17). Desert soils require decades or even centuries to form and stabilize. This process is destroyed instantly by vehicle activity. While in mesic ecosystems tire tracks may fade away quickly, the situation is very different in desert environments. The arid nature of the desert means that such tracks remain for many years, influencing the hydrology of the soil. The ruts channel water, increasing the speed of water runoff and promoting erosion. It also may change the overall direction of flow, preventing water from reaching areas it previously did or causing increased erosion in new areas.

In addition, off-road vehicles compact soil, reduce native plant cover, crush animal burrows, and promote the spread of invasive plant species. Plants with shallow root systems are especially vulnerable to crushing from off-road vehicles and even deep-rooted plants may be damaged. An example of the slow recovery of desert habitats can still be seen in the tracks of military vehicles made by General Patton during in his World War II training exercises in the Mojave Desert, more than 80 years ago, which remain visible today.

The 1980 California Desert Conservation Area Plan referred to off-road vehicles as *"the most pervasive management issue in the area."* Because there are only a handful of rangers patrolling millions of acres of BLM lands, there is little enforcement related to proper off-road vehicle use. This enforcement problem is of particular concern in ecologically sensitive areas along washes, riparian corridors, and dune areas favored by off-road vehicle users. This issue can become particularly confrontational in the Coachella Valley Dune and Algodones Dune areas of the Sonoran Desert where conservation areas are adjacent to designated off-road vehicle areas.

Fig. 12.17. Illegal off-road vehicle damage in Death Valley National Park. National Park Service photo.

Fig. 12.18. Wind power impacts on vegetation, Tehachapi Mountians. Photo by Todd Keeler-Wolf.

Fig. 12.19. Ivanpah solar development in California with Primm, Nevada in the foreground. Photo by Michael Kauffma

Livestock Grazing

Due to the low productivity of the desert, livestock grazing has altered ecosystems. Grazing activities reshape streambeds, trample or consume seedlings of native trees and shrubs, and facilitate the spread of invasive annual grasses. These practices are particularly detrimental to wetland and riparian habitats where fragile soils erode due to frequent animal movement around rivers, springs, and seeps. Feces from domestic animals pollutes surface water important for native species. Grazing issues result not just from domestic livestock but also from feral horses and burros, which exist well beyond carrying capacity in some areas.

Solar and Wind Power Development

Sustainable energy meets its crux in southern California (Figs. 12.18 and 12.19). Year-round solar radiation, consistent wind, cheap land controlled by the federal government, and proximity to major markets for clean power all work together to encourage the expansion of massive energy projects. While renewable energy sources are welcome in the time of rapid climate change, they come with serious environmental costs related to the appropriate placement of solar fields and wind farms to maintain biodiversity. Ground water resources may be impacted by the massive infrastructure needed do establish transmission and transportation corridors required to distribute the generated energy

Proactive land use planning, an ongoing process, will be the key to compatible development of energy resources while at the same time preserving desert ecosystems and biodiversity. Where possible, degraded lands such as abandoned agricultural fields, former industrial sites, brownfields, and existing transportation corridors are appropriate areas for solar development to minimize impacts on wildlife and natural resources.

Conclusion

The conservation and preservation of the natural and cultural resources of the California desert is critical. Congress eloquently expressed its view in the California Desert Protection Act of 1994:

- Preserve unrivaled scenic, geologic and wildlife values associated with these unique natural landscapes;
- Perpetuate in their natural state significant and diverse ecosystems of the California desert;
- Protect and preserve the historical and cultural values of the California Desert associated with ancient Indian cultures, patterns of western exploration and settlement, and sites exemplifying the mining, ranching and railroading history of the Old West;
- Provide opportunities for compatible public outdoor recreation, protect and interpret ecological and geological features and historic, paleontological, and archeological sites, maintain wilderness resource values, and promote public understanding and appreciation of the California desert; and
- Retain and enhance opportunities for scientific research in undisturbed ecosystems.

We must do more and do better, together, to protect these special places.

Further Reading

Baldwin, B.G., S. Boyd, B.J. Ertter., R.W. Patterson, T.J. Rosatti, and D.H. Wilken (eds.) 2002. *The Jepson Desert Manual: Vascular Plants of Southeastern California*. University of California Press, Berkeley. 624 p.

Baldwin, B.G., D. Goldman, D.J. Keil, R. Patterson, T.J. Rosatti, and D.H. Wilkin. 2012. The Jepson Manual. Vascular Plants of California, 2nd Edition. University of Caliornia Press, Berkeley.

Barbour, M, A. Schoenherr and T. Keeler-Wolf. (eds.) 2007. *Terrestrial Vegetation of California*. University of California Press, Berkeley. 730 p.

Blackwell, L.R. 2006. *Great Basin Wildflowers: A Guide to Common Wildflowers of the High Deserts of Nevada, Utah, and Oregon*. Falcon Guide, Globe Pequot Press, Guilford, Connecticut. 208 p.

Bowers, J.E. Jack W. Dykinga, and J.W. Dykinga. 2003. *Desert: The Mojave and Death Valley*. Harry N. Abrams, New York. 143 p.

Bryan, T.S. and B. Tucker-Bryan. 1995. *The Explorer's Guide to Death Valley National Park*. University of Colorado Press, Boulder, 378 p.

Cunningham, B. and P. Cunningham. 2006. *Hiking California's Desert Parks, 2nd edition: A Guide to the Greatest Hiking Adventures in Anza-Borrego, Joshua Tree, Mojave, and Death Valley*. Falcon Guide, Globe Pequot Press, Guilford, Connecticut. 416 p.

Darlington, D. 1996. *The Mojave: A Portrait of the Definitive American Desert*. Henry Holt, New York. 337 p.

Decker, R. and B. Decker. 1999. *Road Guide to Joshua Tree National Park*. Double Decker Press, 48 p.

Decker, R. and B. Decker. 2004. *Road Guide to Death Valley National Park* (Updated Edition). Double Decker Press, 48 p.

Digonnet, M. 2013. *Hiking Western Death Valley National Park: Panamint, Saline, and Eureka Valleys*. Wilderness Press, Birmingham, Alabama. 568 p.

Digonnet, M. 2016. *Hiking Death Valley: A Guide to Its Natural Wonders and Mining Past. Second Edition*. Wilderness Press. Birmingham, Alabama. 550 p.

Digonnet, M. 2019. *Mojave Desert Peaks: Hiking the Crown of the California Desert*. Wilderness Press, Birmingham, Alabama. 600 p.

Digonnet, M. 2021. *Hiking the Mojave Desert: The Natural and Cultural Heritage of Mojave National Preserve. Second Edition*. Wilderness Press, Birmingham, Alabama. 460 p.

Dole, J.W. and B.B. Rose. 1996. *Shrubs and Trees of the Southern California Deserts*. Foot-Loose Press, North Hills, California. 157 p.

Fiero, B. 1986. *Geology of the Great Basin*. University of Nevada Press, Reno. 212 p.

Gildart, B. and J. Gildart.2005. *Death Valley National Park*. Falcon Guide, Globe Pequot Press, Guilford, Connecticut. 160 p.

Grubbs, B. 2006. *Joshua Tree National Park: A Guide to Exploring the Desert Trails and Roads*. Falcon Guide, Globe Pequot Press, Guilford, Connecticut. 112 p.

Hall, C.A. (ed.). 1991. *Natural History of the White-Inyo Range*. University of California Press, Berkeley. 560 p.

Hall, C.A. and V. Doyle-Jones (eds.). 1988. *Plant Biology of Eastern California*. Natural History of the White-Inyo Range Symposium Volume 2, White Mountains Research Station. University of California, Los Angeles.

Houk. R. 2001. *Mojave Desert*. Western National Parks Association, Tucson. 48 p.

Jaffe, D.G.M. and M. Jaffe. 2004. *Mojave National Preserve: A Visitor's Guide*. Western National Parks Association, Tucson. 16 p.

Jaeger, E.C. 1940. *Desert Wildflowers*. Stanford University Press, Stanford. 352 p.

Jaeger, E.C. 1955. *The California Deserts*. Stanford University Press, Stanford. 209 p.

Jaeger, E.C. 1957. *The North American Deserts*. Stanford University Press, Stanford. 308 p.

Kaiser, J. 2008. *Joshua Tree: The Complete Guide* (3rd edition). Destination Press, Shelburne, Vermont. 208 p.

Lanner, R. 1985. *Trees of the Great Basin*. University of Nevada Press, Reno. 215 p.

Larsen, P. and L. Larsen. 2000. *The Deserts of the Southwest: A Sierra Club Naturalist's Guide* (2nd edition). Sierra Club Books, San Francisco. 304 p.

Lightner, J. 2006. *San Diego County Native Plants*. San Diego Flora, San Diego. 320 p.

Lindsay, L. and D. Lindsay. *Anza-Borrego Desert Region: A Guide to State Park and Adjacent Areas of the Western Colorado Desert*. Wilderness Press, Berkeley. 200 p.

MacKay, P. 2013. *Mojave Desert Wildflowers, Including The Mojave National Preserve, Death Valley, National Park, and Joshua Tree National Park*. Falcon Guides, Guilford, Connecticut. 352 p.

Morhardt, S. and A. Morhardt. 2004. *California Desert Wildflowers: An Introduction to Families, Genera, and Species*. University of California Press, Berkeley. 284 p.

Mozingo, H.M. 1987. *Shrubs of the Great Basin: A Natural History*. University of Nevada Press, Reno. 364 p.

Munz, P.A. 2004. *Introduction to California Desert Wildflowers*. Revised Edition. University of California Press, Berkeley. 235 p.

Pavlik, B.M. 2008. *The California Deserts: An Ecological Rediscovery*. University of California Press, Berkeley. 384 p.

Phillips, S.J. and P.W. Comus. (eds.) 2000. *A Natural History of the Sonoran Desert*. University of California Press, Berkeley, and Arizona Sonoran Desert Museum, Tucson. 628 p.

Rae, S. 1999. *Mojave National Preserve*. Olympus Press, Seattle. 240 p.

Robichaux, R.H. (ed.) 1999. *Ecology of Sonoran Desert Plants and Plant Communities*. University of Arizona Press, Tucson. 292 p.

Rundel, P.W. and R. Gustafson. 2005. *An Introduction to the Plant Life of Southern California: Coast to Foothills*. University of California Press, Berkeley, 316 p.

Rundel, P.W. and A.C. Gibson. 1996. *Ecological Communities and Processes in a Mojave Desert Ecosystem: Rock Valley, Nevada*. Cambridge University Press, Cambridge, 376 p.

Sharp, R.P. and A.F. Glazner. 1993. *Geology Underfoot in Southern California*. Mountain Press, Missoula. 224 p.

Sharp, R.P. and A.F. Glazner. 1997. *Geology Underfoot in Death Valley and Owens Valley*. Mountain Press, Missoula. 319 p.

Spellenberg, R. 2012. *Sonoran Desert Wildflowers A Guide to Common Plants*. 2nd edition. Falcon Guide, Globe Pequot Press, Guilford, Connecticut. 256 p.

Stewart, J.M. 1993. *Colorado Desert Wildflowers*. John Stewart Photography, Albuquerque, New Mexico. 120 p.

Stewart, J.M. 1998. *Mojave Desert Wildflowers*. John Stewart Photography, Albuquerque, New Mexico. 210 p.

Trimble, S. 2009. *The Sagebrush Ocean, Tenth Anniversary Edition: A Natural History of The Great Basin*. University of Nevada Press, Reno. 296 p.

Walker, L.R. and F.H. Landau. 2018. A Natural History of the Mojave Desert. University of Arizona Press, Tucson. **344 p.**

Webb, R.H., L. Fenstermaker, J. Heaton, and D. Hughson (eds.). 2009. *The Mojave Desert: Ecosystem Processes and Sustainability*. University of Nevada Press, Reno. 528 p.

Index

NOTE: Page numbers in **bold** refer to key discussions and include photos or other illustrations. Page numbers in *italics* or with *fig.* refer to other photos and figures.

Abies concolor, 238, 239*fig.*
Abronia
  pogonantha, 161, 161*fig.*
  villosa, 160–161, 161*figs.*
Acacia, 107
acacia, catclaw, 107, 107*fig.*
Acamptopappus
  shockleyi, 64–65
  sphaerocephalus, 64, 64fig.
Acanthaceae species, 119–120, 120*fig.*
Acer glabrum, 237, 237*fig.*
Acmispon, 189
  brachycarpus, 189
  rigida, 72, 73*fig.*, 189
  strigosus, 188*fig.*, 189
Acton encelia, 61, 61*fig.*
Adenophyllum
  cooperi, 65, 65*fig.*
  porophylloides, 65
Afton Canyon, 27
Agave, 98–99
  deserti, 98*figs.*, 99
  shawii, 99
  utahensis, 99, 100*fig.*
agaves, 47, 98–99, 98*figs.*
  desert agave, 98*figs.*, 99
  Shaw's agave, 99
  Utah agave, 99, 100*fig.*
Agave subfamily, 98, 209
  See also agaves; yuccas
agricultural development, 28, 29, 106, 244, 257, 258
  livestock and grazing, 244, 255, 261
Algodones Dunes, 29, 158, 160, **166–169**, 259
Algodones Dunes sunflower, 168–169, 169*fig.*
Aliciella latifolia, 194, 194*fig.*
alkali dropseed, 136, 136*fig.*
alkali goldenbush, 146, 148*fig.*
alkali heath, 149, 149*fig.*
alkali mariposa lily, 139, 139*fig.*, 210
alkaline habitats
  alkaline seasonal wetlands, **136–139**, 152
  alkali sinks, **148–152**
  annuals and herbaceous perennials, 113, **152–153**, 178, 180, 188, 204, 205, 210
  See also saline habitats

alkali weed, 152, 153*fig.*
Allenrolfea occidentalis, 150, 150*fig.*, 151, 151*fig.*
Alliona incarnata, 212
Allium, 210
  atrorubens, 210
  fimbriatum, 210, 210*fig.*
  parishii, 210
allscale, 74, 145, 145*fig.*, 147*fig.*
alluvial fans, 15, 15*fig.*
  See also bajadas; washes
Aloe, 48
Amaranthaceae, 143, 212
  desert species, 212, 212*figs.*
Amaranthus, 212
  fimbriatus, 212, 212*fig.*
Amargosa Desert, 25
Amargosa or Mojave nitrophila, 139, 152, 153*fig.*
Amargosa River, 25, 26*fig.*, 28, 130, 131*fig.*, 136, 137*fig.*
  associated riparian and wetland habitats, 25, *126*, 130, 132, 136, 137*fig.*, 141, 152, 256, 258
Amaryllidaceae species, 210, 210*fig.*
Amboy Crater, 13, 14*fig.*, 249*fig.*
Ambrosia, 114–115
  dumosa, 59, 59*figs.*
  ilicifolia, 114
  monogyra, 114, 115*fig.*
  salsola, 114, 115*fig.*
Amelanchier utahensis, 236–237, 236*fig.*
Amphipappus fremontii, 66, 66*fig.*
Amsinckia tessellata, 192, 192*fig.*
Anacardiaceae species, 234, 236, 236*fig.*
Anderson boxthorn, 69, 69*fig.*
Anemopsis californica, 135*fig.*, 136, 136*fig.*
Anisocoma acaulis, 180, 181*fig.*
annuals and herbaceous perennials, 41, 81, **170–213**
  adaptations and strategies of, 45–46, 45*fig.*, 49, 173–175
  alkali associates, 113, **152–153**, 178, 180, 188, 204, 205, 210
  bloom diversity, 171, 172
  borage family, 175, **192**
  broom-rape family, 139, 139*fig.*, **200**
  buckwheat family, 36, 36*fig.*, **204–206**, 207*figs.*
  desert gourds, **125**

dune species, **160–162**, **163–164**, 178, 185–186, 185*fig.*, 191, 203, 203*fig.*, 209, 212–213, 213*fig.*
environmental factors in germination and flowering, 41, 171–173
evening primroses, **200–203**
fire followers, 175, 191, 191*fig.*
geophytes, 39*fig.*, 161, 162*fig.*, **209–210**
impacts of invasives on native species, 253, 255
invasive non-natives, 55, 173, 216, **252–254**, 255, 261
legume family, 164, 164*fig.*, 166, 166*fig.*, 168, 168*fig.*, 174, **184–189**
milkweeds, **208**
mint family, **196**
monkeyflower family, **198–199**
mustard family, 173, **203–204**
native summer annuals and grasses, 173, **211–213**
penstemon family, 175, **197–198**
phacelia family, 175, **189–191**
phlox family, **193–195**
poppy family, 175*fig.*, **183–184**
rare wetlands species, **136**, **138–139**
seed banks and germination, 171–172, 173–175
sunflower family, 168–169, 169*fig.*, 171*fig.*, 173, **178–183**, 211, 211*figs.*
superblooms, **175**
Antelope Valley, 19, 21, 175*fig.*, 176, 188, 257, 257*fig.*
  See also Edwards Air Force Base
Antelope Valley Poppy Preserve, 175*fig.*, 183
Antirrhinum, 197
  filipes, 198, 198*fig.*
Anza-Borrego Desert State Park, 11*fig.*, 29*fig.*, 244, 246, **250**
  annuals and herbaceous perennials, 172, 172*fig.*
  map, 245*fig.*
  palms in, 128*fig.*, 129*fig.*
  rare plant species, 65

wash woodland species, 107–108, 108*fig.*, 110
Anza, Juan Bautista de, 250
Apache plume, 225–226, 225*fig.*
Apocynaceae, 208
 desert species, 208, 208*figs.*
Apodanthaceae, 72
 desert species, 72, 73*fig.*
apricot mallow, 78, 78*fig.*
Arabian schismus, 252–253
Arctostaphylos pungens, 233, 233*fig.*
Arecaceae. *See* palms
Argemone
 corymbosa, 184, 184*fig.*
 munita, 184
Arizona carlowrightia, 119–120
Arizona lupine, 185, 185*fig.*
arrow-leaf, 66, 66*fig.*
arrow weed, 130, 130*fig.*, 160, 165
arroyos, 13, 15, 15*fig.*, 103
Artemisia
 rothrockii, 241, 241*fig.*
 spinescens, 146, 148*fig.*
 tridentata, 218–219, 219*fig.*
Arthrocnemum subterminale, 150
Asclepias
 erosa, 208, 208*fig.*
 subulata, 208
Asclepiadaceae, 208
ashes, 41, 132
 singleleaf ash, 237, 237*fig.*
 velvet ash, 132, 134*fig.*
Ash Meadows/Ash Meadows National Wildlife Refuge, 25, *126*, 132, 136, 137*fig.*
Ash Meadows gumplant, 138, 139*fig.*
ashy silktassel, 236, 236*fig.*
asparagus family (Asparagaceae), 98, 209
 desert species, 47, **54–57**, **98–101**, 161, 162*fig.*, 209
Asteraceae, 35, 46, 58
 annuals and herbaceous perennials, 168–169, 169*fig.*, 171*fig.*, 173, **176–183**, 211, 211*figs.*
 creosote bush scrub–associated woody species, **59–66**
 dune species, 161–162, 161*fig.*, 163*fig.*, 164, 168–169, 169*fig.*
 flower structure, 58–59, 59*fig.*
 Great Basin woody species, 218–219, 218*fig.*, 219*fig.*, **227–230**, 241, 241*fig.*

saline-habitat species, 146, 148, 148*figs.*
wash woodland species, **114–119**
wetland species, 130, 130*fig.*, 136, 138, 138*fig.*
Astragalus, 35, 164, 186
 coccineus, 188, 188*fig.*
 didymocarpus, 187–188, 187*fig.*
 layneae, 187, 187*fig.*
 lentiginosus, 188
 lentiginosus var. *albifolius*, 188
 lentiginosus var. *coachellae*, 166, 166*fig.*
 lentiginosus var. *fremontii*, 188
 lentiginosus var. *micans*, 164, 164*fig.*
 lentiginosus var. *variabilis*, 188, 188*fig.*
 magdalenae var. *peirsonii*, 168, 168*fig.*
 newberryi, 188
Atrichoseris platyphylla, 182, 182*fig.*
Atriplex, 49, 74, **143–146**
 canescens, 146, 147*fig.*, 217, 230
 confertifolia, 144–145, 144*fig.*, 217, 217*fig.*
 hymenelytra, 74, 146, 147*fig.*
 lentiformis, 130, 145–146, 147*fig.*
 parryi, 145, 147*fig.*
 polycarpa, 74, 145, 145*fig.*, 147*fig.*
 spinifera, 145, 145*fig.*

baccharis
 broom baccharis, 118, 118*fig.*
 desert baccharis, 118, 118*fig.*
 shortleaf baccharis, 118
 willow baccharis, 117–118
Baccharis, 117
 brachyphylla, 118
 emoryi, 117
 salacina, 117–118
 salicifolia, 117
 sarothroides, 118, 118*fig.*
 sergiloides, 118, 118*fig.*
Badwater Basin, 17*fig.*, 23, 24*fig.*, 25, 136, 142*fig.*, 151*fig.*, 246–247
Bahiopsis
 parishii, 61–62, 61*fig.*
 reticulata, 61–62
Baileya
 multiradiata, 178, 179*fig.*
 pauciradiata, 178
bajada lupine, 186, 186*fig.*
bajadas, 15–16, 16*fig.*, 19, 103
banana yucca, 56–57, 56*fig.*

barberries
 desert barberry, 232, 232*fig.*
 Fremont's barberry, 232, 232*fig.*
 barberry family species, 232, 232*figs.*
barchans, 156, 156*fig.*
bark beetles, 224
barrel cactus, California, *38*, 45, *88*, 94, 94*fig.*
beavertail cactus, 92, 92*fig.*
Bebbia juncea, 115, 116*fig.*
beehive cactus, 96, 96*fig.*
beleperone, 119, 120*fig.*
belly flowers, 172, 175, 193
 See also annuals and herbaceous perennials
Berberidaceae species, 232, 232*figs.*
Berberis
 fremontii, 232, 232*fig.*
 haematocarpa, 232, 232*fig.*
Bigelow monkeyflower, 199, 199*fig.*
Bigelow's coreopsis, 178, 179*fig.*
Bigelow's crossosoma, 81*fig.*, 82
Bigelow's nolina, 99–100, 101*fig.*
big galleta, 158–159, 158*fig.*
bighorn sheep, 250
Big Morongo Canyon Preserve, 248
Bignoniaceae, 108–109, 213
 desert species, 108–109, 109*fig.*
big saltbush or quailbush, 130, 145–146, 147*fig.*
biodiversity, 35–36, 41, 246, 247, 251
 See also endemism and endemic plants
birdcage primrose, 160, 160*fig.*, 161*fig.*
birds, 119, 173, 197, 224, 240, 248, 256
bird's foot lotus, 189
bitterbrush, 219, 219*fig.*
bitter snakewood, 121, 121*fig.*
black-banded rabbitbrush, 62, 118, 119*fig.*
blackbrush, 215*fig.*, 216, 216*fig.*
blackbrush scrub, **215–216**, 255
Black Mountains, 217
bladderpod, 83, 83*fig.*
bladderpod, slender, 203–204, 204*fig.*
bladder sage, 67, 68, 68*fig.*
blazing star family, 75, 206
 desert species, **75–76**, 206, 207*figs.*
blazing stars
 giant blazing star, 206, 207*fig.*
 sand blazing star, 197, 206, 207*figs.*

yellowcomet, 206, 207*fig.*
BLM (Bureau of Land Management) lands, 244, 246, 248, 249, 259
blue palo verde, 40, 108, 111, 112*fig.*
Boerhavia, 211
    triquetra, 211–212, 212*fig.*
borage family (Boraginaceae), 35, 175, 189, 192, 193
    desert species, **192**, 230–231, 230*fig.*
bottlebrush primrose, 202–203, 202*fig.*
boundary ephedra, 86, 87*fig.*
Bouteloua
    aristidoides, 213
    barbata, 213, 213*fig.*
boxthorns, **69–71**
Brandegea bigelovii, 125, 125*fig.*
Brassica
    incana, 253
    tournefortii, 253, 253*fig.*
Brassicaceae, 35, 173, 200, 203
    invasive species, 253, 253*fig.*
    native desert species, **79**, 152, 153*fig.*, **203–204**
brickellbushes, 116
    California brickellbush, 116, 117*fig.*
    desert brickellbush, 116
    pungent brickellbush, 117, 117*fig.*
    white brickellbush, 116–117, 117*fig.*
Brickellia, 116
    atractyloides, 117, 117*fig.*
    californica, 116, 117*fig.*
    desertorum, 116
    incana, 116–117, 117*fig.*
bristlecone–limber pine forests, **240–241**
bristlecone pines
    Great Basin bristlecone, **240–241**
    Rocky Mountain bristlecone, 240
bristly langloisia, 195
brittlebush, 46, 46*fig.*, 60, 60*figs.*
brittle sage, 68
brittle spineflower, 205, 205*fig.*
broad-flowered gilia, 194
broad-leaved cattail, 135, 135*fig.*
broad-leaved gilia, 194, 194*fig.*
Bromus
    rubens, 216, 252, 252*fig.*, 254, 255
    tectorum, 224, 252, 252*fig.*, 255
broom baccharis, 118, 118*fig.*
broom-rape family, 200
    desert species, 139, 139*fig.*, **200**

broom snakeweed, 63–64, 64*fig.*, 229–230
brown-eyed primrose, 201*fig.*, 202
buckhorn cholla, 91, 91*fig.*
buckthorn family species, 120–121, 121*figs.*, 233–234, 234*figs.*
buckwheat family, 35, 204
    herbaceous species, 36, 36*fig.*, **204–206**, 207*figs.*
    woody species, 36, 37*fig.*, 82*fig.*, 83, 158, 158*fig.*
buckwheats
    California buckwheat, 81*fig.*, 82
    desert trumpet, 204–205, 205*fig.*
    dune buckwheat, 158, 158*fig.*
    flat-topped buckwheat, 204, 205*fig.*
Buddleja utahensis, 231–232, 231*fig.*
budsage, 146, 148*fig.*
bulbs. *See* geophytes
bulrushes, 135, 135*fig.*
Bureau of Land Management (BLM) lands, 244, 246, 248, 249, 259
burrobush, 114, 115*fig.*
bursage, 59, 59*figs.*
Bursera, 122–123
    microphylla, 123, 123*fig.*
Burseraceae species, 123, 123*fig.*
bush seepweed, 150–151, 151*fig.*
butterflies and moths, 57, 109, 200–201, 208, 209
butterflybush, Utah, 231–232, 231*fig.*
button encelia, 60, 61*fig.*
Buxaceae species, 82–83, 82*fig.*

C_3 metabolism, 48*fig.*, 49
    See also photosynthesis
C_4 metabolism, 48*fig.*, 49, 136, 144, 148, 159, 211, 253
cacti (Cactaceae), 210, 224
    adaptations and strategies of, 40*fig.*, 41, 45, 47–48
    desert species, **90–97**
cactus and succulent scrub, **88–101**
    agaves, nolinas, and yuccas, **54–57**, **98–101**
    cacti, **90–97**
    environmental characteristics and distribution, 89
    See also cacti; *other specific taxa*
Cahuilla Basin, 28–29, 33, 134, 167, 250

    See also Coachella Valley; Imperial Valley; Salton Sea; *other specific locations and features*
Cahuilla people, 128, 150, 243, 250
    See also Native American peoples and cultures
calicos
    desert calico, 195, 195*fig.*
    little calico, 195, 195*fig.*
California barrel cactus, *38*, 45, *88*, 94, 94*fig.*
California brickellbush, 116, 117*fig.*
California buckwheat, 81*fig.*, 82
California chicory, 183
California colubrina, 121, 121*fig.*
California coreopsis, 178
California crossosoma, 82
California Desert Conservation Area, 244
California Desert Conservation Area Plan, 259
California Desert Protection Act (1994), 244, 248–249, 261
California Desert Protection Act (2010), 249
California desert regions. *See* desert regions; Great Basin; Mojave desert; Sonoran desert
California encelia, 60
California ephedra, 85–86, 85*fig.*
California evening primrose, 202*fig.*, 203
California fagonia, 81, 81*fig.*
California fan palm, 40–41, **127–130**
California Floristic Province, 35
California juniper, 222, 222*fig.*, 223*fig.*, 224
California Native Plant Society rare plant classification system, 251
California poppy, 175*fig.*, 183–184
California trixis, 120, 120*fig.*
Calliandra eriophylla, 107–108, 108*fig.*
Calochortaceae, 209
    desert species, 139, 139*fig.*, 209–210, 210*fig.*
Calochortus, 209
    flexuosus, 210
    kennedyi, 209, 210*fig.*
    panamintensis, 210
    striatus, 139, 139*fig.*
Calvin cycle, 49
    See also photosynthesis
Calycoseris
    parryi, 180
    wrightii, 180

CAM (crassulacean acid) metabolism, 47–48, 48*fig.*, 49, 99
Camissonia, 200–201, 202
  campestris, 201, 201*fig.*
Camissoniopsis pallida, 202, 202*fig.*
Canterbury bells, desert, 190, 190*fig.*
canyon live oak, 234, 235*figs.*
caper family (Capparidaceae), 84
  desert species, 83, 83*fig.*
Carlowrightia arizonica, 119–120
Carnegeia gigantea, 47, 97, 97*fig.*
Carrizo Badlands, 11*fig.*
Castela emoryi, 122, 122*fig.*
Castilleja, 200
  angustifolia, 200, 200*fig.*
  exserta, 200, 200*fig.*
Castle Mountain Mine, 258–259
Castle Mountains National Monument, 245*fig.*, 249, 259
catclaw acacia, 107, 107*fig.*
cattails
  broad-leaved cattail, 135, 135*fig.*
  narrow-leaved cattail, 135
Caulanthus inflatus, 204, 204*fig.*
caves, 247
ceanothus, Mojave, 233, 234*fig.*
Ceanothus
  greggii, 233
  pauciflorus, 233, 234*fig.*
Ceratoides lanata. See *Krascheninnikovia lanata*
Cercocarpus, 226
  ledifolius, 224, 226–227, 226*fig.*
  ledifolius var. *intricatus*, 227, 227*fig.*
Chaenactis, 178
  fremontii, 181–182, 182*fig.*
Chaetadelpha wheeleri, 163*fig.*, 164
Chamaebatiaria millefolium, 226, 226*fig.*
Chamaesyce, 213
chaparral, 39, 43
  chaparral annuals, 175
  chaparral elements in Great Basin shrublands and woodlands, **232–236**
chaparral tea, 53
chaparral yucca, 57, 57*fig.*
cheatgrass, 224, 252, 252*fig.*, 255
checker fiddlehead, 192, 192*fig.*
cheeseweed, 114, 115*fig.*
Chemehuevi people, 243, 243*fig.*
  See also Native American peoples and cultures
Chenopodiaceae, 49, 150

invasive Russian thistle, 253–254, 253*fig.*
native desert species, **74**, 130, **143–147**, **150–153**, 217, 217*fig.*, 230
chia, 196, 196*fig.*
chicories
  California chicory, 183
  desert chicory, 182–183, 183*fig.*
Chilopsis linearis, 40, 108–109, 109*fig.*, 160
China Lake, 26*fig.*, 27
China Lake Naval Air Weapons Station, 245*fig.*, 250
chinchweed, 211, 211*figs.*
Chloropyron tecopense, 139, 139*fig.*
Chocolate Mountain Aerial Gunnery Range, 245*fig.*, 251
Chocolate Mountains, 23*fig.*, 28, 89
  rare plants, 68, 68*fig.*, 122
chollas, 90
  buckhorn cholla, 91, 91*fig.*
  matted or horse-crippler cholla, 92–93, 93*fig.*
  pencil cholla, 91, 92*fig.*
  silver or golden cholla, 89, 91, 91*fig.*
  teddy bear cholla, *88*, 90, 91*fig.*
Chorizanthe
  brevicornu, 205, 205*fig.*
  rigida, 205–206, 207*fig.*
Chrysothamnus, 228
  viscidiflorus, 228, 228*fig.*
Chuckwalla Mountains, 23*fig.*, 28, 89, 120
Chylismia
  arenaria, 201
  brevipes, 201, 201*fig.*
  claviformis, 201*fig.*, 202
Cima Dome, Dome fire, 255, 255*fig.*
citrus family species, 80, 80*fig.*
Clark Mountains, 22, 23*fig.*, 236, 238
  notable plants and communities, 209, 231, 231*fig.*, **236–239**
Clark's nutcracker, 224, 240
Cleomaceae species, 152, 153*fig.*
Cleomella obtusifolia, 152, 153*fig.*
cliffbush, five-petal, 231, 231*fig.*
cliff goldenbush, 227, 228*fig.*
cliffrose, 225, 225*fig.*
climate, 10–13, 32–35, 41–42
  California Sonoran Desert, 12, 19, 28–29, 30, 32*fig.*, 34, 35, 41
  climate change impacts and vulnerabilities, 56, 254

climate cycles and dune dynamics, 157
cold vs. warm deserts, 30
Great Basin, 12, 19, 30, 32*fig.*, 33, 34, 35
Mojave Desert, 12, 19, 30, 32*fig.*, 33–34, 41
rainfall amounts and timing, 10, 13, 30, 32*fig.*, 33, 41, 209, 211
temperatures, 12, 19, 30, 32*fig.*, 33, 41
See also plant adaptations and strategies
climbing milkweed, 208, 208*fig.*
Coachella Canal, 29
Coachella Valley, 28, 29
  climate, 33, 34
  non-native plants and other human impacts, 253, 257, 259
  palm oases in, 127, 129
  sand dunes, **166**, 259
Coachella Valley milkvetch, 166, 166*fig.*
Coachella Valley Preserve, 166
coffeeberry, hoary, 234, 234*fig.*
Coleogyne ramosissima, 215*fig.*, 216, 216*fig.*
Colorado Desert, 28
  See also Sonoran Desert
Colorado pinyon, 220, 221*figs.*
Colorado River, 26*fig.*, 27, 28, 29, 131*fig.*, 168
  associated riparian and wetland habitats, 130, 256
  diversions, 29, 244
Colubrina californica, 121, 121*fig.*
common reed, 135, 135*fig.*
Condalia, 121
  globosa, 121, 121*fig.*
Condea emoryi, 113–114, 114*fig.*
conifers, 84
  See also bristlecone–limber pine forests; pinyon-juniper woodlands; white fir–pinyon woodland; *specific taxa*
conservation issues, 251–261
  conflicting management objectives, 244, 246
  fire, **254–255**
  groundwater depletion and riparian habitat loss, 132, 256, 258, 261
  invasive plants, 35, **252–254**, **255–256**, 258
  livestock grazing, 261
  mining, **258–259**
  off-road vehicle use, 259, 259*fig.*

solar and wind power development, 260*figs*., 261
urbanization and residential/resort development, **256–257**
See also human impacts
Convolvulaceae species, 152, 153*fig.*
Cooper dyssodia, 65, 65*fig.*
Cooper goldenbush, 62, 62*fig.*
Cooper's paper daisy, 115–116, 116*fig.*
Cooper's rush, 138, 138*fig.*
copperwort, 136, 138, 138*fig.*
Coreopsis. See *Leptosyne*
coreopsis
    Bigelow's coreopsis, 178, 179*fig.*
    California coreopsis, 178
    leafy-stemmed coreopsis, 177–178, 179*fig.*
Coryphantha vivipara, 96, 96*fig.*
cottonthorns, 63, 228–229
    Mojave cottonthorn, 63, 63*fig.*
    See also horsebrushes
cotton-top cactus, 94, 95*fig.*
cottonwoods, 41, 132, 255, 256, 258
    Fremont cottonwood, 130, 133*figs.*
Coves' senna, 113
coyote melon, 125, 125*fig.*
coyotes, 224
coyote willow, 130, 132, 133*figs.*
Crassulaceae, 48
    See also succulents
crassulacean acid (CAM) metabolism, 47–48, 48*fig.*, 49, 99
creambush, small-leaved, 237, 237*fig.*
creosote bush, **50–53**, 59, 142*fig.*, 143, 160, 165
    adaptations and strategies of, 39–40, 40*fig.*, 43*fig.*, 45, 52
    creosote bush scrub and Joshua tree woodlands, **50–87**
    around playas, 142*fig.*, 143
    blazing star family shrubs, **75–76**
    chenopods, 74
    creosote bush, **50–53**
    environmental characteristics and distribution, 51, 217
    Ephedra sp., 47, **84–87**
    fire in, 56, 61, **254–255**
    hibiscus family subshrubs, 78
    invasive grasses in, 254
    Joshua tree and other yuccas, 51, **54–57**
    legume family shrubs and subshrubs, **71–73**
    mustard family subshrubs, **79**
    other shrub species, **80–84**
    perennial grasses, 158–159, 158*fig.*, 159*fig.*
    rose family shrubs, 77
    sages, **67–68**
    spiny boxthorns, **69–71**
    sunflower family shrubs and subshrubs, **58–66**
    See also annuals and herbaceous perennials; creosote bush; Joshua tree
Cressa truxillensis, 152, 153*fig.*
Crossosoma
    bigelovii, 81*fig.*, 82
    californica, 82
crossosomas
    Bigelow's crossosoma, 81*fig.*, 82
    California crossosoma, 82
Crossosomataceae species, 81*fig.*, 82
Croton
    californicus, 159–160, 159*fig.*
    wigginsii, 160
crotons
    sand croton, 159–160, 159*fig.*
    Wiggin's croton, 160
crown-of-thorns, 121–122, 122*fig.*
crucifixion thorn, 122, 122*fig.*
Crucifixion Thorn Natural Area, 122
Cryptantha, 35, 192
    barbigera, 192*fig.*
cryptobiotic crusts, 148
Crystal Spring, 126, 137*fig.*
Cucurbita, 45
    digitata, 125
    palmata, 125, 125*fig.*
Cucurbitaceae, 125
    desert species, 125, 125*figs.*
Cupressaceae species, **220–224**
curl-leaf mountain mahogany, 224, 226–227, 226*fig.*
cyanobacteria, 148
Cylindropuntia, 90
    acanthocarpa, 91, 91*fig.*
    bigelovii, 88, 90, 91*fig.*
    echinocarpa, 91, 91*fig.*
    ramosissima, 91, 92*fig.*
Cyperaceae, 49, 135
    desert species, 135, 135*fig.*

daisies
    Emory rock daisy, 180, 182*fig.*
    nakedstem sunray, 176, 177*fig.*
    Panamint daisy, 176, 177*fig.*
    Pringle's woolly daisy, 177, 178*fig.*
    Wallace's woolly daisy, 177, 178*fig.*
    See also Asteraceae
Dalea, 71
    mollis, 186–187
    mollissima, 186, 186*fig.*
daleas
    hairy prairie clover, 186–187
    Parry dalea, 187
    silky dalea, 186, 186*fig.*
Danaus gilippus strigosus, 208
Danaus plexippus, 208
dandelions
    desert dandelion, *170*, 180, 181*fig.*
    yellow tack-stem dandelion, 180
dark red onion, 210
date palms, 253
death camas, 210
Death Valley ephedra, 85*fig.*, 86
Death Valley golden-eye, 61–62
Death Valley monkeyflower, 199, 199*fig.*
Death Valley region/Death Valley National Park, 10, 18, 21*fig.*, 23, *50*
    ancient lakes, 26*fig.*, 27–28
    annuals and herbaceous perennials, 36, 36–37*figs.*, 171*fig.*, 176, 177*fig.*, 182, 182*fig.*, 199, 199*fig.*, 205
    dune areas, 25, 155*fig.*, 157, **163–165**
    illegal off-road vehicle use, 259*fig.*
    landforms, 14–17*figs.*, 24*figs.*, 26–27*figs.*, 246–247
    map, 245*fig.*
    national monument/park establishment and management, 244, **246–247**
    playas, 141*fig.*, 142*fig.*
    rare and endemic plants, 36, 36–37*figs.*, 67, 67*fig.*, 75, 198, 199, 199*fig.*, 205
    springs and wetlands, 134, *134*
    temperatures, 32*fig.*, 33
    See also Badwater Basin; Saline Valley; *other specific locations and features*
Death Valley sage, 67, 67*fig.*
Death Valley sandpaper plant, 75
Dedeckera, 36
    eurekensis, 37*fig.*

deer, 219
desert agave, 98*figs.*, 99
desert almond, 77, 109, 110*fig.*
desert apricot, 77, 77*fig.*
desert baccharis, 118, 118*fig.*
desert barberry, 232, 232*fig.*
desert brickellbush, 116
desert calico, 195, 195*fig.*
desert candle, 204, 204*fig.*
desert Canterbury bells, 190, 190*fig.*
desert chicory, 182–183, 183*fig.*
desert dandelion, *170*, 180, 181*fig.*
desert ecological communities
    cactus and succulent scrub, **88–101**
    community-level conservation, 251
    creosote bush scrub and Joshua tree woodlands, **50–87**
    desert wetlands, **126–139**
    flowering annuals and herbaceous perennials, **170–213**
    geological influences on, 13–17
    Great Basin shrublands and woodlands, **214–241**
    habitat mosaics, viii–ix
    saline habitats, **140–153**
    sand dunes, **154–169**
    wash woodlands and arroyos, **102–125**
    See also specific communities and habitats
desert environments. *See* environmental conditions
desert gold poppy, 183*fig.*, 184
desert gooseberry, 237, 238, 238*fig.*
desert holly, 74, 146, 147*fig.*
desert ironwood, 40, 108, 108*fig.*, 168
desert lantern, 160, 160*fig.*, 161*fig.*
desert lavender, 113–114, 114*fig.*
desert lily, 161, 162*fig.*, 209
desert lupine, 185–186, 185*fig.*
desert marigold, 178, 179*fig.*
desert mariposa lily, 209, 210*fig.*
desert milkweed, 208, 208*fig.*
desert paintbrush, 200, 200*fig.*
desert panic grass, 158–159, 159*fig.*
desert pavement, 16, 17*fig.*, 178
desert peach, 77, 77*fig.*
desert peppergrass, 78, 78*fig.*
desert pincushion, 181–182, 182*fig.*
desert pupfish, *126*, 134
desert regions, **18–37**
    climate regimes, 30, 32–35, 32*fig.*

First Peoples in, 243
    Great Basin overview, **29–30**
    map, 20*fig.*
    Mojave Desert overview, **19–28**
    plant diversity and endemism, 35–36
    Sonoran Desert overview, **28–29**
    See also specific regions
desert rhubarb, 206, 207*fig.*
desert rock pea, 72, 73*fig.*, 189
desert sage, 68
    See also sages
desert sand verbena, 160–161, 161*figs.*
desert scrub oak, 234, 235*figs.*
desert spurge, 213
    See also spurges
desert stars, 181, 182*fig.*
desert starvine, 125, 125*fig.*
desert sunflower (*Bahiopsis parishii*), 61–62, 61*fig.*
desert sunflower (*Geraea canescens*), 171*fig.*, 176, 177*fig.*
desert tea, 85–86, 85*fig.*
desert thorn, 70, 71*fig.*
desert trumpet, 204–205, 205*fig.*
desert twinbugs, 161–162, 161*fig.*
desert varnish, 16
desert wetlands, **126–139**
    alkaline seasonal wetlands, **136–139**, 152
    environmental characteristics and plant adaptations, 16, 40–41, 45, 47, 127
    grazing impacts, 261
    groundwater depletion and its impacts, 132, 256, 258, 261
    invasive trees in, 132, 134, **255–256**, 258
    marshlands and springs, 16, 25, 29, *125*, **134–139**
    palm oases, 40–41, **127–130**, 145, 250
    rare annuals and herbaceous perennials, **136**, **138–139**
    riparian woodlands, 40, **130–134**, 248, 255–256, 258
desert-willow, 40, 108–109, 109*fig.*, 160
desert woollystar, 195, 195*fig.*
devil's claws
    pink devil's claw, 212–213, 213*fig.*
    yellow devil's claw, 212–213
devil's lettuce, 192, 192*fig.*
devil's spineflower, 205–206, 207*fig.*

Dicoria canescens, 161–162, 161*fig.*
Diplacus
    bigelovii, 199, 199*fig.*
    mohavensis, 199, 199*fig.*
    rupicola, 199, 199*fig.*
Distichlis spicata, 136, 148, 149*fig.*
Dithyrea californica, 203, 204*fig.*
drought and drought stress, 41–42
    See also plant adaptations and strategies; rainfall
drought deciduousness, 39–40, 51–52, 104, 113
dry lakes. *See* playas; *specific dry lakes*
dune broom, 163*fig.*, 164
dune buckwheat, 158, 158*fig.*
dune complexes and communities. *See* sand dunes
dune evening primrose, 160, 160*fig.*, 161*fig.*, 203, 203*fig.*
dwarf conifer woodlands. *See* pinyon-juniper woodlands
dye plants, 71, 121, 151
Dyssodia, 66
dyssodias
    Cooper dyssodia, 65, 65*fig.*
    San Felipe dyssodia, 65

Echinocactus polycephalus, 94, 95*fig.*
Echinocereus
    engelmannii, 94, 95*fig.*
    mojavensis, 95, 95*fig.*
ecological strategies. *See* plant adaptations and strategies
Edwards Air Force Base, 21, 143*fig.*, 217, 245*fig.*, 250
Elaeagnaceae. *See Elaeagnus angustifolius*
Elaeagnus angustifolius, 132, 134, 256, 256*fig.*
elephant tree, 123, 123*fig.*
Emmenanthe penduliflora, 191, 191*fig.*
Emory indigo bush, 72
Emory rock daisy, 180, 182*fig.*
Encelia, 61, 176
    actoni, 61, 61*fig.*
    californica, 60
    farinosa, 46, 46*fig.*, 60, 60*figs.*
    frutescens, 60, 61*fig.*
    virgenensis, 61
encelias
    Acton encelia, 61, 61*fig.*
    button encelia, 60, 61*fig.*
    California encelia, 60
    Virgin River encelia, 61
Enceliopsis
    covillei, 176, 177*fig.*
    nudicaulis, 176, 177*fig.*
endemism and endemic plants, 35–36

Death Valley endemics, 36,
    36–37*figs.*, 67, 67*fig.*,
    205
  dune endemics, 163–164,
    164*figs.*, 168–169,
    168*fig.*, 169*fig.*, 209
  trees and shrubs, 67, 67*fig.*,
    240, 241, 241*fig.*
  wetlands endemics, 138,
    139*fig.*
  See also rare, threatened, or
    endangered plants
energy development, 260*figs.*, 261
environmental conditions, **10–17**
  climate factors, 10–13, 30,
    32–35
  ephemeral blooms and,
    171–173
  landforms and geological
    factors, 13–17
  See also climate; landforms
    and topography;
    plant adaptations
    and strategies; soils;
    *specific communities
    and habitats*
Ephedra, 47, **84–87**
  aspera, 86, 87*fig.*
  californica, 85–86, 85*fig.*
  fasciculata, 86
  funerea, 85*fig.*, 86
  nevadensis, 86–87, 87*fig.*
  torreyana, 86
  trifurca, 86, 86*fig.*
  viridis, 87, 232, 232*fig.*
Ephedraceae. *See Ephedra*
ephedras, 47, **84–87**
  boundary ephedra, 86, 87*fig.*
  California ephedra, 85–86,
    85*fig.*
  green ephedra, 87, 232,
    232*fig.*
  longleaf ephedra, 86, 86*fig.*
  Nevada ephedra, 86–87,
    87*fig.*
ephemerals. *See* annuals and
  herbaceous perennials
Eremalche rotundifolia, 45*fig.*
Eremothera boothii, 202–203,
  202*fig.*
Eriastrum, 195
  eremicum, 195, 195*fig.*
Ericaceae species, 233, 233*fig.*
Ericameria, 62, 118, 228
  cooperi, 62, 62*fig.*
  cuneata, 227, 228*fig.*
  laricifolia, 227–228, 228*fig.*
  linearifolia, 62, 62*fig.*, 228
  nauseosa, 219, 219*fig.*
  palmeri, 62
  paniculata, 62, 118, 119*fig.*
  pinifolia, 62

Eriodictyon angustifolium,
  230–231, 230*fig.*
Eriogonum, 35, 204, 205
  deflexum, 204, 205*fig.*
  desericola, 158, 158*fig.*
  fasciculatum var. *polifolium*,
    81*fig.*, 82
  inflatum, 204–205, 205*fig.*
Eriophyllum, 176
  pringlei, 177, 178*fig.*
  wallacei, 177, 178*fig.*
Erodium cicutarium, 253
Erythranthe guttata, 198, 198*fig.*
Eschscholtz, Johann Friedrich
  Gustav von, 183–184
Eschscholzia
  californica, 175*fig.*, 183–184
  glyptosperma, 183*fig.*, 184
  minutiflora, 183*fig.*, 184
  parishii, 184
Eucnide urens, 76, 76*fig.*
Euphorbia, 48, 213
  albomarginata, 213, 213*fig.*
  micromera, 213
Euphorbiaceae species, 159–160,
  159*fig.*, 213, 213*fig.*
Euphrosyne acerosa, 136, 138,
  138*fig.*
Eureka Dunes, 25, 155*fig.*, 157,
  163–164
Eureka Valley, 163, 246
Eureka Valley dune grass, 37*fig.*,
  163, 163*fig.*
Eureka Valley evening primrose,
  163–164, 163*fig.*
Eurotia lanata. *See Krascheninnikovia lanata*
evening primrose family, 200
  desert species, 160, 160*fig.*,
    161*fig.*, 163–164,
    163*fig.*, **200–203**
evening primroses, **200–203**
  bottlebrush primrose,
    202–203, 202*fig.*
  brown-eyed primrose, 201*fig.*,
    202
  California evening primrose,
    202*fig.*, 203
  dune evening primrose or
    birdcage primrose,
    160, 160*fig.*, 161*fig.*,
    203, 203*fig.*
  Eureka Valley evening primrose, 163–164, 163*fig.*
  golden evening primrose,
    201, 201*fig.*
  Mojave sun cup, 201, 201*fig.*
  pale primrose, 202, 202*fig.*
  sand evening primrose, 201
  yellow evening primrose, 203,
    203*fig.*
evening snow, 193, 193*fig.*

Fabaceae, 35, 40, 46, 47, 71
  annuals and herbaceous perennials, 164, 164*fig.*,
    166, 166*fig.*, 168,
    168*fig.*, 174, **184–189**
  woody species, **71–73**, 103,
    105–108
Fagonia
  laevis, 81, 81*fig.*
  pachyacantha, 81
fagonias
  California fagonia, 81, 81*fig.*
  sticky fagonia, 81
fairyduster, 107–108, 108*fig.*
Fallugia paradoxa, 225–226,
  225*fig.*
fan palms
  California fan palm, 40–41,
    127–130
  Mexican fan palm, 127–128
  See also palm oases
federal lands. *See* public lands;
  *specific parks, monuments,
  and preserves*
Fendlerella utahensis, 231, 231*fig.*
fern bush, 226, 226*fig.*
Ferocactus cylindraceus, 38, 45, 88,
  94, 94*fig.*
fertile islands, 53, 53*fig.*
fiddlehead, checker, 192, 192*fig.*
filaree, redstem, 253
finger-leaved gourd, 125
fire, **254–255**
  in creosote bush scrub
    and Joshua tree
    woodlands, 56, 61,
    254–255
  fire-following annuals, 175,
    191, 191*fig.*
  in Great Basin communities,
    216, 218, 219, 224,
    255
  invasive grasses and, 55, 216,
    224, 253, 254, 255
  palms and, 128, 128*fig.*
First Peoples. *See* Native American
  peoples and cultures
fir, white, 238, 239*fig.*
fish, *126*, 134
fishhook cacti, 96–97, 96*fig.*,
  97*figs.*
five-needle prickly-leaf, 66, 66*fig.*
five-petal cliffbush, 231, 231*fig.*
flat-topped buckwheat, 204,
  205*fig.*
flooding, 103, 103*fig.*, 114
  See also wash woodlands and
    arroyos
flowering annuals and herbaceous
  perennials. *See* annuals and
  herbaceous perennials
food and forage plants
  boxthorns, 69

chia, 196
evening primroses, 200–201
four-wing saltbush, 146
honey mesquite, 106–107
iodine bush, 150
palms, 129
pinyon pines, 224
redstem filaree, 253
sand food, 162
Utah serviceberry, 236–237
winterfat, 230
yuccas and nolinas, 57, 100
foothill vetch, 189
Fort Irwin National Training Center, 245*fig.*, 250
Fouquieria, 124, 250
  splendens, 123–124, 124*fig.*
Fouquieriaceae. See *Fouquieria*
four-o'clock family, 211
  desert species, 160–161, 161*figs.*, 211–212, 212*fig.*
four-wing saltbush, 146, 147*fig.*, 217, 230
foxtail pine, 240
Frangula californica subsp. *ursina*, 234, 234*fig.*
Frankenia salina, 149, 149*fig.*
Fraxinus
  anomala, 237, 237*fig.*
  velutina, 132, 134*fig.*
freckled milkvetch, 188
Fremont cottonwood, 130, 133*figs.*
Fremont desert thorn, 70, 71*fig.*
Fremont indigo bush, 71–72
Fremont phacelia, 190
Fremont's barberry, 232, 232*fig.*
Fremont's chaff-bush, 66, 66*fig.*
fringed amaranth, 212, 212*fig.*
fringed desert onion, 210, 210*fig.*
frost, 34, 104, 173
Funastrum
  cynanchoides, 208, 208*fig.*
  utahense, 208

Garryaceae. See *Garrya*
Garrya flavescens, 236, 236*fig.*
geological setting and processes, 13–17, 30
  See also landforms; Pleistocene lakes and rivers; soils
geophytes, 39*fig.*, 161, 162*fig.*, **209–210**
Geraea canescens, 171*fig.*, 176, 177*fig.*
ghost flower, 197–198, 197*fig.*
giant blazing star, 206, 207*fig.*
giant saguaro *Carnegeia gigantea*, 47, 97, 97*fig.*
giant Spanish needle, 169, 169*fig.*

Gilia latiflora, 194
gilias, 194
  broad-flowered gilia, 194
  broad-leaved gilia, 194, 194*fig.*
Gilmania, 36
  luteola, 36–37*fig.*, 205
glasswort, Pacific, 150
goldenbushes
  alkali goldenbush, 146, 148*fig.*
  Cooper goldenbush, 62, 62*fig.*
  interior goldenbush, 62, 62*fig.*, 228
  Palmer goldenbush, 62
  wedgeleaf or cliff goldenbush, 227, 228*fig.*
  See also rabbitbrushes
golden carpet, 36–37*fig.*, 205
golden evening primrose, 201, 201*fig.*
golden-eyes, 61–62, 61*fig.*
goldenheads, 64–65, 64*fig.*
golden linanthus, 194, 194*fig.*
golden or silver cholla, 91, 91*fig.*
goldfields, 176, 177*fig.*
gold mining, 258–259
Goodding's black willow, 130, 132, 133*fig.*
gooseberry, desert, 237, 238, 238*fig.*
goosefoot family, 49, 150
  invasive Russian thistle, 253–254, 253*fig.*
  native desert species, 74, 130, **143–147, 150–153**, 217, 217*fig.*, 230
gourd family, 125
  desert species, 125, 125*figs.*
grama grasses, 213
  needle grama, 213
  six-weeks grama, 213, 213*fig.*
Granite Mountains, 22, 31*fig.*, 89*fig.*, 102, 224, 233
granites and granitic soils, 13, 14*fig.*, 248
  associated cacti and succulents, 62, 62*fig.*, 98*fig.*, 99, 217
  associated plant communities, 217, 222, 224, 233
  associated woody species, 62, 62*fig.*, 217, 218–219, 219*fig.*, 230, 236, 236*fig.*, 255
grass family, 35
  C_4 metabolism in, 49, 136, 148, 159, 213
  dune species, 37*fig.*, **158–159**, 163, 163*fig.*

invasive grasses, 55, 173, 216, **252–253**, 254, 255, 261
native annual species, 173, 213, 213*figs.*
saltgrass, 148, 149*fig.*
wetlands species, 135, 135*fig.*
gravel ghost, 182, 182*fig.*
Grayia spinosa, 74, 74*fig.*, 146, 217
graythorn, 120, 121*fig.*
grazing, 64, 183, 192, 219, 244, 255, 261
  See also food and forage plants; toxic plants
greasewood, 151–152, 153*fig.*
Great Basin, 12, 12*fig.*, 13, **29–30**
  climate, 12, 19, 30, 32*fig.*, 33, 34, 35
  topography and landforms, 19, 29–30
  See also specific communities, habitats and locations
Great Basin bristlecone pine, **240–241**
Great Basin sagebrush, 218–219, 219*fig.*, 255
Great Basin shrublands and woodlands, 22, 23, 30, **214–241**
  blackbrush scrub, **215–216**, 255
  bristlecone–limber pine forests, **240–241**
  California endemics, 36, 37*fig.*, 240, 241, 241*fig.*
  chaparral elements, **232–236**
  environmental characteristics and subcommunity types, 29–30, 215, 233
  fire in, 216, 218, 219, 224, 255
  pinyon-juniper woodlands, 30, *214*, 217, **220–232**
  sagebrush steppe, 30, 31*fig.*, 216, **217–219**, 255
  shadscale scrub, 30, **216–217**
  white fir–pinyon woodland, **236–239**
  See also annuals and herbaceous perennials; pinyon-juniper woodlands
green ephedra, 87, 232, 232*fig.*
green molly, 217
green rabbitbrush, 228, 228*fig.*
Greenwater Valley, *50*
Grindelia fraxinipratensis, 138, 139*fig.*
Grossulariaceae species, 237–238, 238*figs.*

groundwater availability and depletion. *See* desert wetlands; water resources and availability
Grusonia, 90
　parishii, 92–93, 93*fig.*
　pulchella, 93
gumplant, Ash Meadows, 138, 139*fig.*
Gutierrezia, 64
　microcephala, 63–64
　sarothrae, 63–64, 64*fig.*, 229–230
gymnosperms. *See* conifers; *Ephedra*; *specific conifer taxa*

habitat types. *See* desert ecological communities; *specific communities and habitats*
hairy prairie clover, 186–187
hawk moth, 209
Hedeoma nanum, 196
hedgehog cactus, 94, 95*fig.*
Helianthus
　niveus subsp. *canescens*, 168
　niveus subsp. *tephrodes*, 168–169, 169*fig.*
hemiparasites. *See* parasitic and hemiparasitic plants
herbaceous plants. *See* annuals and herbaceous perennials
Hesperocallis undulata, 161, 162*fig.*, 209
Hesperoyucca whipplei, 57, 57*fig.*
hibiscus family species, 78
Hilaria rigida, 158–159, 158*fig.*
hoary coffeeberry, 234, 234*fig.*
Hoffmannseggia, 111, 113
　glauca, 113
　microphylla, 113, 113*fig.*
hollyleaf bursage, 114
hollyleaf redberry, 234, 234*fig.*
Holmgrenanthe, 36, 197
　petrophila, 36–37*fig.*, 198
Holodiscus discolor, 237, 237*fig.*
honey mesquite, 105–106, 105*fig.*, 106*fig.*, 132, 158
honey-sweet, 212, 212*fig.*
hopsage, 74, 74*fig.*, 146, 217
horsebrushes, 63, 228–229
　long-spine horsebrush, 229, 229*fig.*
　spineless horsebrush, 229, 229*fig.*
　striped horsebrush, 229
　See also cottonthorns
horse-crippler cholla, 92–93, 93*fig.*
Horsfordia
　alata, 78, 78*fig.*
　newberryi, 78
Hosackia, 189

human impacts
　agriculture and grazing, 28, 29, 64, 106, 244, 255, 257, 261
　on desert wetlands, 132, 255–256, 261
　First Peoples settlements and practices, 243
　history of, 243–244
　mining, 243, 258–259, 258*fig.*
　off-road vehicle use, 168, 259, 259*fig.*
　on pinyon-juniper woodlands, 224
　urbanization and residential/resort development, 19, 244, **256–257**
　See also conservation issues; invasive plants; land ownership and management; Native American peoples and cultures
hummingbirds, 119
Hydrangeaceae species, 230–231, 230*fig.*, 231*figs.*
hydrology
　ancient lakes and rivers of desert regions, 19, 25, 26*fig.*, 27–28, 30, 141
　runoff patterns and processes, 15–16, 19, 25, 27, 103, 141, 259
　See also lakes; rivers; water resources and availability; *specific lakes and rivers*
Hydrophyllaceae, 35, 175, 189, 193
　desert species, **189–191**

Ibex Dunes, 163
Imperial Dunes. *See* Algodones Dunes
Imperial Valley/Imperial County, 28, 29, 244, 257
Indian rice grass, 159, 159*fig.*
indigo bushes, 71
　Emory indigo bush, 72
　Fremont indigo bush, 71–72
　Mojave indigo bush, 71, 73*fig.*
　Nevada or spotted indigo bush, 72, 73*fig.*
　Scott indigo bush, 72, 73*fig.*
ink-blite, 150–151, 151*fig.*
interior goldenbush, 62, 62*fig.*, 228
invasive plants, 35, **252–254**
　fire and, 55, 216, 224, 253, 254, 255

grasses, 55, 173, 216, **252–253**, 254, 255, 261
trees in riparian and other wet areas, 132, 134, **255–256**, 258
Inyo Mountains, 22, 23*fig.*, 29, *140*
　conifers in, 240, 241
　endemic plants, 36, 37*fig.*
　Joshua tree in, 54
　plant communities, 216, 218, 238
iodine bush, 150, 150*fig.*, 151, 151*fig.*
ironwood, desert, 40, 108, 108*fig.*, 168
Isocoma acradenia, 146, 148*fig.*
Ivanpah Range, 22, 99, 223*fig.*
Ivanpah solar development, 260*fig.*
Ives phacelia, 191

Jamesia americana, 231, 231*fig.*
Jepson Desert Manual, The, 35
jojoba, 82–83, 82*fig.*
Joshua tree, 21, 21*fig.*, 34*fig.*, 51, 51*fig.*, **54–56**, 57, 248, 254*fig.*
Joshua Tree National Park, 13, 14*fig.*, 21, 90, 174*fig.*, *242*
　establishment and management, 244, **247–248**
　fire in, 254*fig.*, 255
　map, 245*fig.*
　See also Joshua tree; Joshua tree woodlands
Joshua tree woodlands, 51, **54–56**
　See also creosote bush scrub and Joshua tree woodlands
jujube, Parry's, 120–121
Juncaceae species, 138, 138*fig.*
Juncus cooperi, 138, 138*fig.*
junipers
　California juniper, 222, 222*fig.*, 223*fig.*, 224
　Utah juniper, 218*fig.*, 220, 222, 222*fig.*, 223*figs.*, 224, 238
　western juniper, 220*fig.*
Juniperus
　californica, 222, 222*fig.*, 223*fig.*, 224
　occidentalis, 220*fig.*
　osteosperma, 218*fig.*, 220, 222, 222*fig.*, 223*figs.*, 238
Justicia californica, 119, 120*fig.*

Kelso Dunes, 25, 25*fig.*, *154*, 157, **165**, 209
King Clone creosote bush, 52, 53*fig.*

Kingston Range, 22, 23*fig.*, 101*fig.*
  notable plants and communities, **217–219**, 228, 228*fig.*, 231, 231*fig.*, **236–239**
Kochia americana, 217
Koeberlinia spinosa, 121–122, 122*fig.*
Krameria, 80, 81
  bicolor, 80, 81
  erecta, 80, 80*fig.*, 81
Krascheninnikovia lanata, 74, 74*fig.*, 146, 217, 230

lace-leaf phacelia, 189–190, 190*fig.*
Lake Cahuilla, 28, 29, 168
Lake Manix, 26*fig.*, 27
Lake Manley, 26*fig.*, 27–28
Lake Mojave. See Soda Lake
lakes, 19, 25, 26–27*figs.*, 27–28, 29, 30
  See also playas; *specific lakes by name*
Lake Thompson, 19, 26*fig.*
Lamiaceae, 68, 196
  desert species, **67–68**, 113–114, 114*fig.*, **196**
landforms and topography, **13–17**, 25, 25*fig.*, 29
  bajadas, 15–16, 16*fig.*, 19, 103
  basin and range topography, 22–23, 30
  California Sonoran Desert, 28–29
  Great Basin, 29–30
  Mojave Desert, 19, 21–28
  playas, 16, 19, **141–142**, 217
  rain shadows, 12–13, 28, 33
  sand dune dynamics and structure, **155–157**
  washes, 16, 17*fig.*, 102, 103
  See also specific features and locations
land ownership and management
  early mining, ranching, and water supply development, 243–244
  military lands and management, 244, 245*fig.*, 246, 250–251, 259
  protected public lands, 244, 245*fig.*, 246–250, 259
  Tribal lands, 250
  urbanization and residential/resort development, 19, 244, **256–257**
  See also conservation issues; human impacts
Langloisia setosissima, 194–195, 194*fig.*

Larrea
  cuneifolia, 51
  divaricata, 51
  tridentata, 39–40, 40*fig.*, 43*fig.*, 45, **50–53**, 59, 142*fig.*, 143, 160, 165
  See also creosote bush scrub
Lasthenia californica, 176, 177*fig.*
lax flower, 178
Layia, 180
  glandulosa, 180, 181*fig.*
Layne milkvetch, 187, 187*fig.*
leafy-stemmed coreopsis, 177–178, 179*fig.*
legume family, 35, 40, 46, 47, 71
  annuals and herbaceous perennials, 164, 164*fig.*, 166, 166*fig.*, 168, 168*fig.*, 174, **184–189**
  woody species, **71–73**, 103, **105–108**
Lennoaceae species, 162, 162*figs.*
Lepidium
  flavum, 152, 153*fig.*, 204
  fremontii, 78, 78*fig.*
Lepidospartum squamatum, 118–119, 119*fig.*
Leptosiphon, 193
  aureus, 194, 194*fig.*
  breviculus, 194
Leptosyne, 177
  bigelovii, 178, 179*fig.*
  californica, 178
  calliopsidea, 177–178, 179*fig.*
lesser mojavea, 198
lichens, 148
lilac sunbonnet, 194–195, 194*fig.*
lilies. *See* desert lily; mariposa lilies
lily family, 98, 209
  desert species, 139, 139*fig.*, 209–210, 210*fig.*
limber pine, 240*figs.*, 241
limestones and limestone soils, 13, 233, 247
  associated cacti and succulents, 96, 96*figs.*, 99, 100*fig.*
  associated herbaceous species, 36, 36–37*fig.*
  associated woody species, 67, 67*fig.*, 227, 227*fig.*, 230, 230*fig.*, 231–232, 231*figs.*
linanthus
  golden linanthus, 194, 194*fig.*
  Mojave linanthus, 194
  sand blossoms, 193, 193*fig.*
Linanthus, 193
  dichotomus, 193, 193*fig.*
  parryae, 193, 193*fig.*
linear-leaf sandpaper plant, 76
little calico, 195, 195*fig.*

little gold poppy, 183*fig.*, 184
little-leaf mock orange, 230*fig.*, 231
little-leaf palo verde, 111, 112*fig.*
little-leaved mountain mahogany, 227, 227*fig.*
Little San Bernardino Mountains, 21, 28, 36, 89, 248
livestock
  grazing and ranching, 64, 192, 219, 244, 255, 261
  plants toxic to, 63–64, 79, 152, 187, 192, 218, 229–230
Loasaceae, 75, 206
  desert species, **75–76**, 206, 207*figs.*
locoweeds, 35, 164
  Newberry locoweed, 188
  scarlet locoweed, 188, 188*fig.*
  See also milkvetches
Loeseliastrum
  matthewsii, 195, 195*fig.*
  schottii, 195, 195*fig.*
longleaf ephedra, 86, 86*fig.*
long-spine horsebrush, 229, 229*fig.*
Los Angeles Aqueduct, 244
lotebush, 120–121
Lotus, 188–189
lotuses
  bird's foot lotus, 189
  stiff-haired lotus, 188*fig.*, 189
lupines, 185
  Arizona lupine, 185, 185*fig.*
  bajada lupine, 186, 186*fig.*
  desert lupine, 185–186, 185*fig.*
  Mojave lupine, 186, 186*fig.*
Lupinus, 185
  arizonicus, 185, 185*fig.*
  concinnus, 186, 186*fig.*
  odoratus, 186, 186*fig.*
  shockleyi, 185–186, 185*fig.*
Lycium, 69
  andersonii, 69, 69*fig.*
  brevipes, 70, 71*fig.*
  cooperi, 70, 70*fig.*
  fremontii, 70, 71*fig.*
  pallidum, 70
  parishii, 70
  torreyi, 70

Malacothrix glabrata, 170, 180, 181*fig.*
mallow family (Malvaceae) species, **78**
Mammillaria, 96
  dioica, 96–97, 97*fig.*
  grahamii, 97
  tetrancistra, 96, 97*fig.*

manzanita, pointleaf, 233, 233*fig.*
maple, mountain, 237, 237*fig.*
maps
    desert land ownership and management, 245*fig.*
    desert regions, 20*fig.*
    Joshua tree distribution, 55*fig.*
    juniper distribution, 222*fig.*
    Mojave and Sonoran Desert mountain ranges, 23*fig.*
    pinyon pine distribution, 221*fig.*
    Pleistocene lakes and rivers of the Mojave, 26*fig.*
Marina parryi, 187
mariposa lilies, 209
    alkali mariposa lily, 139, 139*fig.*, 210
    desert mariposa lily, 209, 210*fig.*
    Panamint mariposa lily, 210
    twining mariposa lily, 210
marshlands, 29, **134–139**
    See also desert wetlands
Martyniaceae species, 212–213, 213*fig.*
matchweed. *See* snakeweeds
matted cholla, 92–93, 93*fig.*
mealy rosette, 178, 180
Mecca woody-aster, 65
medicinal plant uses
    alkali goldenbush, 146, 148
    creosote bush, 53
    ephedra, 84
    pinyon pines, 224
    rattlesnake weed, 213
    snakeweeds, 63–64
    turpentine broom, 80
    turtleback, 180
    yerba santa, 231
Mediterranean climates, 13, 30
Mediterranean schismus, 252–253
Melianthaceae species, 210
Menodora spinescens, 84–85, 85*fig.*
Mentzelia, 206
    affinis, 206, 207*fig.*
    involucrata, 197, 206, 207*figs.*
    laevicaulis, 206, 207*fig.*
Mesquite Dry Lake, 158*fig.*
Mesquite Dunes, 163, **164–165**
mesquites, 158, 158*fig.*, 159, 160, 164, 256, 258
    honey mesquite, 40, 40*fig.*, 105–106, 105*fig.*, 106*fig.*, 132, 158
    screwbean mesquite, 132, 158, 160, 165
Mexican fan palm, 127–128
Mexican palo verde, 111

military lands and management, 244, 245*fig.*, 246, 250–251, 259
milkvetches, 35, 164
    Coachella Valley milkvetch, 166, 166*fig.*
    freckled milkvetch, 188
    Layne milkvetch, 187, 187*fig.*
    Peirson's milkvetch, 168, 168*fig.*
    shining milkvetch, 164, 164*fig.*
    two-seeded milkvetch, 187–188, 187*fig.*
    See also locoweeds
milkweeds, 208
    climbing milkweed, 208, 208*fig.*
    desert milkweed, 208, 208*fig.*
    rush milkweed, 208
    vine milkweed, 208
Milpitas Wash Wilderness, 17*fig.*
mimicry, 197–198
Mimulus, 199
mining, 243, **258–259**
mint family, 68, 196
    desert species, **67–68**, 113–114, 114*fig.*, **196**
Mitchell Caverns, 247
mock orange family species, 230–231, 230*fig.*, 231*figs.*
mock orange, little-leaf, 230*fig.*, 231
mock pennyroyal, 196
Modoc Plateau, 29–30, 220*fig.*
Mohavea, 197
    breviflora, 198
    confertiflora, 197–198, 197*fig.*
mojavea, lesser, 198
Mojave and Colorado Deserts Biosphere Reserve, 246
Mojave aster, 64*fig.*, 65
Mojave ceanothus, 233, 234*fig.*
Mojave cottonthorn, 63, 63*fig.*
Mojave Desert, 12, **19–28**
    ancient lakes and rivers, 19, 25, 26*fig.*, 27–28
    climate, 12, 19, 30, 32*fig.*, 33–34, 41
    dune areas, 25
    Great Basin plant communities in, 22, 30
    landforms and topography, 19, 21–25
    maps, 12*fig.*, 20*fig.*, 23*fig.*
    mining in, 243, 258–259, 258*fig.*
    Mojave endemics, 36, 36–37*figs.*, 67, 67*fig.*
    photos, 21*figs.*, 22*figs.*, 24–27*figs.*
    plant endemism in, 36

    urbanization and development in, 19, 132, 244, **256–257**, 260*figs.*, 261
    See also specific communities, habitats and locations
Mojave indigo bush, 71, 73*fig.*
Mojave Lake. *See* Soda Lake
Mojave linanthus, 194
Mojave lupine, 186, 186*fig.*
Mojave monkeyflower, 199, 199*fig.*
Mojave mound cactus, 95, 95*fig.*
Mojave National Preserve, 22*fig.*, 31*fig.*, 149*fig.*, 215*fig.*, 223*fig.*, **247**
    Chemehuevi petroglyphs, 243*fig.*
    Dome fire, 255, 255*fig.*
    establishment and management, 244, 246, 247
    Kelso Dunes, 25, 25*fig.*, *154*, 157, **165**, 209
    map, 245*fig.*
    See also specific locations and features
Mojave or Amargosa nitrophila, 139, 152, 153*fig.*
Mojave pennyroyal, 196
Mojave prickly-pear, 92, 92*fig.*
Mojave prickly poppy, 184, 184*fig.*
Mojave River, 25, 26*fig.*, 27, 28, 130, 131*fig.*
    associated riparian and wetland habitats, 130, 256, 258
Mojave sage, 67
Mojave sand verbena, 161, 161*fig.*
Mojave stinkweed, 152, 153*fig.*
Mojave sun cup, 201, 201*fig.*
Mojave Trails National Monument, 245*fig.*, 249, 249*fig.*
Mojave yucca, 56, 56*fig.*
monarch butterfly, 208
Monardella exilis, 196
monkeyflower family, 198
    desert species, **198–199**
monkeyflowers, 198
    Bigelow monkeyflower, 199, 199*fig.*
    Death Valley monkeyflower, 199, 199*fig.*
    Mojave monkeyflower, 199, 199*fig.*
    yellow monkeyflower, 198, 198*fig.*
Monoptilon
    bellidiforme, 181
    bellioides, 181, 182*fig.*
morning-glory family species, 152, 153*fig.*
moths and butterflies, 57, 109, 200–201, 208, 209

mountain desert sage, 67–68
mountain mahoganies, 226
    curl-leaf mountain mahogany, 224, 226–227, 226*fig.*
    little-leaved mountain mahogany, 227, 227*fig.*
mountain maple, 237, 237*fig.*
mountains
    desert mountain ranges mapped, 23*fig.*
    rain shadows, 12–13, 28, 33
    ranges of the Mojave, 22, 23*fig.*
    See also landforms; *specific peaks and ranges*
mule fat, 117
mustard family, 35, 173, 200, 203
    invasive species, 253, 253*fig.*
    native desert species, **79**, 152, 153*fig.*, **203–204**
mustards
    Sahara mustard, 253, 253*fig.*
    shortpod mustard, 253

nakedstem sunray, 176, 177*fig.*
Nama demissa, 191, 191*fig.*
narrow-leaved cattail, 135
narrow-leaved willow, 130, 132, 133*fig.*
narrow-leaved yerba santa, 230–231, 230*fig.*
National Park Service, 246, 249, 259
Native American peoples and cultures, **243**
    burning practices, 128
    Tribal land ownership and management, 250
Native American plant uses
    alkali goldenbush, 146, 148
    bitter snakewood, 121
    chia, 196
    creosote bush, 53
    honey mesquite, 106–107
    indigo bushes, 71
    iodine bush, 150
    pinyon pines, 224
    rabbit thorn, 70
    sand food, 162
    turpentine broom, 80
    turtleback, 180
    Utah serviceberry, 237
    yuccas, 57
needle grama, 213
Nevada
    development and its impacts, 257, 258
    Mojave Desert areas, 22, 25
Nevada ephedra, 86–87, 87*fig.*
Nevada indigo bush, 72, 73*fig.*
Newberry locoweed, 188
New York Mountains, 22, 22*fig.*, 23*fig.*, 215*fig.*
notable plants and communities, 233, 234, 234*fig.*, 235*figs.*, **236–239**
nitrogen fixation, 106, 108, 111, 148, 184–185, 187, 219, 226
Nitrophila
    mojavensis, 139, 152, 153*fig.*
    occidentalis, 152, 153*fig.*
nitrophilas
    Amargosa or Mojave nitrophila, 139, 152, 153*fig.*
    western nitrophila, 152, 153*fig.*
Nolina, 98, 99
    bigelovii, 99–100, 101*fig.*
    parryi, 100, 101*fig.*
nolinas, 99
    Bigelow's nolina, 99–100, 101*fig.*
    Parry's nolina, 100, 101*fig.*
non-native plants. *See* invasive plants
notch-leaved phacelia, 190, 190*fig.*
Nyctaginaceae, 211
    desert species, 160–161, 161*figs.*, 211–212, 212*fig.*

oaks
    canyon live oak, 234, 235*figs.*
    desert scrub oak, 234, 235*figs.*
ocotillo, 123–124, 124*fig.*, 250
odora, 65, 65*fig.*
Oenothera, 200, 203
    californica, 202*fig.*, 203
    californica subsp. *eurekensis*, 163–164, 163*fig.*
    deltoides, 160, 160*fig.*, 161*fig.*, 203, 203*fig.*
    primiveris, 203, 203*fig.*
off-road vehicle use, 168, 259, 259*fig.*
Olancha dunes, 157
olive family (Oleaceae) species, 83–84, 84*fig.*, 132, 134*fig.*, 237, 237*fig.*
Olneya tesota, 40, 108, 108*fig.*, 168
Onagraceae, 200
    desert species, 160, 160*fig.*, 161*fig.*, 163–164, 163*fig.*, **200–203**
onions. *See* wild onions
Opuntia, 90, 91–92
    basilaris, 92, 92*fig.*
    chlorotica, 92, 93*fig.*
    polyacantha var. *erinacea*, 92, 92*fig.*
Orcutt's woody-aster, 65
Orobanchaceae, 200
    desert species, 139, 139*fig.*, **200**

Orocopia Mountains, 23*fig.*, 68, 120
Orocopia sage, 68, 68*fig.*
Ovis canadensis nelsoni, 250
Owens Lake, 25, 26*fig.*, 27
Owens River, 25, 26*fig.*, 27, 244
Owens Valley, 22–23, 25, 27, 29, 30, 33, 216
owl's clover, purple, 200, 200*fig.*

Pacific glasswort, 150
paintbrush, desert, 200, 200*fig.*
Palafoxia arida var. *gigantea*, 169, 169*fig.*
pale primrose, 202, 202*fig.*
pale wolfberry, 70
Palm Canyon, 127*fig.*, 128*fig.*
Palmer goldenbush, 62
Palmer's penstemon, 197, 197*fig.*
palm oases, 40–41, **127–130**, 145, 250
palms
    California fan palm, 40–41, **127–130**
    date palms, 253
    Mexican fan palm, 127–128
palo verdes, 110–111, 168, 250
    blue palo verde, 40, 108, 111, 112*fig.*
    little-leaf palo verde, 111, 112*fig.*
    Mexican palo verde, 111
Panamint daisy, 176, 177*fig.*
Panamint Dunes, 157, 163
Panamint Lake, 26*fig.*, 27
Panamint mariposa lily, 210
Panamint Mountains, 23, 23*fig.*, 29, *214*, 216
    pines in, 240, 241
    rare plants, 67, 67*fig.*, 171*fig.*, 176, 177*fig.*, 210
Panamint plume, 78
Panamint Valley, 23, 27, 246
    See also Death Valley region/Death Valley National Park
pancake prickly-pear, 92, 93*fig.*
Panicum urvilleanum, 158–159, 159*fig.*
Papaveraceae, 183, 200, 203
    desert species, **183–184**
paper-bag bush, 67, 68, 68*fig.*
Papilionoideae, 184–185
    desert species, 164, 164*fig.*, 166, 166*fig.*, 168, 168*fig.*, **184–189**
parasitic and hemiparasitic plants, 200
    rhatanies, 80–81, 80*fig.*
    sand food, 162, 162*figs.*
    Tecopa salty birds-beak, 139, 139*fig.*
    Thurber's pilostyles, 72, 73*fig.*

Parish's boxthorn, 70
Parish's golden-eye, 61–62, 61*fig.*
Parish's gold poppy, 184
Parish's onion, 210
Parish's pickleweed, 150
Parkinsonia, 110–111, 168, 250
    aculeata, 111
    florida, 40, 108, 111, 112*fig.*
    microphylla, 111, 112*fig.*
parks. *See* public lands; *specific parks and preserves*
Parry dalea, 187
Parry pinyon, 220, 221*fig.*
Parry's jujube, 120–121
Parry's nolina, 100, 101*fig.*
Parry's saltbush, 145, 147*fig.*
Patton, George S., 259
peach boxthorn, 70, 70*fig.*
pea subfamily, 184–185
    desert species, 164, 164*fig.*, 166, 166*fig.*, 168, 168*fig.*, **184–189**
Pectis papposa, 211, 211*figs.*
Pectocarya, 192
    recurvata, 192*fig.*
Peirson's milkvetch, 168, 168*fig.*
pencil cactus, 91, 92*fig.*
pennyroyal, Mojave, 196
Penstemon, 35, 197
    palmeri, 197, 197*fig.*
penstemon family, 35, 175, 197
    desert species, **197–198**
penstemons, 197
    Palmer's penstemon, 197, 197*fig.*
pepper-grass, yellow, 152, 153*fig.*, 204
Peritoma arborea, 83, 83*fig.*
Perityle emoryi, 180, 182*fig.*
Petalonyx, 75
    linearis, 76
    nitidus, 75–76, 75*fig.*
    thurberi, 75, 75*fig.*
    thurberi subsp. *gilmanii*, 75
petroglyphs, 243*fig.*
Peucephyllum schottii, 63, 63*fig.*
Phacelia, 35, 189, 191
    campanularia, 190, 190*fig.*
    crenulata, 190, 190*fig.*
    distans, 189–190, 190*fig.*
    fremontii, 190
    ivesiana, 191
    pedicillata, 190
    rotundifolia, 191, 191*fig.*
phacelia family, 35, 175, 189, 193
    desert species, **189–191**
phacelias, 35, 189, 191
    desert Canterbury bells, 190, 190*fig.*
    Fremont phacelia, 190
    Ives phacelia, 191
    lace-leaf phacelia, 189–190, 190*fig.*
    notch-leaved phacelia, 190, 190*fig.*
    round-leaf phacelia, 191, 191*fig.*
    specter phacelia, 190
Philadelphus microphyllus, 230*fig.*, 231
phlox family, 35, 193
    desert species, **193–195**
Pholisma
    arenarium, 162
    sonorae, 162, 162*figs.*
photoinhibition, 43
photosynthesis, 48*fig.*, 49
    vs. CAM and C_4 metabolism, 47–48, 48*fig.*, 49
    leaf adaptations to maximize photosynthetic rates, 42–43
    See also stem photosynthesis
Phragmites australis, 135, 135*fig.*
phreatophytes, 40, 40*fig.*, 47, 105–106, 159, 160, 258
Phrymaceae, 198
    desert species, **198–199**
Physaria tenella, 203–204, 204*fig.*
physical environment. *See* climate; environmental conditions; geological setting; landforms and topography
pickleweeds, 150
    Parish's pickleweed, 150
pigweed family, 212
    desert species, 212, 212*figs.*
Pilostyles thurberi, 72, 73*fig.*
pima rhatany, 80, 80*fig.*, 81
Pinaceae species, **220–224**, 238, 239*fig.*, **240–241**
pincushion cactus, 96, 96*fig.*
pincushions, 178, 181–182
    desert pincushion, 181–182, 182*fig.*
pineapple cactus, 96, 96*fig.*
pine-bush, 62
pines, 224, 240
    Colorado pinyon, 220, 221*figs.*
    foxtail pine, 240
    Great Basin bristlecone, **240–241**
    limber pine, 240*figs.*, 241
    Parry pinyon, 220, 221*fig.*
    Rocky Mountain bristlecone, 240
    singleleaf pinyon, 220, 221*figs.*, 224, 238
pink devil's claw, 212–213, 213*fig.*
pink velvet mallow, 78, 78*fig.*
Pinus
    aristata, 240
    balfouriana, 240
    edulis, 220, 221*figs.*
    flexilis, 240*figs.*, 241
    longaeva, **240–241**
    monophylla, 220, 221*figs.*, 224, 238
    quadrifolia, 220, 221*fig.*
pinyon jay, 224
pinyon-juniper woodlands, 30, *214*, 217, **220–232**
    dominant tree species, **220–222**
    environmental characteristics and distribution, 220, 222
    fire in, 224
    seed dispersers, 224
    woody shrub associates, 217, **224–232**
    See also annuals and herbaceous perennials
pinyon pines, 224, 240
    Colorado pinyon, 220, 221*figs.*
    Parry pinyon, 220, 221*fig.*
    singleleaf pinyon, 220, 221*figs.*, 224, 238
    See also pinyon-juniper woodlands; white fir–pinyon woodland
Plagiobothrys, 192
plant adaptations and strategies, **38–49**
    C_4 metabolism, 48*fig.*, 49, 136, 144, 148, 159, 211, 253
    drought deciduousness, 39–40, 104, 113
    energy regulation adaptations, 44–46
    fire adaptations, 254–255
    growth forms, 39–41
    leaf morphology and adaptations, 41, 42–46
    limiting environmental factors, 41–42
    photosynthesis maximization, 42–43
    phreatophytes, 40, 40*fig.*, 47, 105–106, 159, 160, 258
    stem adaptations, 46–47
    succulence and CAM metabolism, 47–48, 48*fig.*, 49, 99
    winter deciduousness, 39, 104, 105, 132
    See also stem photosynthesis; *specific communities and habitats*; *specific taxa*
Plantaginaceae, 35, 175, 197
    desert species, **197–198**

plant communities. *See* desert ecological communities; *specific communities by name*
plant diversity, 35–36, 41, 246, 247, 251
See also endemism and endemic plants
plant families
key California desert families, 35
See also specific families
playas, 16, 19, **141–142**, 217
Pleistocene fauna, 213, 218–219
Pleistocene lakes and rivers
Great Basin, 30
map, 26*fig.*
Mojave Desert, 19, 25, 26*fig.*, 27–28
Sonoran Desert, 28, 29, 168
See also playas
Pleurocoronis pluriseta, 66, 66*fig.*
Pluchea sericea, 130, 130*fig.*, 160, 165
Poaceae, 35
C_4 metabolism in, 49, 136, 148, 159, 213
dune species, 37*fig.*, **158–159**, 163, 163*fig.*
invasive grasses, 55, 173, 216, **252–253**, 254, 255, 261
native annual species, 173, 213, 213*figs.*
saltgrass, 148, 149*fig.*
wetlands species, 135, 135*fig.*
pointleaf manzanita, 233, 233*fig.*
poison oak, 236
Polemoniaceae, 35, 193
desert species, **193–195**
pollinators, 57, 58, 81, 95, 160, 197
Polygonaceae, 35, 204
herbaceous species, 36, 36–37*fig.*, **204–206**, 207*figs.*
woody species, 36, 37*fig.*, 82*fig.*, 83, 158, 158*fig.*
popcorn flowers, 192
poppies
California poppy, 175*fig.*, 183–184
desert gold poppy, 183*fig.*, 184
little gold poppy, 183*fig.*, 184
Parish's gold poppy, 184
poppy family, 183, 200, 203
desert species, 175*fig.*, **183–184**
Populus, 41, 132, 255, 256, 258
fremontii, 130, 133*figs.*
Porophyllum gracile, 65, 65*fig.*

precipitation
rainfall amounts and timing, 10, 13, 30, 32*fig.*, 33, 41, 209, 211
snow, 30, 34*fig.*
prickly-pears, 90, 91–92
Mojave prickly-pear, 92, 92*fig.*
pancake prickly-pear, 92, 93*fig.*
prickly poppies, 184, 184*fig.*
prince's plume, 78, 78*fig.*
Pringle's woolly daisy, 177, 178*fig.*
Proboscidea
althaeifolia, 212–213
parviflora, 212–213, 213*fig.*
pronghorn antelope, 218–219
Prosopis, 158, 158*fig.*, 159, 160, 164, 256, 258
glandulosa var. *torreyana*, 40, 40*fig.*, 105–106, 105*fig.*, 106*fig.*, 132, 158
pubescens, 132, 158, 160, 165
Providence Mountains, 22, 22*fig.*, 23*fig.*, 247
rare and notable plants, 209, 231, 231*fig.*
Prunus
andersonii, 77, 77*fig.*
fasciculata, 77, 109, 110*fig.*
fremontii, 77, 77*fig.*
Psathyrotes
annua, 178, 180
ramosissima, 178, 179*fig.*, 180
Psilostrophe cooperi, 115–116, 116*fig.*
Psorothamnus, 71–72, 73*figs.*, 110
arborescens, 71, 73*fig.*
emoryi, 72
fremontii, 71–72
polydenius, 72, 73*fig.*
schottii, 72, 73*fig.*
spinosus, 47*fig.*, 71, 72, 110, 111*fig.*
public lands and land management, 244, 245*fig.*, 246–250, 259
military lands and management, 244, 245*fig.*, 246, 250–251, 259
See also specific parks and preserves
pungent brickellbush, 117, 117*fig.*
purple desert sage, 67, 67*fig.*
purple mat, 191, 191*fig.*
purple owl's clover, 200, 200*fig.*
Purshia
stansburiana, 225, 225*fig.*
tridentata, 219, 219*fig.*
pygmy-cedar, 63, 63*fig.*

quailbush, 130, 145–146, 147*fig.*
Quercus
chrysolepis, 234, 235*figs.*
turbinella, 234, 235*figs.*

rabbitbrushes
black-banded rabbitbrush, 62, 118, 119*fig.*
green rabbitbrush, 228, 228*fig.*
yellow or rubber rabbitbrush, 219, 219*fig.*
See also goldenbushes
rabbit thorn, 70
Racetrack playa, 141*fig.*
Rafinesquia
californica, 183
neomexicana, 182–183, 183*fig.*
rainfall
amounts and timing of, 10, 13, 30, 32*fig.*, 33, 41, 209, 211
ephemeral blooms and, 41, 171–172, 173, 175
rain shadow deserts and effects, 11–12, 28, 33
runoff patterns and processes, 15–16, 19, 25, 27, 103, 141, 259
sediment transport and deposition processes, 13, 15, 141, 256
temporary lakes, 26–27*fig.*, 27
rare, threatened, or endangered fauna, *126*, 134, 250, 253
rare, threatened, or endangered plants, 251
annuals and herbaceous perennials, 36, 36*fig.*, **136**, **138–139**, 176, 177*fig.*, 187, 198, 199, 199*figs.*
cacti, 92–93, 93*fig.*, 97, 97*fig.*
CNPS classification system, 251
creosote bush scrub associates, 65, 68, 68*fig.*, 70, 75, 76
dune species, 160, **162–164**, 166, 166*fig.*, **168–169**
Great Basin woody species, 230–231, 230*fig.*, 234, 235*figs.*
key threats, 251
wash woodland species, 113, 119–120, 121–122, 122*figs.*
wetlands species, **136**, **138–139**, 152
See also conservation issues; *specific locations*

rattlesnake weed, 213, 213*fig.*
rattleweeds, 187
   See also Astragalus
red brome, 216, 252, 252*fig.*, 254, 255
Red Rock Canyon State Park, *170*, 244, 248–249, 248*fig.*
redstem filaree, 253
red willow, 130, 132, 133*fig.*
reed, common, 135, 135*fig.*
Rhamnaceae species, 120–121, 121*figs.*, 233–234, 234*figs.*
Rhamnus ilicifolia, 234, 234*fig.*
rhatanies, 80, 81
   pima rhatany, 80, 80*fig.*, 81
   white rhatany, 80, 81
rhubarb, desert, 206, 207*fig.*
Rhus aromatica, 234, 236, 236*fig.*
Ribes
   cereum, 237–238, 238*fig.*
   velutinum, 237, 238, 238*fig.*
riparian woodlands, 40, 104, **130–134**, 248, 258
   invasive trees in, 132, 134, **255–256**, 258
rivers
   ancient lakes and rivers of the Mojave, 19, 25, 26*fig.*, 27–28
   modern rivers of the Mojave, 25
   See also marshlands; riparian woodlands; *specific rivers*
rocklady, 36–37*fig.*, 198
rock nettle, 76, 76*fig.*
Rocky Mountain bristlecone pine, 240
Rogers Dry Lake, 19, 21, 250
Rosamond Dry Lake, 19, 143*fig.*, 250
rose family
   creosote bush scrub species, 77
   Great Basin species, 216, 216*fig.*, 219, 219*fig.*, **225–227**, 236–237, 237*figs.*
   wash woodland species, 109, 110*fig.*
Rothrock's sagebrush, 241, 241*fig.*
round-leaf phacelia, 191, 191*fig.*
rubber rabbitbrush, 219, 219*fig.*
Rumex hymenosepalus, 206, 207*fig.*
rush, Cooper's, 138, 138*fig.*
rush milkweed, 208
rushpea, 113, 113*fig.*
Russian olive, 132, 134, 256, 256*fig.*
Russian thistle, 253–254, 253*fig.*
Rutaceae species, 80, 80*fig.*

sagebrushes
   budsage, 146, 148*fig.*
   Great Basin sagebrush, 218–219, 219*fig.*, 255
   Rothrock's sagebrush, 241, 241*fig.*
sagebrush steppe, 30, 31*fig.*, 216, **217–219**, 255
sages, **67–68**
   bladder sage, 67, 68, 68*fig.*
   brittle sage, 68
   chia, 196, 196*fig.*
   Death Valley sage, 67, 67*fig.*
   desert sage, 68
   Mojave sage, 67
   mountain desert sage, 67–68
   Orocopia sage, 68, 68*fig.*
   purple desert sage, 67, 67*fig.*
   thistle sage, 196, 196*fig.*
saguaro, 47, 97, 97*fig.*
Sahara mustard, 253, 253*fig.*
Salicaceae. See *Populus*; *Salix*
Salicornia pacifica, 150
saline habitats, **140–153**
   alkaline seasonal wetlands, **136–139**, 152
   alkali sinks and saline scrub, **148–153**
   annuals and herbaceous perennials, 113, **152–153**, 178, 180, 188, 204, 205, 210
   environmental characteristics and plant adaptations, 49, 141, **143–144**, 146, 148, 149–150
   playas, 16, 19, **141–142**, 217
   saltbush scrub, *142*, **143–148**, 180
Saline Mountains, 163
saline soils, 19
   See also saline habitats
Saline Valley, *10*, 26–27*fig.*, 27, *140*, 163, 246
Salix, 41, 132, 255, 256, 258
   exigua, 130, 132, 133*fig.*
   gooddingii, 130, 132, 133*fig.*
   laevigata, 130, 132, 133*fig.*
Salsola tragus, 253–254, 253*fig.*
saltbushes, 49, 74, **143–146**
   four-wing saltbush, 146, 147*fig.*, 217, 230
   Parry's saltbush, 145, 147*fig.*
   quailbush or big saltbush, 130, 145–146, 147*fig.*
   shadscale, 144–145, 144*fig.*, 217, 217*fig.*
saltbush scrub, *142*, **143–148**, 180
saltcedar, 132, 255–256, 256*fig.*, 258
saltgrass, 136, 148, 149*fig.*
Salton Sea, 28–29, 168, 246

Salton Sea Basin. *See* Cahuilla Basin
Salvia, **67–68**
   carduacea, 196, 196*fig.*
   columbariae, 196, 196*fig.*
   dorrii, 67, 67*fig.*
   eremostachya, 68
   funerea, 67, 67*fig.*
   greatae, 68, 68*fig.*
   mojavensis, 67
   pachyphylla, 67–68
   vaseyi, 68
San Andreas fault, 19, 127, 129, 166
San Bernardino Mountains, 19, 23*fig.*, 25, 28, 30
sandbar willow, 130, 132, 133*fig.*
sand blazing star, 197, 206, 207*figs.*
sand blossoms, 193, 193*fig.*
sand croton, 159–160, 159*fig.*
sand dunes, 25, **154–169**
   Algodones Dunes, 29, 158, 160, **166–169**, 259
   annuals and herbaceous perennials, **160–162**, **163–164**, 178, 185–186, 185*fig.*, 191, 203, 203*fig.*, 209, 212–213, 213*fig.*
   Coachella Valley dunes, **166**
   Death Valley dune areas, 25, 155*fig.*, 157, **163–165**
   dune cacti, 93
   dynamics and structure of, **155–157**
   Kelso Dunes, 25, 25*fig.*, *154*, 157, **165**, 209
   plant adaptations and strategies, **157–160**
   sound emissions, 157
sand evening primrose, 201
sand food, 162, 162*figs.*
sandpaper plants, 75
   Death Valley sandpaper plant, 75
   linear-leaf sandpaper plant, 76
   shiny-leaf sandpaper plant, 75–76, 75*fig.*
   Thurber sandpaper plant, 75, 75*fig.*
Sand to Snow National Monument, 245*fig.*, 249*fig.*
sand verbenas
   desert sand verbena, 160–161, 161*figs.*
   Mojave sand verbena, 161, 161*fig.*
San Felipe dyssodia, 65
San Gabriel Mountains, 19, 23*fig.*, 26*fig.*, 27, 30, 224

San Jacinto Mountains, 23*fig.*, 28, 89
San Jacinto Wilderness, 250
Santa Rosa and San Jacinto National Monument, 245*fig.*, 246, 249–250
Santa Rosa Mountains, 28, 68, 89
Santa Rosa Wilderness, 250
Sapindaceae species, 237, 237*fig.*
Saratoga Springs, 134, *134*
Sarcobatus vermiculatus, 151–152, 153*fig.*
Saururaceae species, 135*fig.*, 136, 136*fig.*
scale broom, 118–119, 119*fig.*
scale-bud, 180, 181*fig.*
scarlet locoweed, 188, 188*fig.*
schismus, 254
    Arabian schismus, 252–253
    Mediterranean schismus, 252–253
Schismus, 254
    arabicus, 252–253
    barbatus, 252–253
Schoenoplectus
    acutus, 135
    americanus, 135, *135*
Sclerocactus polyancistrus, 96, 96*fig.*
Scott indigo bush, 72, 73*fig.*
screwbean mesquite, 132, 158, 160, 165
Scrophulariaceae, 35, 197
    desert species, 231–232, 231*fig.*
Scutellaria mexicana, 67, 68, 68*fig.*
Searles Lake, 26*fig.*, 27
sedge family, 49, 135
    desert species, 135, 135*fig.*
sedimentary deposits, 13, 14*fig.*, 248, 248*fig.*
    dune deposits, 157
sediment transport and deposition, 13, 15, 141, 256
See also sand dunes
Senegalia, 107
    greggii, 107, 107*fig.*
Senna, 113
    armata, 113, 113*fig.*
    covesii, 113
serviceberry, Utah, 236–237, 236*fig.*
shadscale, 144–145, 144*fig.*, 217, 217*fig.*
shadscale scrub, 30, **216–217**
Shaw's agave, 99
Sheep Range, 22
shining milkvetch, 164, 164*fig.*
shiny-leaf sandpaper plant, 75–76, 75*fig.*
Shockley goldenhead, 64–65
shortleaf baccharis, 118
shortpod mustard, 253
shrubs, 39, 39*fig.*

adaptations and strategies of, 39–40, 45–47
See also specific communities, habitats, and taxa
Sierra Nevada, 19, 22, 23, 23*fig.*, 218
silktassel, ashy *Garrya flavescens*, 236, 236*fig.*
silky dalea, 186, 186*fig.*
silver cholla, 91, 91*fig.*
Simaroubaceae species, 122, 122*fig.*
Simmondsia chinensis, 82–83, 82*fig.*
singleleaf ash, 237, 237*fig.*
singleleaf pinyon, 220, 221*figs.*, 224, 238
six-weeks grama, 213, 213*fig.*
skeletonweed, Wheeler's, 163*fig.*, 164
skunkbush, 234, 236, 236*fig.*
slender bladderpod, 203–204, 204*fig.*
slender pore leaf, 65, 65*fig.*
slender spiderling, 211–212, 212*fig.*
small desert star, 181
small-leaved creambush, 237, 237*fig.*
Small Tract Act, 244
smoke tree, 47*fig.*, 71, 72, 110, 111*fig.*
snakeweeds, 64
    broom snakeweed, 63–64, 64*fig.*, 229–230
    sticky snakeweedd, 63–64
snakewood, bitter, 121, 121*fig.*
snapdragon, twining, 198, 198*fig.*
snow, 30, 34*fig.*
Soda Lake, 25, 26*fig.*, 27, 135*fig.*, 149*fig.*
soils, 13, 15–16
    cryptobiotic crusts, 148
    nitrogen fixation, 106, 108, 111, 148, 184–185, 187, 219, 226
    off-road vehicle use impacts, 259, 259*fig.*
    playa and saline soils, 19
    succulents and, 89
    wash soils, 103
See also granites and granitic soils; limestones and limestone soils; saline habitats; sediment transport and deposition
solar and wind power development, 260*figs.*, 261
Sonoran Desert, 12, 12*fig.*, 20*fig.*, 51, 89

geography and climate, 12, 19, 28–29, 30, 32*fig.*, 33, 34, 35, 41
Mojave-Sonoran boundary, 21
urbanization and development impacts, 257
See also specific communities, habitats and locations
Spanish needle, giant, 169, 169*fig.*
spectacle-pod, 203, 204*fig.*
specter phacelia, 190
Sphaeralcea ambigua, 78, 78*fig.*
sphinx moth, 200–201
spiderlings, 211
    slender spiderling, 211–212, 212*fig.*
spineflowers
    brittle spineflower, 205, 205*fig.*
    devil's spineflower, 205–206, 207*fig.*
spineless horsebrush, 229, 229*fig.*
spinescale, 145, 145*fig.*
spiny boxthorns, **69–71**
spiny menodora, 84–85, 85*fig.*
spiny senna, 113, 113*fig.*
Sporobolus airoides, 136, 136*fig.*
spotted indigo bush, 72, 73*fig.*
Spring Mountains, 22, 23*fig.*
springs and spring complexes, 16, 25, *125*, 134, 136, 137*fig.*
See also desert wetlands; marshlands
spurges, 213
    desert spurge, 213
    rattlesnake weed, 213, 213*fig.*
Stanleya
    elata, 78
    pinnata, 78, 78*fig.*
state lands, 246
    University of California research centers, 247
See also Anza-Borrego Desert State Park; Red Rock Canyon State Park
stem photosynthesis, 46–47
stem photosynthetic trees and shrubs, 46–47, 47*fig.*, **84–87, 110–113**, 114, 115, 115*fig.*, 116*fig.*, 119–120
sticky fagonia, 81
sticky snakeweed, 63–64
stiff-haired lotus, 188*fig.*, 189
stinkweed, Mojave, 152, 153*fig.*
Stipa hymenoides, 159, 159*fig.*
striated queen butterfly, 208
striped horsebrush, 229
Suaeda nigra, 150–151, 151*fig.*

subshrubs, 63
  adaptations and strategies of, 39, 39*fig.*, 46
  See also specific communities, habitats, and taxa
succulents
  adaptations and strategies of, 39*fig.*, 41, 47–48, 149–150
  alkali sink species, 150–151, 150*fig.*, 151*fig.*
  soil preferences, 89
  See also cacti; cactus and succulent scrub
summer annuals, 173, **211–213**
sunflower family, 35, 46, 58
  annuals and herbaceous perennials, 168–169, 169*fig.*, 171*fig.*, 173, **176–183**, 211, 211*figs.*
  creosote bush scrub associates, **59–66**
  dune species, 161–162, 161*fig.*, 163*fig.*, 164, 168–169, 169*fig.*
  flower structure, 58–59, 59*fig.*
  Great Basin woody species, 218–219, 218*fig.*, 219*fig.*, **227–230**, 241, 241*fig.*
  saline-habitat species, 146, 148, 148*figs.*
  wash woodland species, **114–119**
  wetland species, 130, 130*fig.*, 136, 138, 138*fig.*
sunflowers
  Algodones Dunes sunflower, 168–169, 169*fig.*
  desert sunflower, 171*fig.*, 176, 177*fig.*
  Helianthus niveus subsp. *canescens*, 168
  See also woolly sunflowers
superblooms, **175**
  See also annuals and herbaceous perennials
Swallenia, 36
  alexandrae, 37*fig.*, 163, 163*fig.*
sweetbush, 115, 116*fig.*
Sweetwater Mountains, 241
sycamores, 41
Syntrichopappus fremontii, 177, 179*fig.*

tack-stem dandelions, 180
Tamaricaceae. *See* tamarisk
tamarisk or saltcedar, 132, 255–256, 256*fig.*, 258

Tamarix
  parviflora, 132
  ramosissima, 132, 255–256, 256*fig.*, 258
Tecopa salty birds-beak, 139, 139*fig.*
teddy bear cholla, *88*, 90, 91*fig.*
Tegeticula sp., 57
Tehachapi Mountains, 19, 23*fig.*, 26*fig.*
  wind development, 260*fig.*
Telescope Peak, 23, 24*fig.*, 240*fig.*, 247
temperatures
  frost and snow, 30, 34, 34*fig.*, 104, 173
  mean temperatures for desert locations, 32*fig.*, 33
  warm vs. cold deserts, 12, 12*fig.*, 19, 30
  See also climate; plant adaptations and strategies
tent caterpillars, 109
Tetradymia, 63, 228–229
  argyraea, 229
  axillaris, 229, 229*fig.*
  canescens, 229, 229*fig.*
  stenolepis, 63, 63*fig.*
Thamnosma montana, 80, 80*fig.*
thistle sage, 196, 196*fig.*
Thousand Palms Canyon, 166
Thurber sandpaper plant, 75, 75*fig.*
Thurber's pilostyles, 72, 73*fig.*
Thymophylla pentachaeta, 66, 66*fig.*
Tidestromia subfruticosa var. *oblongifolia*, 212, 212*fig.*
tidytips, 180
  white tidytips, 180, 181*fig.*
topography. *See* landforms and topography
tornillo or screwbean mesquite, 132, 158, 160, 165
Torrey wolfberry, 70
Toxicodendron diversilobum, 236
Toxicoscordion
  brevibracteatum, 210
toxic plants, 63–64, 79, 152, 187, 192, 210, 218, 229–230
trees
  adaptations and strategies of, 39*fig.*, 40–41
  dendrochronology, 241
  invasive non-natives, 132, 134, **255–256**, 258
  See also specific communities, habitats, and taxa
Trichoptilium incisum, 178, 179*fig.*
Trixis californica, 120, 120*fig.*
tumbleweed (Russian thistle), 253–254, 253*fig.*

turpentine broom, 80, 80*fig.*
turpentine bush, 227–228, 228*fig.*
turtleback, annual, 178, 180
turtleback, 178, 179*fig.*, 180
Twentynine Palms, 245*fig.*, 251
twinbugs, desert, 161–162, 161*fig.*
twining mariposa lily, 210
twining snapdragon, 198, 198*fig.*
two-seeded milkvetch, 187–188, 187*fig.*
Typha
  domingensis, 135
  latifolia, 135, 135*fig.*
Typhaceae species, 135, 135*fig.*
UNESCO Mojave and Colorado Deserts Biosphere Reserve, 246
unicorn-plant family species, 212–213, 213*fig.*
University of California research centers, 247
urbanization and development, 19, 132, 244, **256–257**, 260*figs.*, 261
U.S. Bureau of Land Management (BLM) lands, 244, 246, 248, 249, 259
U.S. Department of Defense, military lands and management, 244, 245*fig.*, 246, 250–251, 259
Utah agave, 99, 100*fig.*
Utah butterflybush, 231–232, 231*fig.*
Utah juniper, 218*fig.*, 220, 222, 222*fig.*, 223*figs.*, 224, 238
Utah serviceberry, 236–237, 236*fig.*

vehicle use, off-road, 168, 259, 259*fig.*
velvet ash, 132, 134*fig.*
vetch, foothill, 189
Viguiera, 62
vine milkweed, 208
Virgin River encelia, 61
volcanic formations and soils, 13, 14*fig.*, 247, 248, 249*fig.*
  associated plants, 182, 182*fig.*, 226, 226*fig.*, 231–232, 231*fig.*

Wallace's woolly daisy, 177, 178*fig.*
washes, 16, 17*fig.*, *102*, 103
Washingtonia
  filifera, 40–41, **127–130**
  robusta, 127–128
wash-oases, 129
wash woodlands and arroyos, **102–125**, 160
  Algodones Dunes wash-woodland communities, 168

colonizer shrubs, **114–119**
desert gourds, **125**
drought-deciduous shrubs, **113–114**
environmental factors and plant adaptations, 40, 41, 103, 104, 105, 110, 113–114, 123–124
stem photosynthetic trees and shrubs, **110–113**, 114, 115, 115*fig.*, 116*fig.*, 119–120
subtropical outliers, **119–124**
winter deciduous trees and shrubs, **105–110**
See also annuals and herbaceous perennials
water resources and availability
adaptive strategies of plants and, 40–41, 40*fig.*, 44–45, 104, 105–106
groundwater depletion and riparian habitat loss, 132, 256, 258, 261
groundwater resources, 25, 29, 103, 104, 127
rivers of the Mojave, 25
water quality, 261

water supply development,

244

See also desert wetlands; hydrology; lakes; rainfall; rivers; wash woodlands and arroyos
wax currant, 237–238, 238*fig.*
weather. *See* climate; rainfall
wedgeleaf goldenbush, 227, 228*fig.*
weeds. *See* invasive plants
western juniper, 220*fig.*
western nitrophila, 152, 153*fig.*
wetlands. *See* desert wetlands; wash woodlands and arroyos
Wheeler's skeletonweed, 163*fig.*, 164
whispering bells, 191, 191*fig.*
white brickellbush, 116–117, 117*fig.*
white fir, 238, 239*fig.*
white fir–pinyon woodland, **236–239**
white-flowered tack-stem, 180
White Mountain Peak, 31*fig.*
White Mountains, 22, 29, 218, 224, 238, 240, 241
endemic plants, 36, 37*fig.*
white rhatany, 80, 81
Wiggin's croton, 160

wilderness areas, 17*fig.*, 246, 247, 250
wildfire. *See* fire
wildflowers. *See* annuals and herbaceous perennials
wild onions, 210
dark red onion, 210
fringed desert onion, 210, 210*fig.*
Parish's onion, 210
willow baccharis, 117–118
willows, 41, 132, 255, 256, 258
Goodding's black willow, 130, 132, 133*fig.*
red willow, 130, 132, 133*fig.*
sandbar, coyote, or narrow-leaved willow, 130, 132, 133*fig.*
windmills, 212
winterfat, 74, 74*fig.*, 146, 217, 230
wolfberries
pale wolfberry, 70
Torrey wolfberry, 70
woodlands. *See* Great Basin shrublands and woodlands; riparian woodlands; wash woodlands and arroyos; *specific tree species*
woody-asters, 65
Mecca woody-aster, 65
Mojave aster, 64*fig.*, 65
Orcutt's woody-aster, 65
woody plants
adaptations and strategies of, 39–41, 45–47
See also shrubs; trees; *specific communities, habitats, and taxa*
woolly sunflowers, 176
Pringle's woolly daisy, 177, 178*fig.*
Wallace's woolly daisy, 177, 178*fig.*

Xeralictus bees, 197
Xylorhiza
cognata, 65
orcuttii, 65
tortifolia, 64*fig.*, 65

yellowcomet, 206, 207*fig.*
yellow cups, 201, 201*fig.*
yellow devil's claw, 212–213
yellow evening primrose, 203, 203*fig.*
yellow-heads, 178, 179*fig.*
yellow monkeyflower, 198, 198*fig.*
yellow pepper-grass, 152, 153*fig.*, 204
yellow rabbitbrush, 219, 219*fig.*
yellow syntrichopappus, 177, 179*fig.*
yellow tack-stem dandelion, 180

yerba desierto, 231, 231*fig.*
yerba mansa, 135*fig.*, 136, 136*fig.*
yerba santa, narrow-leaved, 230–231, 230*fig.*
Yucca, 55
baccata, 56–57, 56*fig.*
brevifolia, 21, 21*fig.*, 34*fig.*, 51, 51*fig.*, **54–56**, 57, 248, 254*fig.*
schidigera, 56, 56*fig.*
yucca moths, 57
yuccas, **54–57**, 98, 100–101
banana yucca, 56–57, 56*fig.*
chaparral yucca, 57, 57*fig.*
Joshua tree, 21, 21*fig.*, 34*fig.*, 51, 51*fig.*, **54–56**, 57, 248, 254*fig.*
Mojave yucca, 56, 56*fig.*

Zabriskie Point, 23, 24*fig.*
Ziziphus, 121
obtusifolia, 120, 121*fig.*
parryi, 120–121
Zygophyllaceae
desert species, **50–53**, 81, 81*fig.*
See also Larrea

NOTES

NOTES

NOTES

NOTES

Explore Your Natural History

Backcountry Press is an independent publisher of web and print media exploring natural history, ecology, and the western landscape.

Our small business focuses on quality products that enhance the human experience and relationship to the natural world.

We co-create and offer:
- Print and digital book
- Live and on-demand webinars (including some for Arborist CEUs)
- Prints and posters

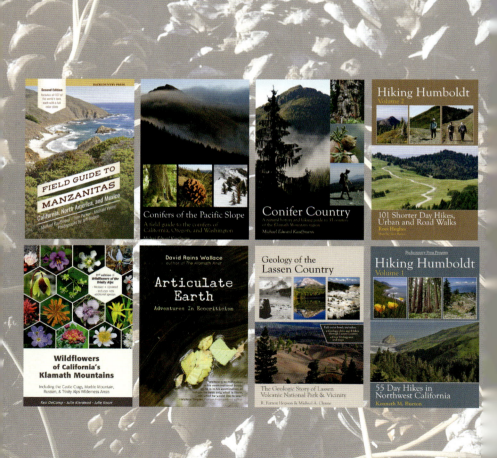

BACKCOUNTRY PRESS
Humboldt County, CA

Follow our work

The first comprehensive look at the natural history within the Klamath Mountains Geological Province

Edited by
Michael Kauffmann
and
Justin Garwood

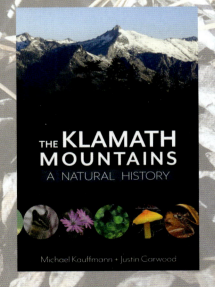

Fall 2022

Phil Rundel is Distinguished Professor Emeritus in the Department of Ecology and Evolutionary Biology at the University of California, Los Angeles (UCLA). He has written extensively on the ecology of California desert plants as well as from the winter-rainfall Atacama Desert of northern Chile and arid Succulent Karoo of South Africa.

Rundel and Gustafson have previously coauthored two books - *Introduction to the Plant Life of Southern California: Coast to Foothills* (University of California Press, 2005) and *Hawaiian Plant Life: Vegetation and Flora* (University of Hawai'i Press, 2014).

Robert Gustafson is the retired Botanical Collection Manager of the Los Angeles County Museum of Natural History, and internationally known for his rare plant photography. He is the coauthor with Sy Sohmer of P*lants and Flowers of Hawai'i* (University of Hawai'i Press, 1989).

Michael Kauffmann is and educator, author, and ecologist based in Humboldt County, California where he lives with his partner Allison and their two boys Sylas and Asa. Michael and Allison started Backcountry Press in 2012 with the goal of connecting more people with the wonders of the natural world.

Michael is the author of *Conifer Country* (2012), *Conifers of the Pacific Slope* (2013), and *Field Guide to Manzanitas* (2015). He is the co-editor of the forthcoming *The Klamath Mountains: A Natural History* (2022).